CAVS
From Fitch to Fratello

*The Sometimes Miraculous, Often Hilarious
Wild Ride of the Cleveland Cavaliers*

Joe Menzer
Burt Graeff

SAGAMORE PUBLISHING
Champaign, IL 61820

Production Manager: Susan M. McKinney
Dust jacket and photo insert design: Michelle R. Dressen
Proofreader: Phyllis L. Bannon

Library of Congress Catalog Card Number: 94-68644
ISBN: 1-57167-006-8

Printed in the United States

To my three first-round draft picks: Jules, June and Stacy

—B.G.

To my lovely and very patient wife, Sarah;
my former coach in basketball and ongoing mentor in life, Dad;
one of the game's biggest fans, Mom;
and hopefully two of its future stars, Andrew and Elizabeth.

—J.M.

CONTENTS

ACKNOWLEDGMENTS

When inspiration for this book first came upon me one summer morning in 1992, I was thinking of writing it by myself. But when I happened to mention the general idea to Burt Graeff in the middle of a golf round barely one week later, his response was, "Hey, I'd love to write it with you."

I'm not sure I was asking him to do so at the time, but in retrospect, it was the greatest game plan that could have been devised for a project such as this. When this silver anniversary season of 1994-95 is through, Burt Graeff will have covered the Cleveland Cavaliers on a daily basis for nearly 20 of their 25 years of existence. His recollection of past events, particularly humorous and sometimes even bizarre anecdotes, was remarkable. His ability to incorporate these treasured memories into our numerous interview sessions served as an invaluable sort of cattle prod to move even the less-willing sources down their own memory lanes with greater clarity than otherwise possible.

Speaking for the both of us, we must also thank each and every person we interviewed, but especially Bill Fitch, Nick Mileti, Joe Tait, Jim Lessig, Wayne Embry, Lenny Wilkens, Gordon Gund, Mike Fratello, Chuck Daly, Bill Needle, Bill Nichols, Doug Clarke, Rich Rollins, Don Delaney, Harry Weltman, George Karl, Ron Harper, Phil Hubbard, Jim Chones, Mark Termini, Austin Carr, Stan Albeck, Marc Hoffman, Sheldon Ocker, Craig Ehlo and even Ted Stepien, who was gracious and generous with his time, even though history may judge him one way and his own selective memory judges him another. Others, such as Nate Thurmond, Foots Walker, World B. Free, Mark Price, Brad Daugherty and Larry Nance, always were or have been and continue to be more than accommodating to reporters in the locker room. Most of the material gathered on them was pieced together through years of observing them at close quarters and interviewing them probably hundreds of times.

Paul Tepley deserves a nod for all the great photos accompanying the copy in this book, and also deserves credit for being perhaps the only man alive who has seen as many Cavaliers games as Joe Tait and Burt Graeff. As his photos attest, he has been shooting the team on a regular basis since its inaugural season in 1970-71.

The only art not belonging to Tepley comes courtesy of talented *News-Herald* photographer Chuck Crow, who supplied the color photo of Mike Fratello on the cover; and courtesy of the Cavaliers themselves, who permitted use of the classic 20-year-old photo of Bill Fitch coaching in a leisure suit during the Miracle of Richfield season. This picture of Fitch could not have been acquired without the generosity of Cavs public relations director Bob Price, who assisted on this project in other ways he may not even have realized. Simply being one of the best PR men in the NBA was assistance enough as we went about our jobs of gathering information while covering the team on a daily basis.

Thanks also to our literary agent, Shari Lesser Wenk, who put up with countless phone calls from desperate novice authors in search of direction from a veteran of the book world. She always pointed us the right way. And to Joe Bannon Jr., who enticed Sagamore Publishing to buy what was at the time not much more than a rather raw idea.

And finally, to our families for putting up with all the added hours of work involved in putting together this manuscript. My wife, Sarah, helped with the proofreading, and served as a sounding board on idea after idea, many worse than the ones before them. Burt's daughter, who recently and proudly became Mrs. Stacy Jantz, also assisted with the proofreading and organization of raw chapter material.

This book was intended from the start to be an accurate portrayal of the history of a franchise whose past can best be described as often hilarious, occasionally exhilarating, sometimes miraculous, but usually heartbreaking. We firmly believe we achieved our goal of putting together a truthful account of what has transpired on the court and behind closed doors over the last 24 years.

We hope all who read it will agree, while also engaging in a chuckle or two along the way.

—Joe Menzer

FOREWORD

In this modern day of sports journalism, there is usually a championship in hand or some juicy inside story to tell before a book is written. What we have here in *CAVS: From Fitch to Fratello*, however, is a chronicle of a team that has never won a title and has kept its linen reasonably clean over the 25 years it has been in business.

Burt Graeff and Joe Menzer take you on an interesting journey from the moment Coach Bill Fitch laid down those storied bubblegum cards on a hotel room bed to prepare for the expansion draft to the first season for Coach Mike Fratello, who did a wonderful imitation of General George Armstrong Custer at the Little Big Horn . . . except that he dodged the arrow. The Cleveland Cavaliers have certainly had their moments, from the debut at the dingy Cleveland Arena to the prairie at Richfield Township, where the Coliseum served well for more than 20 seasons, to the inception of the absolute finest of facilities in the new Gund Arena.

There are not many of us who have taken the entire trip with the Cavs. . . from the wine-and-gold through the orange-and-blue to the current black-blue-orange. Even I had to step aside as play-by-play broadcaster for a couple of seasons in the early 1980s, while Ted Stepien worked ever so hard at dismantling the franchise in Cleveland. What would you expect from someone who to this day cannot understand why it would be silly for the owner of a team to dress in full uniform and warm up with his players on opening night?

Two groups figure most prominently in the history of this team: Nick Mileti and his group of investors, who brought NBA basketball to Northeastern Ohio; and the Gund brothers, who saved the team and then financed the rebuilding of the franchise. You will meet all concerned in the course of this book, and receive their unique perspectives on this team.

There are other names to be recalled as well. Gary Suiter heads the list of characters, while Walt Wesley with his 50 points and Rick Roberson with his 25 rebounds top the performance charts. Austin Carr, Nate Thurmond and Bobby "Bingo" Smith have had their numbers retired for their contributions to the history of the team, which during one magical season in 1975-76 bordered on the miraculous. Larry Nance's number 22 also will be retired during a ceremony this season.

In the humble opinion of this observer, there is another player who deserves recognition both as a character and a performer. His name: World B. Free. He was as unique as his name—and for awhile in the early '80s, he was the only reason to buy a ticket to watch the Cavs play ball. Free carried the team on his back during those transition days from Stepien to Gund. Number 21 should be retired as well.

As you read this book, you will find the name Michael Jordan mentioned on more than a few occasions, too. One of the unique aspects of Cavaliers history is that one particular player from another team figures so prominently. Twice, Michael ended Cavs seasons with a single shot. The first killed the team, the second put it out of its misery.

This is the story of a team that started 2-37 in its first season and came within a single shot of possibly playing for the championship in more recent times. If you have questions about this franchise and its history, they will hopefully be answered within these pages.

So read on, and then keep your eye on the bouncing ball at Gund Arena as the Cavaliers continue to write the chapters yet to come.

—Joe Tait

CHAPTER ONE

"Birth of a Franchise"

Only in America. Only in America, says Nick Mileti.

Only in America can a guy who is the son of Sicilian immigrants, a guy who was raised on the East Side of Cleveland in a two-bedroom house with a $32-a-year real estate tax bill, a guy who was making 50 cents a week working at a drug store before he was 10 years old, a guy who was a cheerleader in high school, grow up to accrue enough money to buy a National Basketball Association team.

"Amazing," said Mileti, "but it happened."

Mileti knew virtually nothing about sports or sports promotion when the Alumni Chapter of Bowling Green State University met one day in 1967 at the Mid-Day Club in Cleveland.

"We had a strong Bowling Green alumni group in Cleveland," said Mileti, "and we wanted to promote a sporting event that people would rally around."

Mileti brought a Bowling Green basketball schedule with him. "How about this game with Cazzie Russell and Michigan?" Mileti asked BGSU Athletic Director Doyt Perry.

Perry laughed. "No, no, no," he said. "We're not going to give up the homecourt advantage for that game."

Mileti spotted another game on the schedule. Niagara at Bowling Green. Perry said fine. "On that same day," said Mileti, "I telephoned the people at the Cleveland Arena. We set up a meeting."

Mileti met with John Lemmo, who was running the Arena. "I was concerned if they would have any dates available," said

Mileti. "I looked on the wall of Lemmo's office where the schedule of Arena events was posted. I was blinded by nothing but white.

"There was nothing scheduled for the Arena. They had no dates for anything. We struck a deal."

What Mileti didn't realize was who was playing on the Niagara team that season. "We got lucky for two reasons," said Mileti. "One, they had a guy named Calvin Murphy playing for them. Two, they had a player named Manny Leaks."

Leaks, a 6-9 center, was from East High School in Cleveland. "He was very popular," said Mileti. "He must have sold 5,000 tickets by himself." The game sold out the 10,000-seat building. Bowling Green, coached by Bill Fitch, defeated Niagara, coached by Frank Layden. The success of the game piqued the interest of Mileti, a former city prosecutor in the Cleveland suburb of Lakewood.

"I couldn't figure out what was going on here," said Mileti. "Here we were sitting in the eighth-largest market in the United States, we had this arena with 10,000 seats and nothing was going on in it. When I saw all that white on the wall, I realized something had to be done. I couldn't figure out what the problem was, though."

Mileti soon found out. "The reason was that there was the most incredible document in the history of mankind," said Mileti. "One group owned the (Cleveland) Barons and another group owned the Arena.

"They were mutually self-destructing. The Barons (a minor league hockey club) had games booked every weekend (during their season), but four. Two went to the Ice Follies, two went to the Ice Capades. The circus could not even get in because of the commitment to the Barons. The Arena had an agreement that if the Barons were ever sold, they could buy them for one dollar.

"The Barons never got sold and the Arena never got full. It was just incredible. It dawned on me that what had to be done is they had to be married. You had to own them both."

Mileti bought the Arena and Barons in September 1968. The selling price was $1.5 million. "The first phone call I received," said Mileti, "was from Irving Feld, who is now dead. He owned the Barnum and Bailey Circus and wanted to come to Cleveland.

"People don't realize how important this sort of thing was to me. Here we were giving the kids a chance to see the circus."

He ultimately would give the city of Cleveland much, much more. The NBA in 1968 consisted of 14 teams. There were reports that as many as 12 of them were losing money. Nonetheless, shortly after buying the Arena, Mileti telephoned NBA commissioner Walter Kennedy.

"Why? Well, there was a combination of reasons," Mileti said. "First of all, cities like Milwaukee had an NBA team. Seattle had a team. Phoenix had a team. I mean, these were nice cities, but they were $2 cities, especially in those days. They were very small cities.

"Here we were, this huge town, this humongous town … my town. And we didn't have a team. It made no sense to me. It was easy making this call. It was clear to me that we should have an NBA team. And he (Kennedy) was not discouraging at all."

At the time, other cities bidding for franchises included Portland, Buffalo, Minneapolis, Memphis and Kansas City. "The way this worked," said Mileti, "was interesting. I had no idea who the other cities involved were. The league was playing one against the other. It's not like it is today. For some time, I had no idea who the other cities competing against us were."

Kennedy told writers at the time that he was impressed with Mileti's presentation. "The Cleveland group scored high in all categories," said Kennedy. "An NBA arena must seat 10,000 and Cleveland's does. It is also well-maintained, despite its age.

"As far as we can see, the Cleveland group has good financial backing, but let me also say that just because a group has money doesn't necessarily make them good owners. We are very interested in Cleveland."

This was not Cleveland's first shot at the NBA. In the league's inaugural season, 1946-47, the Cleveland Rebels of Ed Sadoski, Frank Baumboltz, Melvin Riebe and Ken Sailors were 30-30 in the Western Division. The next year, they were disbanded.

In the 1960s, the Cincinnati Royals of Oscar Robertson, Jerry Lucas and Connie Dierking played 10 to 12 games yearly at the Cleveland Arena. The Arena was not to be confused with the modern buildings of today. It was a dump. It was dark inside. It was damp. Occasionally, but only occasionally, hot water came out of the showers. Visiting players nicknamed it the Black Hole of Cleveland.

The visiting teams stayed at a hotel across the street from the Arena. Rarely did anyone change from street clothes to their uniforms at the Arena. Instead, they changed clothes at the hotel, played the game, then returned to the hotel to shower.

Boston Celtics great John Havlicek once said the reason he did not use the facilities at the Arena was that he feared picking up an incurable disease. The irony in this, of course, is that Havlicek and the rest of the Celtics played in Boston Garden, which also was a dump. In how many arenas, for instance, have fans sitting courtside been hit with rats falling from the ceiling? It has happened in Boston Garden.

At least the city of Cleveland had a team, and that had not come about easily or by accident. Bidding for an NBA team was one thing. Getting it was another.

"We went through some hard negotiating with the league," said Mileti. "There were times when I seriously wondered if we would get it. There was no way I was going to go into this thing just on any terms. The NBA knew where we stood. We wanted to be equal partners."

Lakers owner Jack Kent Cooke wanted the three expansion teams — Cleveland, Buffalo and Portland — to be put in the same division and play each other 12 times a year for the first several years. "I wouldn't go along with that at all," said Mileti. "If I was going to do that, why not just start my own league?"

In January 1970, the *Cleveland Press* reported that Mileti would drop his bid. The *Press* said the planned ownership group would not go along with the conditions placed on getting the franchise. "We simply cannot accept a deal like this," an unidentified member of the group told the newspaper. "The setup would be an artistic failure and an economic bomb."

"I was discouraged," said Mileti, who brought back $100,000 in earnest money he had deposited with the league after a January meeting in Philadelphia. "There was no way I could accept the NBA's plan the way it stood. After what happened in Philadelphia, I had some serious doubts. Gradually, though, the owners began to see we weren't just going to go for anything."

At about this time, Mileti began some serious discussions with the renegade American Basketball Association. "At one point," he said, "I went to Minneapolis and met with (ABA) commissioner George Mikan. I remember looking at a film presentation he made. He had a very clever thing in that film.

"The league had a 3-point line. He kept saying how important, how much of a revolutionary thing this was. They were very aggressive with me. They wanted Cleveland."

Mileti, though, did not want the ABA.

"I always wanted to go in the NBA," he said, "because of the original principals that I thought we should have major league sports in Cleveland."

Cleveland, Buffalo and Portland were awarded NBA franchises in February 1970. The cost to join the league was $3.7 million, which is what many of today's NBA players make in one season and a long way from what the league's most recent franchises — Toronto and Vancouver — will pay to enter the league for the 1995-96 season. Those teams will pay $125 million apiece.

Mileti made an earnest deposit of $100,000 at the time of the agreement. Several days later, another $650,000 was paid. An additional $750,000 was paid before the June college draft and $2.2 million was paid over the next four years.

A portion of the financing for the Cavaliers, the Cleveland Arena and the Barons hockey club evolved out of a friendship Mileti developed while serving in the Army. Leo McKenna, an Army buddy, was an investment counselor and an officer of the C.F. Kettering Company of Dayton, Ohio when Mileti made his bid to the NBA.

The Kettering firm was created as a vehicle to invest the fortunes amassed by C.F. Kettering, inventor of the automobile self-starter. Kettering, said McKenna, had a 49 percent interest in the Cleveland Arena and Barons, about a 5 percent interest in the Cavaliers. "I think this is a good business venture," McKenna said at the time, "and that's how I advised the Kettering people."

A major portion of the financing came as a result of a public sale of stock. Mileti received a check for more than $2 million when 400,000 shares were sold at $5 a share. "Going public was not an easy thing to do," said Mileti, "but that turned out to be our basic funding."

Mileti needed every penny. In the first four years of the franchise's history, the team lost a total of $790,000. There were four double-figure crowds in the first two years of play at the Arena. "It was the nature of what we had here," said Mileti. "It was a league in transition."

The team played in front of some incredibly small crowds at the Arena in the early years. At one such game, United Press International writer Dick Svoboda was typing the lead to his story late in the fourth quarter. The sound of his typewriter could be heard 10 rows in back of him. "Shut that damn machine up," yelled a fan. "It's making too much noise."

For $3.7 million, Mileti did not get much talent to start out with the first season. The expansion draft yielded guys like Walt Wesley and Luther Rackley.

"In the expansion draft," said Mileti, "the existing teams were allowed to freeze eight players. The expansion teams then picked one of the remaining players. Another player was frozen and we picked again. It meant we were getting the ninth and tenth players off these rosters. It also meant that the last player we picked (Don Ohl) was retired."

The 1970 college draft was considered to be one of the NBA's all-time best. It was a draft that included the likes of Bob Lanier, Dave Cowens, Rudy Tomjanovich, Pete Maravich and Nate Archibald. "All of the non-playoff teams from the previous season picked ahead of us, though," said Mileti.

The expansion teams drafted seventh, eighth and ninth. The Cavaliers, picking seventh, selected high-scoring Iowa guard/forward John Johnson. Making matters worse, the ABA was gobbling up players such as Spencer Haywood, Charlie Scott and Rick Mount.

"We did not get a marquee player," said Mileti, "which is why Bill Fitch once said that war is hell and expansion is worse. It was impossible to win. We went 15-67 in our first season for a good reason. The only reason we won 15 games is because we (the three expansion teams) kept beating each other."

It was on October 14, 1970, when the Cavaliers played their first NBA game. They lost, 107-92, in Buffalo. "I remember that first game very well," said Mileti. "We made a television deal to have the game shown on delayed tape. I remember bringing the tape back to Cleveland and saying to myself that I should throw it into Lake Erie."

He didn't. Mileti was too proud. He was one of three children born to James and Josephine Mileti. James Mileti worked in a factory.

"We lived in a little house on a little lot on the east side of Cleveland. There were a lot of flowers," said Mileti. "The sidewalks were literally swept."

Mileti was born during the time of the Great Depression — 1931. "It was a time when potatoes were given away to people on the street corners," he said. "My daddy, though, would not take a single potato. He was too proud. He worked. My mother worked. Whoever came home first did the cooking. That's just how it was done."

The Mileti house had two bedrooms. "My two sisters (Kimberly and Sally) slept in one room," said Mileti, "and I slept in the other room with my parents. The house was small, but it never entered my mind that it was small. My perception was that was never like that. In speeches years later, I often quoted Sam Levinson, who said, 'I did not know I was deprived. I was having too much fun.' And I was."

Mileti did not get into sports because of an athletic background. "I was a cheerleader in high school (John Adams)," he said. "Oh, I did play CYO, Class F and Class D baseball when I was a kid. I played third base and we were the Kenny Keltners because he was my hero. I did make it to Class C ball as a kid, but when I saw how fast those pitches were coming, my baseball career was over."

There was never much money around, but Mileti didn't care. "What did you need it for? All the kids in that neighborhood would do was find an old golf ball, an old tennis ball, a racquet and play games in the streets that we made up. I had a great childhood. Loving parents, wonderful schools like Corlett, Moses Cleaveland and John Adams," Mileti said.

Mileti the kid did more than just play games in the streets of Cleveland. Before he was 10 years old, he was working in a drug store for 50 cents a week. "Zabornick's," he said. "Hey, I always worked about three jobs. I'd come home and tell my mother that I had some great news for her. She'd ask what, honey, and I'd say I had another job."

Mileti was the first in his family to attend college when he enrolled at Bowling Green in the early 1950s. "My dad always told me that someday I was going to wear a white shirt," said Mileti. "In his mind, there was never any doubt that I was going to college."

He worked his way through Bowling Green, too, graduating in 1953. "I had at least three jobs there all the time," he said. "I worked as a house boy. Great job. Got all my meals for free. I cleaned, I dusted.

"My fraternity brothers had a band and I booked that. I worked at gas stations. I worked for a brewery. I was driven to do things, and it all seemed very natural."

Mileti was more than just a promoter in the arena of sports. "I'm as proud of the civic things I've done in Cleveland as anything," he said. "I've always been motivated to touch people's lives in a positive way, and I think I have. Take something like bringing Sunday night band concerts to the elderly of Lakewood. They'd draw more than 5,000. It meant so much to those people. That was the same principal as sports, only a different venue."

Yet, Mileti had his critics. There was an outcry from the city of Cleveland when he announced in 1973 he would move the Cavaliers to a $36-million building in Richfield, 30 miles from the downtown area.

"It was needed, so I did it," said Mileti. "I felt I wanted to serve the greatest number of people. I will never forget something (former Cleveland Press and current *News-Herald* sports columnist) Bob August wrote. He said that if you wanted to go to the Cleveland Arena from the north, you had to use a boat or the Australian crawl. I used the example that there were 2 1/2 million people within an hour's drive of the Arena.

"With the Coliseum, those same 2 1/2 million just turned their cars around. Another 2 1/2 million from places like Youngstown, Alliance and Mansfield and so on could join the party. It meant half the state of Ohio was within an hour's drive. This did not mean I had any problems with the people in downtown

Cleveland. This was not a matter of someone asking for abatement or some other deal and them saying no. The truth of the matter was that I thought this was the best possible location for the facility."

Frank Sinatra opened the Richfield Coliseum in October 1974.

"I made one miscalculation on the Coliseum and it was a major miscalculation," said Mileti. "I thought the area between Cleveland and Akron would fill in. I thought every intersection along the way would look like many of those in the suburbs around Cleveland."

It didn't happen.

"People moved, but they moved to places like Arizona, Florida and California. That's what happened. You never had the population growth in the Cleveland area that you had in the past," Mileti said.

Health problems were part of the reason why Mileti moved to California in 1979. He sold his stock in the team to Columbus investor Louis Mitchell in 1980.

"The last two winters have been murder on my legs," Mileti said in December 1978 when he announced he was moving to the West Coast. He was 47 and had been hospitalized 10 days for treatment of a dead spot on his hip bone. Mileti, who eventually had surgery to replace both hip bones, points to the Miracle of Richfield season — 1975-76 — as the highlight of 11 years as owner of the Cavaliers.

"Sports can drive a community," he said. "It can marry its ethnic, social and economic fiber. It can give a community pride and purpose. Jonas Salk can invent all the vaccines in the world, and he will never get a parade.

"The Miracle of Richfield was a dream that had become reality. It was clear to me that this was going to happen. I just never knew when. I will say this much — it can never happen again. That was a certain kind of magic. All of Northeast Ohio had a chance to share in my private dream. Coming from my neighborhood, that was a hell of a thing.

"I can remember walking in the Theatrical (a downtown Cleveland bar) and people jumping on their feet and screaming and applauding. I choke up talking about it now. Think of the impact that had on a guy coming from my neighborhood."

Soon after selling the team in 1980, Mileti regretted getting out. "That was a mistake," he said. "If I had it to do all over again, I wouldn't have sold. I missed it too much.

"I missed the guys, I missed the action. It took off so well and that was wonderful. The main thing is that I should have kept my foot in the door."

Today, Mileti is president of the Las Vegas Posse, a Canadian Football League team. He occasionally visits Cleveland and has driven past Gateway, the complex that includes a baseball stadium used by the Indians and the arena that is the new home of the Cavaliers.

"I feel proud when I drive by that complex," he said. "It is a magnificent accomplishment. I feel so proud of the role I had directly, or indirectly, or both, in it. That vote (to build the complex) would never have gone through without the Cavaliers. If I don't create the Cavaliers, there is no arena. If I don't save the Indians (Mileti owned the Indians for three years in the early 1970s when there was speculation they would move to New Orleans), there is no stadium.

"Not bad for a kid from the neighborhood."

Only in America.

CHAPTER TWO

"The Name is Fitch, Not Houdini"

"Sometimes," Bill Fitch once said, "I wish my parents had never met."

Well, they did meet, and on March 19, 1970, Nick Mileti announced he had whittled out one name from the 100 or so who had applied to coach the Cavaliers. Bill Fitch became the team's first coach. "He's far and away the best man for the job," Mileti said at the time of the announcement. "Here's a guy who had gone through what we had in mind here. He started from scratch and built a winner in Minnesota. Minnesota played the closest to a pro style of any Big Ten team. He recruited a fantastic freshman class and now some other guy will step in and get the credit in a few years."

Fitch, 35, came to Cleveland with no previous coaching experience at the NBA level. He was Irish, he was born in Cedar Rapids, Iowa, he was a former Marine, he had 12 years of coaching at the collegiate level on his resume, and he was funny. Oh, boy, was he funny.

"Just remember," he said on the day he was hired, "the name is Fitch, not Houdini."

He talked about playing baseball and basketball at Coe College in Cedar Rapids, and he talked about how he turned to coaching. "After entering Coe," he said, "I was thinking that I might become a lawyer, a doctor or a minister."

One day, though, he went to a counselor. "I have half a mind I want to become a coach," he told the counselor.

"Then," said the counselor, "that is the way you should go, because half a mind is what it takes to become a coach."

Fitch's first taste of coaching came at Creighton University in the mid-1950s. He was the head baseball coach and an assistant basketball coach. One of the baseball players he tutored was Bob Gibson, who went on to become a Hall of Fame pitcher for the St. Louis Cardinals. Fitch's role in developing Gibson? Plenty, he said. "I deserve a lot of credit," Fitch said. "Bob was left-handed when I got him."

Fitch coached basketball at Coe College, North Dakota, Bowling Green, and was at Minnesota when Mileti approached him about the Cavaliers job. Fitch said the Minnesota freshman class was the best recruited in the school's history. "We had everything covered except how to block a foul shot," he said.

Despite never having coached in the NBA, Fitch maintained he knew what to expect.

"The history of expansion teams shows it is death for coaches," he said. "The coach suffers through the first two years building a team and then the owner fires him and brings in someone else to reap the harvest. I don't think Nick Mileti is that kind of owner and that's why I'm here. Nick believes in this city and will fight anyone who doesn't."

On the day he was named coach, Fitch was asked about his offense. "I will use the KISS offense —Keep It Simple, Stupid," he said. "Maybe the GMA, too—General Milling Around. By the way, the GMA works a lot better if you have a good 7-footer."

Asked why he accepted Mileti's offer, Fitch said, "I get to make my own mistakes instead of inheriting someone else's."

Asked about his first-year goal, he said, "To keep my job." His philosophy? "Three things," he said. "The first is to win. So are the second and third."

He did have one complaint. "I just put in a blacktop driveway (at home in Minneapolis) so my three girls can play basketball," he said.

Several nights after being named the Cavaliers coach, Fitch left the Cleveland Arena at the same time a roller derby crowd was emptying out. He listened to a complaining woman.

"Next season," said Fitch, "they are going to be talking about me that way. They are going to be asking where this dummy got an idea he was a basketball coach. They are going to say he couldn't coach the Wheaties box top team."

Nearly 25 years after being named the Cavaliers' first coach, Fitch talked about how he got the job. "I had been offered to coach a couple of teams in the ABA," he said, "but I was worried about the financial status of these teams. Nick (Mileti) called one day and asked if I would be interested in the Cavaliers.

"I told him I didn't think so. I had never really given serious thought to leaving college coaching. Plus, I had re-cruited the best freshman class Minnesota ever had. What it boiled down to, though, is that Nick turned out to be the biggest factor. He painted a great picture. So many people thought the NBA would not go in Cleveland. He always thought of Cleve-land as being a great garden to be planted . . . a great place to put a pro basketball franchise. It turned out he was right about that."

Fitch and Mileti first met in 1967. Fitch was coaching at Bowling Green, and Mileti, a Bowling Green graduate, wanted to bring the school's game against Niagara University to the Cleve-land Arena. "Nick was trying to drum up interest there and I had lunch with him on the day we played Niagara," Fitch said.

In 1967, the star of Niagara's team was Calvin Murphy, a 5-9, 165-pound guard from Norwalk, Connecticut. He was an expert baton twirler who, by the way, also averaged 38 points a game.

"It was my first time in the Cleveland Arena," said Fitch. "The locker rooms then were separated by a false parti-tion. We heard everything they were saying beforehand, which didn't mean a hell of a lot. I knew they could hear me as well. So I stood up and gave the bullshit sign and said all these things we were going to do to Murphy in terms of doubling him, playing him man to man, two-timing him. Everything. Then, we zoned."

Fitch's first assistant coach with the Cavaliers was Jim Lessig, who had previously served as an assistant to Fitch at Bowling Green and Minnesota. The bulk of the Cavaliers first squad would come from the college draft and from the league's expansion draft.

Lessig said that figuring out the college draft was much easier than figuring out the expansion draft. "We spent a great deal of time trying to gather information for the college draft, which we felt we had some knowledge on because we could check with other college coaches we knew," said Lessig. "But we were really stymied by the NBA's expansion draft, because we just couldn't get the statistics we needed to research for it. What made it stranger is that we couldn't get that information out of the NBA office."

What made it even stranger, though, is how Fitch and Lessig got much of their information on the expansion draft. "We were back in Minnesota," said Lessig, "and I had gone out one night to buy milk. My son, who was about 10 at the time, asked for a quarter to buy some bubblegum."

With the bubblegum came a set of NBA cards. "I saw the cards," said Lessig, "and I asked what he had there. He told me they were NBA player cards. Well, I didn't even know they made NBA player cards. I picked one up and flipped it over. Not only did each card have the player's career stats on the back, but also his most recent year's stats. There was everything, really, that we were looking for."

Lessig immediately telephoned Fitch. "Bill told me to go back to that store and buy as much bubblegum as I could," said Lessig. "I went back and bought about $15 or $20 worth. We laid the cards all out on our family room floor. There were about 120 players in the NBA at the time and I think we had about 97 of their cards. We also had enough bubblegum to take care of us for about five years."

The expansion draft, which was held in New York, eventually helped stock the Cavaliers, Buffalo and Portland.

"Representatives from each team were put in separate rooms," said Lessig. "We took those bubblegum cards in a shoe box and we used them extensively to make our draft picks— vowing that we would never tell anyone, because it would have been embarrassing. At the very least, people would have said that by the way we played, it looked like we drafted these guys off bubblegum cards."

The Cavaliers' first college draft was 10 rounds. It became one of the NBA's best drafts ever, yielding names such as Bob Lanier, Rudy Tomjanovich, Pete Maravich, Dave Cowens and Nate Archibald. The expansion teams, though, did not pick near the top. Selecting seventh in the first round, the Cavaliers settled for John Johnson, a high-scoring forward/ guard from the University of Iowa. The second-round pick was Dave Sorenson, a center/forward from Ohio State. Fitch eventually took six forwards, three guards and one center.

Explaining why he took so many forwards, he said, "If we're going to have inexperience, I'd just as soon have it at the forwards. I'm hoping we can pick some experienced guards when we pick from the team's existing pool of players. If we're going to lose the ball, I want to at least get it over half-court."

The expansion draft followed. So did names such as Walt Wesley, Bobby (Bingo) Smith, McCoy McLemore, Luther Rackley, John Warren, Len Chappell, Bobby Lewis, Johnny Egan and Don Ohl. Not a household name among them.

Fitch's first pick in the expansion draft was Wesley, a 6-11, 225-pounder from the University of Kansas who averaged 7.5 points in four previous seasons with the Cincinnati Royals. He was as skinny as a broom handle. Fitch immediately announced that Wesley would be put on a diet that included a milkshake (with two eggs), graham crackers and milk before going to bed. "There is no way," said Fitch, "he can go up against guys like (Wilt) Chamberlain (275 pounds) or (Willis) Reed (240 pounds). He just can't."

After drafting Wesley and Rackley, who both played the previous season with the Royals, Fitch was asked why. "I wanted two guys who could look (Lew) Alcindor in the jaw," he said.

Nineteen players reported to Fitch for a rookie/free agent camp at Baldwin-Wallace College, Berea, Ohio, in September 1970. Asked to assess the situation, Fitch said, "I'm not afraid of the long haul. It's the short haul that worries me."

Training camp was busy. Real busy. "I have no idea how many guys we ran through that rookie/free agent camp," said Lessig. "We tried to give everyone a look. Some of these guys obviously couldn't play high school basketball. That's how bad they were. It was a real weeding-out process."

The surviving rookies and veterans reported to Fitch and Lessig in October 1970. "I don't think any of these veterans, guys like Egan and McLemore, had ever been through the kind of camp Bill ran," said Lessig. "We practiced two hours in the morning, two in the afternoon, and watched film at night."

After the third day, Egan and McLemore went to see Fitch in the dormitory where the team stayed.

"I've never been through anything like this, " Egan told

Fitch. "When I was with the Lakers, we'd practice two hours in the morning and play golf in the afternoon."

Fitch thought about Egan's remarks. "You're no longer with the Lakers," he told Egan. "We practice two hours in the morning, two hours in the afternoon and watch film at night.

"If I had Chamberlain and West, we'd do it the Lakers' way, too."

Fitch found a way to stop the complaining about two-a-day practices. "Wesley pulled a groin muscle one day," Fitch said. "He wanted to miss practice. We had a terrific team doctor (Nick Sekerak) at the time. He had this long needle he used to insert into the groin and fan the cortisone. Several of the players were standing around when Doc pulled that needle out and shot Walt in the groin. They all watched. No one ever missed a practice again."

Bingo Smith was a 6-5 small forward from Tulsa who played the previous season in San Diego. He reported to camp at 235 pounds, about 20 more than Fitch wanted. "I called Bingo the Redpop King," said Fitch. "He loved that red pop. The refrigerator in his room at Baldwin-Wallace looked like one of those you'd see in the commercials. Need some munchies? Just go to Bingo's room. I like to tell the story about how I caught him with that red pop once, grabbed him and said, 'I'm either going to kill you or make a ball player out of you.' To this day, Bingo says he still didn't know which it was going to be."

Dave Sorenson was a baby-faced 6-8, 227-pounder from Ohio State. He had a nice jump shot from 17 feet, but not much else. He was slow afoot, didn't rebound, and was Fitch's whipping boy.

"Fitch was relentless on Sorenson," said Bill Nichols, who covered the first training camp for The *Cleveland Plain Dealer*. "He never got off the kid's case. Like everyone else, Dave had a few training camp bumps and bruises. Fitch would always say that you had to play through them, that you had to play hurt. He was always saying that you've got to play hurt. Dave got even, though."

He got even not long after one of the Cavaliers' first exhibition games. "It was against the Buffalo Braves and it was in upstate New York," said Fitch. "The scorer's table at the gym we played in sat up high. Mendy Rudolph, who was the head of the officials at the time, was there watching the game. He looked like a judge sitting up there. Anyway, the officiating was atrocious and I was getting hot. At one point in the game, I walked over to Mendy. I started raising hell."

While raising hell, Fitch banged his hand on the table. "I broke a bone in the hand," said Fitch, "but at the time, I didn't know it." The Cavaliers took a bus back to Cleveland. About halfway home, the bus stopped at a restaurant. As he was leaving the restaurant, Fitch rubbed his hand and complained that there was some pain. Among those who heard the complaining was Sorenson. Sticking his head into the group around Fitch, Sorenson said, "Just remember, Bill, you've got to coach hurt in this league."

Everyone laughed. "Dave got me and he got me good," said Fitch. "The other thing I recall about that incident, though, is what someone told me Mendy said not long after I smacked my hand on the table. He turned to a radio guy next to him and said, 'That guy will never make it through 82 games.' "

The zaniest character of the Cavaliers' first training camp was Gary Suiter, a 6-9, 235-pound free agent center/forward from Midwestern University, Wichita Falls, Texas.

He made quite an impression immediately. Trainer Ron Culp was sent to pick Suiter up at the Cleveland airport for the start of camp. Culp waited as the airplane emptied, but no Suiter emerged. The airline personnel insisted Suiter had boarded the plane for Cleveland. But no Suiter got off after it arrived.

Culp summoned the cleaning crew. They got on the plane. In the back, sound asleep, was Suiter.

Fitch had never heard of Suiter until one day when he got a telephone call in Minneapolis. "He called me even before it was announced that I had the job in Cleveland," said Fitch. "He somehow found out that I was one of the leading candidates for the job. I put the call off. Not long after that, I was talking to (Pistons coach) Butch van Breda Kolff and he mentioned Suiter. He said the guy was a big body and might be worth bringing to training camp. We needed some size, so I did."

Big mistake. "This guy drove Bill nuts," said Lessig. "He was always bugging Bill to give him playing time. He was relentless. Finally, Bill gave in."

Fitch decided to start Suiter in the team's second exhibition game. It was played in Dayton, Ohio and it was played against the Phoenix Suns. One problem. No one could find Suiter.

"That was the only time that I can remember," said Lessig, "when we had a pre-game meal. Suiter was nowhere to be found. Bill sent Ron (Culp) to see if he could find him."

Culp found Suiter sprawled out on the floor near his hotel room. "He'd been sleeping," said Lessig, "the alarm had gone off, he jumped out of bed and started to run out the door. He hit his head on the door jam and knocked himself out cold. That was the way it started with Gary Suiter."

Fitch nearly cut Suiter on the spot. "The guy was strange," said Lessig. "No one wanted to room with him. Bill used this to his advantage. Bill informed them that on a given night, whoever made the most turnovers would have to room with Suiter that night. Bill joked that that was why we didn't make that many turnovers. The thing about Suiter, though, is that he was a big kid and he was strong. We played Seattle in an exhibition game in Canton. Things weren't going well. We put Suiter in and he got something like 20 rebounds in the second half. We didn't have anyone who could do anything like that, so we kept him."

Fitch said there was no way he could cut Suiter. "He blocked Connie Hawkins twice down the stretch of the exhibition game in Dayton," said Fitch. "Then he eats the Sonics alive in Canton. He was the star of the game twice. How the hell could I cut him?"

During training camp, Suiter lived in a run-down hotel near the Cleveland Arena. "Wesley, Rackley and Bingo lived somewhere in Shaker Heights," said Fitch, "and they'd pick him up for practice every day. He told them he needed a ride and they went out of their way to help. Once, Rackley is driving by himself and he sees Suiter standing on the corner. He picks him up and takes him to practice. Not long after, Wesley and Bingo come by. They are waiting and waiting and waiting for Suiter. He never shows up. They come to practice late, I fine both of them and they are hot.

"A few days after that, I hear all this commotion in the locker room at Baldwin-Wallace. I walk into the shower area and there's Bingo and Suiter. They are both bare-ass naked and Suiter has his fists up. Bingo is looking like Cassius Clay. They're ready to go at it. I turn to one of the players and ask what the hell is going on here."

"Coach," said the player, "Bingo just found out that Suiter's had his car here all along."

The Cavaliers' first regular-season game ever was played in Buffalo. Again, no Suiter. "We were in the pre-game meeting," said Lessig. "Everyone was dressed and ready to go. Suiter was missing. Once more, Ron (Culp) was dispatched to find him."

Culp eventually found Suiter. He was wearing his warmups and was standing in line at a concession stand. He was waiting to buy a couple of hot dogs and a coke.

"The stories go on and on," said Lessig. "I can remember seeing him in front of the (Cleveland) arena on game nights trying to sell his tickets. He'd go into barber shops around town trying to exchange his tickets for a haircut."

Fitch cut Suiter not long after teammate Larry Mikan said he caught him going through his luggage. "This should not have surprised me," said Fitch. "I mean, here was someone who'd wait for guys to leave a restaurant and then pick up the tips they put down. Here is someone who once went over to the Goodyear tire store and ran up $700 in long distance phone calls on one of their phones. Larry caught him going through his luggage and that was it. Suiter couldn't understand why I cut him. He said he would not have gotten mad if Larry had gone through his luggage."

On the day Suiter was cut, Fitch saw him making a telephone call at the Cavaliers' Cleveland Arena offices. "I told him that call better not be long distance," said Fitch. "He assured me it wasn't."

Minutes later, one of the league's general managers called. "Where's Gary Suiter? I just talked to him," the GM said. Fitch was furious. "I physically threw him down the stairs and out onto the street," said Fitch.

The coaches were not the only ones Suiter annoyed. "He'd always be coming up to me when I was doing my story after a game," said *Plain Dealer* writer Bill Nichols. "He'd beg me to tell the coach that he could take them to a championship. I once had breakfast with his parents in Phoenix. Nice people. Wouldn't you know it, though, his dad told me that if they

played Gary more, he could help them win a championship. What a guy. He once went to (Buffalo coach) Dolph
Schayes and asked if he could use a good white forward. He
was once cut by (Houston coach) Tex Winters. He kept writing
letters to Winters, though. So many that Winters sent him a
registered letter telling him to stay away. The last I heard of
Gary Suiter is when he was cut at the halftime of an Eastern
League game."

Suiter appeared in 30 games before Fitch cut him. "Suiter
hung around town for a long, long time after that," said Lessig.
"He would call me every night. He would call Bill every night,
begging to be put back on the team."

Not long after Suiter was cut, Lessig got a telephone call. It
was from a funeral home located across the street from the
Cleveland Arena.

"The guy on the phone asked if we had a Gary Suiter on our
roster," said Lessig. "He said Suiter came into his place a few
days ago saying there was a death in the family and wanted to
know if he could use the telephone to make all the proper
arrangements. Suiter, it turned out, used the telephone to call
every general manager in the league, begging for a tryout."

There was more.

"Bill told Suiter when he came to Cleveland that if he
made the team, he would pay for Suiter's wife to come from
Texas," said Lessig. "Well, after he cut him, Suiter came in
and said Bill owed him $400. He said Bill had promised him he
would fly his wife to Cleveland. Bill told him that he's never seen
his wife and that he didn't even know if he was married. Suiter
told him he was married and that his wife was right here in
Cleveland. Bill told him to bring her in, that he was not going to
pay him until he saw her."

Suiter went to the Wine and Roses, a go-go bar located next
to the Cleveland Arena. He picked up a prostitute, had her pose
as his wife, and brought her in to Fitch.

"It was obvious that she was not his wife," said Lessig. "Bill
asked to see her driver's license. She did not have one. Bill
decided that Suiter was probably paying this woman by the
hour. He told them to come back the next day. He did this
about three times, figuring that any money Suiter had was
going to go to her. Bill finally paid him. Just because of persever-
ance and ingenuity, Bill paid him."

Fitch said that Suiter's name still comes up occasionally. "It comes up often when I talk to Cotton Fitzsimmons," said Fitch. "We'll be arguing about something and I'll stop the conversation and say, 'Lowell, just remember something. The two greatest people ever to come out of Midwestern were you and Gary Suiter.' He has no comeback for that."

After the Cavaliers dropped their first six games, Fitch was addressing the media when he paused and said, "Hear that drip? I think it's an ulcer."

The expansion teams of 1970-71 played each other 12 times, making it even more remarkable that the Cavaliers compiled a 15-67 record. They lost their first 14 games, won one, then lost 12 more before winning again.

The eleventh straight loss, 141-87, came in Philadelphia. The 54-point defeat remains the largest in club history. "I remember the national anthem being played before that game," said Fitch. "I gave (Sixers) coach Jack Ramsay the victory sign. He gave me half of it in return." After the game, Fitch fined each player $54 for what he called "a total team effort in reverse."

The Cavaliers continued losing. "It did begin to cross my mind that we might not ever win," said Fitch.

On the night of the 14th loss, Fitch, Lessig, and play-by-play radio broadcaster Joe Tait left the hotel and walked over to the Civic Center in downtown San Francisco, where the game between the Cavaliers and San Francisco Warriors would be played. It was raining.

Approaching the players' entrance, Fitch, Lessig and Tait were asked by a security guard for their NBA passes. Lessig and Tait showed theirs. Fitch had left his back in the hotel room.

"I've got to see a pass," said the security guard.

"I don't have mine," said Fitch. "I left it back at the hotel. I'm the coach of the Cleveland Cavaliers."

The security guard was not convinced. "I've got to see some credentials," he told Fitch. "How do I know that you are the coach of the Cleveland Cavaliers?"

Fitch paused. Looking at the security guard, he asked, "Do you know what the Cavaliers' record is?"

"Yes," said the security guard. "They are 0-14."

"Then," said Fitch, "let me ask you something else. Do you think I would tell you I am the coach of the Cleveland Cavaliers if I really am not?"

The security guard smiled. "Go right on in," he said.

The 15th straight defeat followed. The Warriors crushed the Cavaliers, 109-74. The loss tied an NBA record for defeats to start a season and left them two shy of the league's all-time losing streak. Fitch's thoughts? "We have a built-in pressure in reverse," he said. "Instead of trying to win 15 in a row, we're trying to keep from losing 16 in a row."

The solution? "Put Nate Thurmond on our team," said Fitch, "and we'd be still playing the game against the Warriors and holding our own against any team in the league." Ironically, the Cavaliers did get Nate Thurmond. It was five years later, though.

On the morning after the 15th loss, the Cavaliers traveled to Portland. It was an off-day. After practice, Fitch and Lessig went for a walk in downtown Portland. "We were always looking for something to do," said Lessig. "We went for a walk and passed a curio shop."

Fitch spotted what looked like a human skull in the window of the shop. Gnawing on the skull was a fake rat. "It wasn't a real skull, but it looked like one," said Lessig.

Fitch paid $8 for it. That night, Fitch pulled the skull out of the trainer's bag and put it under the seat he was sitting on. "I let the guys come over and touch it for good luck," said Fitch. At one point in the game, Portland's Shaler Halimon threw a towel over the skull. "One of the wire services took a picture of Bill and the skull," said Lessig. "It was in papers all over the country."

So was the Cavaliers' first-ever victory—105-103 over the Blazers.

"I don't know where the skull is today," said Fitch. "Nick (Mileti) either has it or he lost it in his divorce."

The Cavaliers were 1-26 at the start of December when a Cincinnati newsman came up with a new name for the team: The Cadavers. It was at that time when veteran guard Bobby Lewis was asked if he'd have trouble forgetting the first 27 games. "Not when you've lost 26 of them," he said. Asked what he figured the worst the Cavaliers could do in the next 27 games, he said, "0-27. That's what the NBA has taught me."

In a mid-December game at the Cleveland Arena, the defending NBA champion Knicks beat the Cavaliers, 108-84. Coming off the New York bench to score 17 points was current Chicago Bulls coach Phil Jackson.

Jackson set 17 school records several years earlier at the Fitch-coached University of North Dakota. Jackson had led Williston High School in Williston, North Dakota, to successive state high school championships when he first met Fitch.

Fitch, who badly wanted Jackson to attend North Dakota, spoke at the Williston High School awards banquet. "He wanted me to come to North Dakota and there were no two ways about it," said Jackson. "In fact, he wanted me so bad, he chained me to a chair at that banquet, put a lock on it, and told me I couldn't have the key until I promised to come to North Dakota."

Not true, Fitch recently said. "I handcuffed him to a half-back," said Fitch. "Our football coach wanted that kid. I told both of them that I'd give them the key when they agreed to come to North Dakota.

"I still remember that night. I drove through the worst snowstorm to get there. People were being marooned for days before they could be found. I had to go all the way across that damn state. Went into a ditch twice. When I finally got there, they couldn't believe I made it. I drove all over in those days. I'd go into Missouri, Iowa and Illinois, looking for kids who flunked geography."

If nothing else, the early Cavaliers were entertaining. They made people laugh. One of the most famous baskets in club history occurred in the 30th game of the first season. The Cavaliers were playing Portland at the Cleveland Arena and trailed, 84-81, at the half.

Walt Wesley controlled the jump ball to start the third quarter, tipping it to teammate Bobby Lewis. Streaking for the basket was teammate John Warren. He was screaming for the ball. Lewis got a nifty bounce pass to him and Warren barely eluded Portland center Leroy Ellis, who was trying to block the shot, for a layup.

One problem. Warren put the layup, the layup Ellis was trying to block, into the wrong basket. "All I know," said Warren, "is that I started running and Ellis was right with me.

Lewis was stunned. "I looked up and saw Johnny going," said Lewis. "In fact, I had to make a super pass to get it to him."

There was more. Minutes later, Portland coach Roland Todd sent Dale Schleuter in to replace Jim Barnett. Schleuter, though, neglected to tell Barnett, who stayed in the game. Six-man teams are not allowed in the NBA.

"When the two teams came back out on the floor," said play-by-play man Tait, "I started doing my matchups. Here comes Schleuter and I have no one to match him up with. I start yelling that they've got six men on the floor. Well, at that time, I was doing the games from a seat near the Cavaliers bench.

That caught Fitch's attention. "What did you say?" Fitch turned, screaming at Tait.

"They have six men on the floor!" said Tait. Fitch let the officials know and got a technical free throw out of it.

It was Blazers coach Rolland Todd who summed every-thing up best. "The last time I saw anything like that," he said, "was in a junior high game—where you'd expect to see it."

A gathering of 2,022 witnessed more than just a mundane 109-102 loss. "It looked like the Mets out there tonight," said Fitch. "Only (Mets manager) Casey (Stengel) had a dugout to hide in."

Years later, Fitch said, "Ellis could have been called for goal-tending, or a foul. I wish to hell they would have called a foul. The funny thing about all this was that the next day we're showing films. Everyone's dumping all over John. Bingo (Smith) especially. I told everyone that we were going to take a look at that film again."

And what did the film show? "It showed Bingo in one corner," said Fitch. "He's waving his arms and screaming for the ball."

Lessig reflected on the play years later. "It was unbeliev-able that this happened to us," he said. "If it had happened to anyone else, it would not have been that big a deal. But it happened to the Cleveland Cavaliers.

"On the film, and Bill always thought this was funny, was Walt. He started to go the right way, then turned and started to follow them the wrong way, then turned again. Bill later said that it was at about that time Walt figured he had gotten some bad Gatorade at halftime. He didn't know which way to go."

During one road trip in 1970-71, Fitch walked up to a United Airlines counter and asked, "Where do we go to surrender?"

Wesley and Rackley shared the pivot duties in that first season. Wesley averaged a career-high 17.7 points and 8.7 rebounds. Rackley averaged 7.6 points and 5.3 rebounds. "Walt was the original black hole," said Fitch. "Once the ball went into him, it never came out. The players sometimes got upset. I always told them that if they passed as bad as Walt Wesley, would you pass?"

Fitch constantly tried to put weight on Wesley. "I tried everything," said Fitch. "I even had him room with Bingo for awhile. Nothing worked." The highlight of Wesley's career came in February 1971. In a game against Cincinnati, he scored a club-record 50 points. It still stands. "Walt was a good person," said Fitch. "I was really proud of him on that night."

The Wesley-Rackley duo was broken up the next season. Rackley was traded to the Knicks. "I saw (Knicks coach) Red (Holzman) not long after the trade," said Fitch. "I asked him how Rack was doing."

"He's doing fine," said Holzman. "He knows two plays now. One of them is yours. I think the other is mine."

The Cavaliers' first victory over a non-expansion team in 1970-71 was a 114-101 decision over Philadelphia. It pushed their record to 6-36.

The game was scheduled for a 7 p.m. tipoff at the Cleveland Arena. But the DC-3 the Sixers were to travel on for the trip to Cleveland developed mechanical problems, and the team left Philadelphia aboard two nine-seaters at 5:50 p.m. The game did not start until 8:15. Afterward, Fitch smiled and said, "You don't know how much it cost me to keep that plane in Philly."

Asked how he might delay the start of the next game, he said, "I'm calling United tomorrow. Or maybe this time WE won't show up."

Fitch, who refunded each player the $54 he took from them for losing by 54 points earlier in Philadelphia, was excited about finally beating an established team. "I feel so good," he said, "that I might go home and kiss my wife and not beat her. In fact, I might go out and celebrate Thanksgiving, Christmas and New Year's Eve all in one evening."

No one, though, was more excited than Joe Cooke, a 6-2 rookie guard from Indiana. He hit 5 of 6 shots and scored 13 points. "This is great," he said. "This tells us we can beat anyone in the league now." Yes, he did say the Cavaliers could now beat anyone in the league.

Cooke still holds a special place in Fitch's heart. "It's because he still owes me some money," said Fitch. "He called me one time from prison. He was in for drugs or something. Said he needed some money and he'd repay me. I sent it to him. I'm still waiting for the money."

The Cavaliers were 6-46 in 1970-71 when Fitch said, "This team is going to make more records than Frank Sinatra ever did."

Rookie John Johnson was named to the All-Star Game in 1971. The Cavaliers were 9-48 when he got the news. Asked about all the losing, he said, "There are times when I feel like just crying, and there are other times when I feel just like going out and belting someone and getting thrown out of the league. It's not easy to lose."

One of the Cavaliers' most popular players in their first season was Bobby Washington, a 6-foot, 175-pound point guard. He quickly became a crowd favorite for his hustle. He was billed The Little General by the local news media.

"I saw Bobby playing in a Continental League game when I was out scouting in Milwaukee," said Lessig. "I telephoned Bill and told him I think I've found a point guard for us. We signed him for the minimum—I think it was about $20,000 at the time. We were paying Egan about five times as much and this kid was better. So we traded Egan to San Diego.

"The fans loved Bobby Washington. He penetrated. He was scrappy. The thing I remember most about him is that he threw up before every game. Every game. He broke his leg badly the second season that we had him (1971-72) and he never really recovered from that."

The Cavaliers developed a near cult-like following in their first season. The *Cleveland Plain Dealer* labeled them the Lovable Losers. The *Cleveland Press* hailed them as the Madcap Mob. They had celebrity-like status wherever they went. One New York newspaper held a contest, asking its readers to guess when the Cavaliers would win their first game.

"I was doing a lot of scouting at the time," said Lessig. "Every time I'd go to New York, the crowd went nuts when the Cavaliers score was announced."

The Cavaliers made their first New York appearance in November 1970. There were 19,279 fans at the Garden, the biggest crowd the Cavaliers would play in front of all season and more than they played in front of their first eight home games at the Cleveland Arena.

"We made quite an entrance," said Lessig. "At that time, the guys didn't come out to do layup drills right away. They wandered out on their own to take some practice shots. Anyway, Walt Wesley comes out. He spots the ball rack at midcourt. The rack had six balls at the top and six at the bottom. Walt walks over to get a ball. For some reason, he tries to get one out of the bottom rack, instead of taking one off the top. Why, I have no idea. Anyway, the ball he tries to get is stuck. He yanks at it. The whole rack falls over and 12 balls are bounding everywhere. The Garden went nuts."

Fitch was asked once how he felt about people always coming up to the tall players and asking, "Are you guys basketball players?"

"With the guys I had then," said Fitch, "I wanted to know the answer to that one, too."

Wilt Chamberlain was in the league when the Cavaliers broke into it. He was 34 and no longer the dominant player he was when he was averaging more than 30 points a game.

"I liken Shaquille O'Neal to Chamberlain," said Fitch years later. "Both are just so strong. Both have problems shooting free throws. In one of the games we played the Lakers during that first season, he was trailing on a play when they got the ball. Someone threw a pass back to him and he was looking at an easy dunk. He lost his balance near the basket, though, and got too far underneath it. The ball hit the front of the rim and Wilt got knocked on his ass."

What did Fitch do? "I got up as fast as I could, looked down the bench and said, 'Don't anyone laugh!' "

There was another thing Fitch recalled about that game. "Jerry West," said Fitch. "He came in with a broken nose and was wearing a bird cage, a mask. He came all the way to play in that game and then went back home. No one was going to pass up the opportunity to play us."

Lessig recalled a game late in the first season. "We were down by something like 90-60," he said. "Bill called a timeout. He gets down on one knee and is trying to collect his thoughts for something to say. John Johnson breaks the silence by saying, 'Come on guys, we're only down by 10. We can still get them.'

"I looked at Bill. He looked at me. Neither of us said anything."

CHAPTER THREE

"Building a Contender"

It took four years to build the Miracle of Richfield team that would become the most loved in the history of the franchise. It took drafting Austin Carr in 1971, Jim Brewer in 1973, Campy Russell in 1974 and Clarence (Foots) Walker in 1974. It took Bill Fitch making shrewd trades for Jimmy Cleamons in August 1972, Jim Chones in May 1974 and Dick Snyder in May 1974.

Carr was one of the greatest scorers in the history of college basketball when the Cavaliers made him the top pick of the 1971 draft. In three seasons at Notre Dame, he averaged 34.6 points a game, second only on the NCAA career scoring list behind Pete Maravich. He holds the NCAA Tournament single-game scoring record, getting 61 points against Ohio University in 1970. He once scored 46 points against UCLA, inflicting the Bruins with their only defeat in 89 games over three seasons.

On the eve of the 1971 draft, Fitch did not know if he should go with Carr, UCLA forward Sidney Wicks or Kentucky State center Elmore Smith. "We took Austin," said Fitch, "because bottom line, he was the best player available. And, Cleveland was the number-two Irish alumni city in the United States. We needed a factor on the floor. Every team has to start somewhere. He was every bit as good a prospect as anyone — Sidney Wicks, Elmore Smith included."

There were other considerations. The renegade ABA was making inroads, signing stars such as Spencer Haywood, Rick Barry, Dan Issel, Artis Gilmore and Charlie Scott. "Austin's contract (a five-year, $1.5 million deal) was in the vault," Fitch said. "He had already been signed by the league (NBA). Plus, we had already made a deal up front to get some additional cash ($300,000) from Portland. Portland wanted Wicks and wanted to make sure we were not going to take him."

"That was a surprise to me," said Carr. "It was my understanding that the Cavaliers wanted a center and they were going to take Elmore Smith."

The Blazers, picking second, got Wicks. Buffalo, picking third, took Smith.

Carr's nine-year career with the Cavaliers was star-crossed. He broke his right foot before his first training camp in 1971. He reinjured the foot later in the season, missing 39 games as a rookie. He subsequently missed half of the 1974-75 season after undergoing knee surgery.

"The injuries hurt me and hurt my career," Carr said. "I rehabbed five times for various injuries. If injuries had not played such a major part in my career, I feel I would have scored 20,000 points (he scored 10,265 points). I spent half of my career coming off the bench. I always felt I got cheated because of the injuries.

"All I could do, though, was play the hand that was dealt me. I got as much out of everything that I could. I always felt fortunate to get back onto the floor after the type of injuries that I had."

Carr was 44 when he participated in the NBA's last Legends Classic during the All-Star Game weekend in February 1993 at Salt Lake City, Utah. At the time, he recalled a conversation he had with his 10-year-old son, Jason. "Every so often," said Carr, "Jason will ask me about what kind of player I was. It's hard explaining it and I don't have any films to show him. I once told him that before I had all the injuries, the only difference between Michael Jordan and me is that I don't do all the dunking Michael does."

Jason Carr's reaction? "Oh, dad," he said, "I don't believe it."

"I don't think he has any idea what kind of player I was," said Carr.

Fitch does. "I always said that Austin was a superior player even though he went through all that he did," said Fitch. "Had he not been injured, he might have been mentioned with Oscar (Robertson) and some of the other great guards of our time. He was that much of a scoring machine."

Chones, a long-time color commentator on the Cavaliers television network, agrees. "Austin Carr is a sad story," said Chones. "His knees were always hurting. He had the worst knees of any guy I ever played with. He'd have to put heat packs on them before practices and games and ice all the time afterwards. We'd always bitch at him about the ice. Water would be draining from the ice bags he'd wear after practice. He'd be walking around the locker room and everything was always wet. Here's a guy who, if it was not for his injuries, would be talked about with all the greatest guards to ever play in this league. He could still make the big shots, he could still drive left. He didn't have the knees, though."

Carr averaged 21.2 points in the 39 games he played in as a rookie in 1971-72. The Cavaliers were slowly shaking the joke-of-the-league image they firmly established in their inaugural season. They went from 15 victories to 23.

The antics that punctuated the first season were fewer. There were some, though. The Cavaliers played a game against Atlanta at the Cleveland Arena. Early on, Fitch became annoyed with the officiating. The annoyance grew. Finally, Fitch stood up. He grabbed the chair on which he was sitting, wound up, and threw it 15 feet in the direction of official Bob Rakel. The entire windup and toss were captured on film by *Cleveland Press* photographer Paul Tepley.

"Bobby Knight's chair toss was nothing next to mine," said Fitch. "Mine was a hell of a lot farther. His slid. Mine carried. The whole thing began with a first-quarter foul call. He (Rakel) had been on me and (Hawks coach) Cotton (Fitzsimmons) to shut up. I turned away and crossed my hands so I wouldn't get a technical. I said out loud that this official is going to kill me. Well, he (Rakel) came all the way from the foul line extended and was standing right behind me. He hits me with a technical. Now, I'm hot. He starts walking away and that's when I put the chair on him. I could have hit him. I always said that someone needed to throw a chair at him and I was going to do it. I wanted to shake him up."

Fitch was fined $5,000 for the incident. The league wiped out $3,000 of it. "At the time," said Fitch, "it was the biggest fine ever levied. There were some terrific one-liners to come out of it. Cotton said it was a good thing we weren't sitting on sofas."

Fitch and Jimmy Rodgers, his assistant coach, watched film of the toss the next day. "I told Jimmy," said Fitch, "that was his raise for next season I threw out there."

Fitch still has mementos of the early years at his home outside Houston. Among them is the chair he threw at Rakel.

"I've still got a lot of things," he said. "There was a game when Walt Bellamy tripped John Johnson. John slid on the (Cleveland) arena floor. One of the spikes that held the floor down was sticking up. While sliding, he got hung up on it. Stopped him cold and it ripped a huge hole in the shirt. I've still got that shirt."

A touch of professionalism came to the Cavaliers before the start of their third season when Fitch announced the acquisition of Lenny Wilkens from Seattle. Wilkens and journeyman forward Barry Clemens came to Cleveland in exchange for Butch Beard, a 24-year-old guard who played one season (1971-72) with the Cavaliers after serving a hitch in the Army. The trade stunned Wilkens. He learned about it from his wife, Marilyn, who reached him while he was playing golf. Wilkens was regarded as an icon in Seattle, and he at first refused to report to the Cavaliers.

"Basically," said Fitch, "(Sonics owner) Sam Schulman had stuck it in Lenny's ear. They had gotten rid of him as a coach and hired Tom Nissalke. There was a lot of unpopularity there. There was the Wilkens camp and the non-Wilkens camp. Lenny had been very popular. He had almost retired as a player, but I felt he still had something left. They had a chance to get Beard, who was a young, promising player, and they went for it."

Fitch and Mileti met with Wilkens in Seattle. "We had to talk him into coming," said Fitch. "He was not upset about coming to Cleveland or coming to a down team. And it wasn't that he wanted more money. It was that his home was out there, his family was out there and his feelings were hurt. He was bitter. It was a matter of time healing the wounds. I told him that he was not done as a player — that here was a chance to continue his career."

Wilkens joined the Cavaliers in late October 1972. They were 0-7 when he reported. Two weeks later, Wilkens and the Cavaliers played one of the most intriguing games in the history of the franchise. It was in Seattle, which was still in turmoil over the trade that sent Wilkens to the Cavaliers.

"It was one of the most memorable games I've ever done," said Cavaliers long-time play-by-play voice Joe Tait. "People in the Seattle front office were ready for what was going to happen. They had the whole place (Seattle Center Coliseum) papered with pro-Sonics signs. There were signs like 'Sonics Power,' 'Back the Sonics,' 'Stay behind Coach Tom' (Nissalke).

"A half hour before the game, though, you couldn't see those signs. They were covered with pro-Lenny signs. The other thing I remember about the game is that Lenny had been bothered with some leg problems. When the Cavaliers came out, though, the place went insane. They screamed every time he touched the ball in the layup drills.

"There was no way that crowd was going to let the Cavaliers lose the game. It's funny, because the Cavaliers had not received that kind of support even in their own building."

The Cavaliers didn't lose. They won, 113-107. Wilkens had 22 points, nine rebounds and nine assists, narrowly missing a rare triple-double.

The franchise's first-round pick for the third season was Dwight Davis, a 6-8, 220-pound forward from the University of Houston. "The guy could jump like a deer," said Fitch. "He was a great kid, one of the most emotional I ever coached."

Davis averaged 9.2 points and 7.2 rebounds as a rookie and, for the third straight year, the Cavaliers increased their number of victories. They won 32 and lost 50. Just how emotional a player Davis was surfaced in a game during the 1974-75 season. The Cavaliers were on their way to suffering their seventh straight loss in a game at the Coliseum against Buffalo. A couple of fans, who made the drive to Richfield from Buffalo, were about 15 rows in the stands behind the Cavaliers bench. They had been spending much of the evening throwing back beers and heckling Davis. With four minutes remaining in the third quarter and the Cavaliers trailing, 66-62, Fitch replaced Davis with Jim Brewer. Davis was not happy about being lifted and barked his displeasure toward Fitch as he went to his seat.

What really set Davis off, though, was a remark made by one of the two guys from Buffalo. Within seconds of the remark, Davis was up in the stands and confronting the fan, James Grochala of Niagara Falls, N.Y. Grochala was stunned.

"I didn't cuss him or anything," said Grochala. "All I did was tell him he can't do the job. That he should sit down. He became irrational. He asked me what I had said. He asked me if I wanted to fight. I told him that if he wanted to hit me, go ahead. I'll just get my lawyer."

Davis, who said he'd rather forget the incident than talk about it, was escorted out of the stands by Fitch. "I was as surprised as the guy up in the stands," said Fitch. "I looked up there and about 60 seconds later, I said to myself, 'Hey, that's Dwight Davis up there.' He learned his lesson. When I saw pictures of me throwing that chair, it cured me. He did something a lot of guys would like to do, but don't."

The Cavaliers' lone step backward in the first six seasons occurred in 1973-74. Carr was terrific in leading the team with a 21.9 scoring average and making his only All-Star Game appearance. Wilkens had an excellent final season as a player, averaging 16.4 points. The last year at the Cleveland Arena, though, produced just 29 victories because of a trade that sent John Johnson and Rick Roberson to Portland for the draft rights to Jim Brewer, a Paul Silas-type power forward.

With the 6-8 Brewer and 6-9 Steve Patterson playing the pivot, the Cavaliers were regularly beaten in the middle.

For the first time since his arrival in Cleveland, Fitch took some heat from the media. The media and fans expected more and were not getting it. As is the case with many professional coaches, Fitch did not take the criticism well.

"Bill could be tough, real tough, on writers," Tait said. "It goes back a long way. When Bill was coaching at North Dakota, some poor sucker there wrote something he didn't like. Not long after, the team was taking a bus trip somewhere and the writer went along. It was in a horrible blizzard. The bus made a stop somewhere along the way. Everyone piles out as though they are going to stop and get something to eat. The writer goes to the john, Fitch has everyone get back on the bus and they take off. The guy was snowed in for four days. Fitch had pre-arranged the whole thing."

Cleveland Plain Dealer writer Bill Nichols felt Fitch's wrath. "I had written something that bugged him," said Nichols, "and we weren't on the best of terms. Anyway, we're on this trip to play the Nets in New Jersey. At that time, they were playing their home games in Piscataway, which was impossible for even people who lived in New Jersey to find. He told everyone, players included, that he did not want them checking luggage. He wanted to get to the Newark airport, board the bus and take off for Piscataway.

"Not long after we land, trainer Charlie Strasser tells me that my carry-on bags have been inadvertently checked in. I go to the baggage claim. While I'm waiting on my bags, I looked up just in time to see the bus pulling away. I found out later that everyone sprinted to the bus to take off without me. Jim Mueller, one of the TV guys, asked Fitch if they were going to wait for me. Fitch told him, 'Hell no.' Bottom line was, I didn't get to the hotel until about 2:30 in the afternoon. It took four hours to get there. I was steamed. For the most part, I got along with Bill Fitch famously in the early years. Then, it got to the point where he was coaching too long and I was covering them too long. Years later, he and I got along fine."

Four major pieces to the Miracle of Richfield team were added before the 1974-75 season, the first at the Coliseum in Richfield. Acquired in a trade with the Los Angeles Lakers was Jim Chones, who would take care of the problems in the middle. Acquired from the Seattle SuperSonics was Dick Snyder, a guard with a radar-like shooting touch from the outside. Tabbed in the first round of the draft as part of the Seattle trade was Campy Russell, a flashy forward from the University of Michigan. Selected in the third round of the draft was Clarence (Foots) Walker, a little-known point guard from West Georgia College.

"I had known Jim Chones for a long time," Fitch said. "When I was at Minnesota, I had recruited him. He finally told me he had narrowed his choices to Wisconsin or Marquette. I told him to go to Marquette. That way, I'd only have to face him once a year.

"The Lakers owned Jim's NBA rights and they never thought he'd be a player. He was regarded as kind of a Peck's bad boy in the ABA. The ABA was such a mystery, though. There were a lot of half-truths. It was very easy to be branded as a bum. A lot of these young kids were making big money. They were being called spoiled brats. Anyway, the Lakers were sitting there with Chamberlain and others. They had no need for Jim Chones. As it turned out, this ranked up there as a very good deal."

Chones was 24 when the Cavaliers acquired him in May 1974. He had been a center of attention from the time he led St. Catherine High School in Racine, Wisconsin, to 26 straight victories. He was the oldest of six children and was a freshman at Marquette when his father, a foundry worker, died of lung cancer at 43.

"When my father died," said Chones, "it dropped us into a hole so big you can't imagine. We didn't have anything. Other kids laughed and made jokes about our family. I know what being homeless is like. My mother worked making salads at a restaurant."

The ABA changed everything for Chones.

"The (New York) Nets wanted me to leave in the middle of my sophomore season," said Chones. "It was a tough decision. I loved my teammates, but I loved my family more. We didn't have a thing. I know what it's like to eat biscuits with gravy and sugar on top."

Chones became the second player — Spencer Haywood was the first — to leave college and sign an ABA contract.

"They offered me five years at $175,000 a year. I got a $500,000 signing bonus and deferred payments of $37,500 for the next 15 years," he said. "At the time, it was the best contract in sports. I ended up losing a lot of money, though. Bad investments, bad advice. That wasn't unusual at the time. I sued two attorneys who beat me out of money."

Chones left the ABA after two seasons. "They (the ABA) couldn't afford to pay me any more. The Lakers worked out a deal with them," Chones said. "When they traded me to Cleveland, I didn't know what to expect. I hadn't watched a lot of television, so I wasn't hip to the Cleveland jokes. If I had been, I would have been upset. I'd known Fitch, though, and that's the main reason I wanted to go there. I knew about his wise-cracking. I also knew he was a strong leader and was very loyal to his players. He hated to trade players, he hated to get rid of people. He and I got along real well.

"Our situation was more like a father hollering at his son. We knew where each other stood. When I got there, the team was terrible. Luke (Witte) was a journeyman. So was Steve Patterson.

We didn't have much. My biggest frustration was not starting right away. He (Fitch) started Patterson, then went to Luke. I beat up Luke so many times in practice that Fitch had to move me up. I remember one practice when Patterson and I got into it. He was giving me all this UCLA garbage. I told him that if he didn't end it, I'd knock him out. He asks me if I know who I'm talking to. I told him that I did and really took it to him in that practice. The next day, I was starting. My thing was to start. I could not come off the bench.

"Things started to look up when I came. I gave them a center who could shoot from the outside, but who could also go inside and run the floor. I knew how to play. I knew how to pass."

Eleven days after acquiring Chones from Seattle in May 1974, Fitch made another deal. He exchanged first-round draft picks with Seattle, also getting Snyder. The Sonics would get the third pick in the draft; the Cavaliers the eighth. "That turned out to be the best trade I made while I was in Cleveland," said Fitch. "Tom Burleson was out there and, next to (Bill) Walton, he was the center at the time. I didn't think Burleson would be much of an NBA center, though. He didn't have much of a body. He reminded me a lot of Shawn Bradley today. I thought he would always have a body problem.

"(Sonics coach) Bill Russell wanted a center in Seattle. He thought he could do a lot with Burleson. They gave us $250,000, Dick Snyder and the eighth choice in the draft. I thought we could get Campy (Russell) with that pick. Nick (Mileti) was so happy that we got the $250,000. I told him that if we held out, I thought we might get able to get more than $250,000. He told me not to press it, just make the deal."

Fitch did. The Sonics, picking third, took Burleson. Portland, picking first, took Walton. Philadelphia, picking second, took Marvin (Bad News) Barnes. The Cavaliers came away with Snyder and Russell.

"In Dick Snyder," said Fitch, "we were getting a veteran who could shoot and defend guys like Bill Bradley in New York. In Campy, we got a potential young star."

Snyder, a 6-5, 210-pounder, was an eight-year veteran when he came to the Cavaliers. He was 30 and a graduate of Davidson College. Snyder grew up in North Canton, Ohio and wanted to attend Ohio State. OSU coach Fred Taylor, though, said Snyder was not good enough to play in the Big Ten. It was Snyder who got the last laugh on Taylor. He played on the Davidson team that ended OSU's 50-game homecourt winning streak at St. John Arena in Columbus. While Snyder was not good enough, in Taylor's estimation, to play in the Big Ten, he was good enough to average 13.8 points in eight NBA seasons when the Cavaliers acquired him.

"Dick Snyder had tremendous range on his shots," said Chones. "He couldn't handle the ball and you didn't want him passing it to you, though. I used to turn my back to him when I thought he was going to pass me the ball. I knew I'd have to make a great catch to get it. He'd either throw it at your knees or throw it at your feet or else he'd throw it at your head, and you'd have to leap out of the gym to get it."

Fitch said that getting an additional $250,000 from Seattle was just as important to the franchise as getting Snyder and eventually Russell.

"Nick (Mileti) did it with mirrors in those early years," said Fitch. "We weren't drawing. We didn't have much money. I remember once when (Tom) Boerwinkle was available in Chicago. He was making $60,000. I went to Nick one day and said we could get this guy. Nick said, 'I don't know how to tell you this, but we've got problems of our own. It looks like we may have to move Lenny (Wilkens) or Austin (Carr).' They were the only two players we had at the time who were worth anything to anyone. We made it through some real hard times, and Nick never got the credit he deserved. A good business can make millions. But what he did was make something go with nothing."

The last acquisition before the start of the 1974-75 season came in the third round of the 1974 draft. Using the 38th pick of the draft, Fitch selected Foots Walker, a 6-0, 172-pound point guard from West Georgia, an NAIA school.

"I found out about Foots through a friend of mine," said Fitch. "And (NBA Scouting Director) Marty Blake was real high on him. I always kidded Marty that if he liked a guy, I would not take him. A few of us listened to Marty. Others thought he was a comic. I loved Foots Walker. How could you not love the guy? He reminded me of that bunny in the battery commercial. He just never wore down."

Walker played six seasons for the Cavaliers, coming off the bench behind Jimmy Cleamons most of the time. Fitch used to tell people that when he'd signal for Walker to go into a game, he told him two words: "Sic 'em."

Walker was raised in Long Island, N.Y. As a youngster, he broke his leg in three places playing softball. "The doctors told me I'd never be able to run again like I once did," said Walker. "I wore a cast from my toes to my waist for one year. Every time I'd go to the doctor, he'd take the cast off, put another one on and say the leg wasn't ready yet. Finally, I got sick of the doctor and sick of the cast. One day, I jumped into a tub of hot water and peeled the cast off. I never went back to the doctor and the leg never bothered me again."

Walker's energy was boundless. Once, in a game at Portland, Cleamons was having a horrible first quarter. He couldn't do anything right. Fitch signaled for Walker. Over the next five minutes, Walker was everywhere. He was double-teaming, he was getting the team out on the break, he was tossing in 15-footers.

During a break in play, Fitch noticed Walker with his right hand up. He wanted out. Fitch was stunned. When Foots Walker put his hand up wanting out, something must be wrong. There was. Walker had literally run out of his sneakers. The soles were nearly flapping. He needed a new pair, which is why his hand was in the air. "I had never seen anything like that," said Fitch. Walker regularly went through a pair of shoes every two or three games.

"When they talk about overachievers," said Chones, "they talk about Foots Walker. This guy should not have played in the NBA. He was 147 pounds when he came to us. I roomed with him for a while. He's the biggest overachiever I've ever played with."

Adding Chones, Snyder, Russell and Walker to a team that already had Bingo Smith, Austin Carr, Jimmy Cleamons and Jim Brewer set the stage for the Cavaliers' best-season ever — a 40-42 record in 1974-75. What turned out to be the biggest game in the franchise's history was played on April 3, 1975 at the Coliseum. An NBA-record crowd of 20,239 watched the Cavaliers defeat the New York Knicks, 100-95. Mileti and Fitch openly wept when listening to the rousing ovation accorded the team for the introduction of the starting lineup. The victory in the 81st game of the season kept alive the team's playoff hopes. A victory three days later against Kansas City in Omaha, Nebraska, or a Knicks loss to the Buffalo Braves meant a playoff spot for the Cavaliers.

"Buffalo, though, went into the tank (a playoff spot assured, they lost, 105-93)," said Fitch. It meant the Cavaliers had to win in Omaha. They didn't. Falling behind by 14 points late in the game, they rallied behind Snyder and Brewer to pull within 95-94 with three seconds left. They inbounded the ball, but Fred Foster's 20-foot shot at the buzzer was partially blocked.

The stage, though, had been set for a miraculous season. The Cavaliers reported to Fitch at the Coliseum for the 1975-76 season in late September 1975. On the day they reported, he put them on a bus headed for Cleveland. The bus stopped at the old, run-down Cleveland Arena. "I wanted to open their eyes," said Fitch.

He did. Fitch and the entire team went into the arena. The 17 players and coaches looked around.

"When are they going to turn on the lights?," asked Butch Beard.

Austin Carr looked around. "Right there," he said, pointing, "is where the bench and scorers' table used to be."

Wrong, said Bingo Smith. "It was right there," he said pointing to another spot.

Steve Patterson interrupted. "Wait a minute," he said. "If anyone knows where the bench was it was me. It was right there." End of discussion.

The tour of the building John Havlicek once said he refused to dress in for fear of picking up an incurable disease was over after nine minutes. "We've got a lot to be thankful for," said Fitch, who then boarded the bus back to the Coliseum.

CHAPTER FOUR

"Miracle of Richfield"

The Miracle of Richfield season started out anything but miraculously. The pieces looked to be in place, but the Cavaliers were a puzzle. They were 6-11 nearing the quarter pole.

"Nothing was clicking," said Jim Chones. "It was almost like we were tired from the year before, when we had come so close to making the playoffs. There were some petty jealousies. Players were bitching about the time they were getting. Guys were questioning Fitch. All the things that eventually can tear a team apart were being set in place."

All of that changed on a day in late November. Fitch made a trade that not only turned the season around, but turned the franchise around. He sent Steve Patterson and Eric Fernstein to the Chicago Bulls for Rowland Garrett and Nate Thurmond.

"At the time," said Fitch, "the Bulls had two centers—Nate and Tom Boerwinkle. Nate wasn't scoring any points and they were losing. He was playing the high post in Dick Motta's offense and he didn't like it. He was a low-post player. They were in need of making a change. I thought I had a couple of young guys they could use. The timing was right to make the trade."

Thurmond, who played his first 11 seasons in San Francisco with the Warriors, was 34 at the time of the trade to the Cavaliers. "They said I was as much a fixture in the Bay Area as the Golden Gate Bridge," he said when dealt from the Warriors to Chicago. "Well, the bridge is still there and I got traded."

He knew he didn't have many years left if he was to get a championship ring. Fitch knew it, too. "I was ready to quit if I didn't play well the rest of that season," said Thurmond. "I wanted to play 14 seasons. If I had not played well, I was going to retire." The Bulls were 3-11 when they traded Thurmond. "I was being used as the scapegoat for their poor start," said Thurmond.

Thurmond lived in San Francisco, was a bachelor, made nearly $300,000 a year and enjoyed the good life. He owned a 1965 Rolls Royce. The license plate: Nate-42. He lived in an apartment that overlooked the city. He owned a restaurant—The Beginning. On the walls of the restaurant were pictures of his parents, who raised him in Akron, Ohio, not pictures of basketball-related awards. "I wanted something to always remember my beginnings from," he said. The restaurant's menu was principally soul food.

"I consider myself to be an adventurous person," he said. "About 35 percent of the people who come into my restaurant are white, which goes to show that I am not the only adventurous one in town. Of course, you can look at it from the standpoint that black people have been cooking for white people for so many years that it's probably no big deal."

Thurmond's late father, Andrew, worked at the Firestone Tire and Rubber company in Akron for 29 years. His mother, Leala, is a retired beautician. Thurmond attended Akron Central High School, where one of his teammates was the late Gus Johnson.

Central, though, never made it to the finals of the Ohio state basketball tournament. "It was disappointing," said Thurmond, "because Gus and I always wanted to play against (Jerry) Lucas. That's all people ever talked about at that time."

Fitch had a specific idea of what Thurmond's role with the Cavaliers would be. "When we got him," said Fitch, "I told Nate that I was going to play him about 18, 19 minutes a game. That's because we had this young turk in Jim Chones; he'd probably be able to play forever. He was the final piece.

"How soon did I know he'd be the final piece? I knew before we got him that he'd be it. I have always been a basketball junkie. I was one before I got into the league. When I was still coaching in college, we'd often come into some NBA town the day before our game and I'd go and watch the NBA game. Nate was the only guy I ever saw who could play the superstar centers

. . . the guys like Abdul-Jabbar and Chamberlain. I've been lucky in my coaching career. I've had some great centers. (Hakeem) Olajuwon (in Houston) was the greatest athlete I ever had in the pivot. (Dave) Cowens (in Boston) got as much out of a small body (6-9,230) as any center I've ever seen. (Ralph) Sampson (in Houston) was a big mystery. He was never as good as people thought he'd be, but he achieved some things while I had him.

"Nate Thurmond was a racehorse. He was a pure-bred. The first time he walked into our locker room, he had the respect of everyone on our team. That's the kind of person he was.

"I love Nate. He's on television every now and then in San Francisco. I can listen to him talk forever. He's got such an analytical mind. He was like that as a player. He was and is a real gentleman. He looks now the same as he did then. That's one thing about looking old when you're 30. You don't change. He had feet that looked like Hiroshima. He had those hammer toes. He once told me that his feet were so bad because as a kid, his family could not afford gym shoes and he had to wear hand-me-downs. He played in shoes that were a size too small; his brother (Ben) had smaller feet than he did.

"The funny thing about Nate is that he never tried to be a leader. He just was one. One of the reasons I really liked that team is because we developed a spirit and love for one another that you find in championship teams."

Austin Carr recalled one of the first games after Thurmond joined the team. "We were sitting around in the locker room before the game," Carr said. "Nate told us that he didn't have too many years left —one, maybe two—to get a championship ring. He said that we had the ability to win a championship, but there was a problem. We didn't believe in ourselves. That hit home. From that moment, we all changed. From then on, we all wanted to win one for that big guy. It became a crusade to win a championship for him. He had the unique ability of making guys believe in themselves."

With Thurmond playing behind Chones, the Cavaliers showed signs of being the playoff team that they were predicted to be. They won their first two games after the trade, then lost three straight. They were feeling their way around. Fitch elected to go with a starting lineup of Chones, Bingo Smith and Jim Brewer on the front line. Jimmy Cleamons and Dick Snyder were the backcourt starters. Coming off the bench were Thurmond, Carr, Foots Walker and Campy Russell. On paper it looked good. On the court, it started to look even better. The Cavaliers won seven straight, 10 of their next 11. In a 123-103 victory over the Kareem Abdul-Jabbar-led Los Angeles Lakers at The Forum in Los Angeles, Thurmond had nine points, nine rebounds, three assists and three blocked shots in 19 minutes.

"Coming here is like getting a new life to me," said Thurmond. "In Chicago, they told me I was through and the last thing an athlete wants to hear is that he is washed up. I know I can't run as fast as I used to. I know I can't jump as high as I used to. I do know, though, that I can help this team. I know defense. I want to make these guys believe in it. They all listen to me when I tell them about it. They have received me unbelievably well."

Particularly Chones, who occasionally was on the court at the same time as Thurmond.

"I loved playing with Nate," said Chones, "because you didn't have to rebound. See, Nate got every rebound. He got every defensive rebound. There were no offensive rebounds for them (the opposing team). The only time I saw a guy get an offensive rebound off Nate was Maurice Lucas. He's the only guy. When the ball went off the rim, you just turned around and started going the other way. Nate was from the old school. He prided himself on getting all the defensive rebounds. All you had to do was screen your man off."

Another veteran, Snyder, was becoming impressed. "This team is capable of running full-tilt for four quarters," he said. "It wasn't that way early in the season. By the time the fourth quarter came, we walked the ball upcourt because we were tiring."

But by mid-December, they were clicking. They were clicking because Fitch convinced everyone that his role was important, whether it was coming off the bench and playing 18 minutes or starting and playing 20. All four principals on the bench—Carr, Russell, Walker and Thurmond—could have started for just about any team in the league.

"The big difference, though, was Nate Thurmond," said Chones. "He was just what we needed. He was the key. He gave us a physical player and he was a guy who knew how to win. He was fearless. He played the same way whether he had five fouls or he had three fouls. He played with the same intensity in the first quarter or the fourth quarter. He was truly a leader, not so much verbally, but rather by example. And he was so physically dominating, even at his old age. He still dominated all the centers in the league. They couldn't shoot in his face. They weren't as aggressive as they'd be against other centers.

"When we got Nate, we were off to the races. The funny thing about all this is that when we got him, I was very paranoid. I was always paranoid and when we got Nate, I thought it was to get someone to take my place. I didn't have the confidence of these young kids today. Fitch told me not to worry. That he didn't bring Nate in here to take my job. I learned so much from Nate Thurmond, the way he carried himself. He had arrogance. He was cool. He was just one of those old cool guys. He kept us from being so childish.

"He was a pro in every sense of the word. I could see in the first day of practice with him that there was something different. He was a lot older, more mature. This is a guy who hung around Wilt. Every once and a while, he'd talk about Wilt and his eyes would light up. He demanded respect. He could hurt you. He had an upper body that looked like it came off a bodybuilder. And, he was just so suave."

Thurmond did little things, little things that Fitch remembered nearly 20 years later. With six seconds left in an 111-88 rout of Buffalo, Fitch was tapped on the knee. It was Thurmond.

"Let me go in there and get the big guy (Chones)," Thurmond said. "He's played a helluva game."

Fitch was stunned. "Imagine," he said, "a 13-year veteran who has already cooled off wanting to go back in just to make sure one of his teammates gets the recognition he deserves. The guy is just one beautiful person."

The Cavaliers won some improbable games during the regular season. They trailed, 51-34, after shooting 27 percent in the first half of a February game at Philadelphia. While Fitch extolled the team in the locker room at the half, a 650-pound bear named Victor wrestled anyone who wanted to wrestle him at midcourt.

"Six years ago," said Fitch, after the Cavaliers rallied from a 19-point deficit to win, 92-87, "if someone had told me I had my choice of coming out for the second half or wrestling that bear, I'd have wrestled him. Yes, I told these guys at the half that they could still win. The difference with this team, though, is that it just didn't sit there and listen. It got into the discussion and talked like it could do it."

In a March game at Portland, they trailed, 32-13, after 9 1/2 minutes and won, 113-100, when Carr, Thurmond, Walker, Russell and rookie John Lambert came off the bench to score 65 points.

"We hit rock bottom when we were down 32-13," said Fitch. "It was just like when you get a big boil — after a while it gets so bad, it finally bursts. At that point, I was willing to try any combination out there, even if it included running my grandmother in."

They came from five points down with two minutes left to beat the Bullets, 106-104, in a January game. It was a game in which many of the fans at the Coliseum left with two minutes remaining. "Those people probably wish they had stuck a potato in their exhaust pipes when they heard what happened," said Fitch.

They won a double-overtime game in Phoenix, 128-124, after Fitch was ejected. Carr sent the game into overtime by making two free throws with 0:00 on the clock. Fitch watched the game on television in the visitor's locker room. Upon entering the locker room after being tossed, he wrote the time (9:17 p.m.), the score of the game (Phoenix, 65-54). He also wrote: We will win this game.

"That game was huge," said Cavaliers play-by-play voice Joe Tait. "Two nights later, we came back to beat the Lakers at home (99-98) for our seventh in a row. At that point, you started to think that maybe there was something going on here."

Chones could sense something big was about to happen. "Everyone knew their roles, that was the thing," said Chones. "Jim Brewer was the consummate team player. Dennis Rodman is doing now what Brewer did for us in Cleveland. He never got the respect he deserved for what he did. He rebounded, he guarded smaller players, he guarded bigger players. He did it all for us. Jimmy Cleamons was a true leader. I think he's the best leader this franchise has ever had. He's just as good a leader as Mark Price is today and better. Clem was more verbal. He was always up, always ready to go. Fitch would cuss him out at times, but it never seemed to bother Clem. Campy (Russell) was a great talent, but he never reached his potential. He could have been a great player, but he had bad work habits. When he finally started to work hard, it was too late. Then, he tore up his knee and never recovered from it."

The Cavaliers finished the season with their best record ever—49-33. They were 43-22 after acquiring Thurmond and they won what remains to date their only Central Division title.

What followed were 36 of the most stirring days in the history of the franchise—the Miracle of Richfield. "You could not write enough about these guys," said *Plain Dealer* reporter Bill Nichols. "The Washington series was the greatest sporting event I will ever see in my life. The town was ready for something like this. I can only compare it to the '48 Indians. It was a month of nothing but frenzy."

The Cavaliers' first-ever playoff series became, and still is, considered the most memorable in franchise history. They met the Washington Bullets in a best-of-seven series that went seven games. Three of the games were decided by two points or less. All three were decided in the final seconds. Another went into overtime.

The Bullets (48-34) finished one game behind the Central Division-winning Cavaliers (49-33). They were coached by K.C. Jones and were a veteran team that had won 60 games, the Central Division title and had taken the Celtics into the East Finals the previous season before losing, 4-2, in a seven-game series.

They were one of the league's top defensive teams. Thanks to an interior that included 6-foot-9, 235-pound gazelle-like Elvin Hayes and 6-7, 245-pound tank-like Wes Unseld, opposing teams shot a league-low 44.2 percent against them and averaged 100.4 points. Only the Chicago Bulls (99.8) and Cavaliers (99.2) gave up fewer points.

They had a couple of snipers from the field in guard Phil Chenier and Dave Bing. Chenier, 25, was averaging a team-leading 19.9 points a game. Bing, 35, in the twilight of what would be a brilliant career, was averaging 16.2 points in 36 minutes a game.

How good was this group? Hayes, Unseld and Bing later were elected into the Basketball Hall of Fame.

Twenty years later, Chones reflected on the Washington series. "We knew we could beat the Bullets," Chones said, "because we had Nate. There was no way we were going to be intimidated by anyone. We had gained respect because of Nate." Brewer agreed. "What Nate brought to us," said Brewer, "was a maturity. A maturity on how you went about playing and the business of basketball. How you practiced. Up until he came, the leadership on our team was not very strong."

Fitch remained undaunted. "No matter what happens in these playoffs," he said, "I will still say we had a great season. Nothing can take away what we've accomplished so far. I'm not thinking in terms of losing. The Bullets are an excellent team. They can destroy you. They can also be beaten, though."

GAME 1: They can be beaten, huh? It did not look like it in Game 1.

An NBA playoff-record crowd, 19,994, rocked the Coliseum. Twenty minutes before— yes, before— the Cavaliers came out for their pre-game drills came the chant, "We want the Cavs! We want the Cavs! We want the Cavs! We want the Cavs!" It was not a polite request. It was a demand. It was nearly 20,000 wild-eyed, frenzied people demanding that a team they had fallen in love with come out and kick ass. It was so loud that the chalkboard Fitch used to diagram plays on in the locker room shook. "A couple of players had to hold it down for him," Austin Carr said.

Ten minutes before the tipoff came another relentless chant: "Let's go Cavs! Let's go Cavs! Lets go Cavs!" It cascaded from the upper loges into the players' ears. A guy in the stands hoisted a sign. It read: We Believe.

No one was believing after the first quarter. The Bullets' experience showed immediately. So did the Cavaliers' stage fright. With Hayes, Unseld, Chenier and Bing leading the way, the Bullets jumped out to a 37-19 lead in the first quarter. They shot 63 percent from the field, they owned the boards, 13-8, and they cakewalked to a 100-95 victory.

Hayes (28 points, 18 rebounds, three blocked shots) put the defensive clamps on a jittery Brewer, who missed 7 of 8 shots to score two points. Bing, hardly acting his age, hit 10 of 16 shots to tear up Snyder, who had a quiet eight points.

THE POST-GAME AUTOPSY: Fitch: "We didn't play as badly as it looked. If we were three games down, I wouldn't count these guys out. We've been one game and out for so long that we're not about to wave the white flag. We are either going to win this thing with a fight or lose it with a fight."

Snyder: "I've looked forward to this for a long time. I missed the playoffs for seven years and I'm not about to chuck it after one game."

Brewer: "We got our taste of the playoffs. We know what to expect. This thing is far from over."

Bing: "We're capable of playing even better. We didn't play well here all year, but this is for the money and the pride."

Hayes: "The playoffs are like starting over. They make an average player become good, a good player become great and a superstar become even greater. People try to tell you it's just another game, but it's not. I've seen teams come into the playoffs and be entirely different. The pressure is there. It's always on you. It's totally different.

"The noise? Listen, we've been here before. The noise just comes in and grasps you. I'm not taking anything away from the Cleveland fans, because they're great, but it's nothing like playing the Knicks at the Garden in a playoff game."

GAME 2: The series moved to the Capital Centre in Landover, Maryland. "We had to win there," said Nate Thurmond. They did, 80-79, when Bingo Smith hit what was labeled as the biggest shot in the six-year history of the franchise. Six seconds remained and the Bullets led, 79-78, when Bing was called for palming the ball. Time out, Cavaliers.

Taking the inbounds pass after the timeout, Smith dribbled a couple of times, rose up with defender Leonard (Truck) Robinson laying too far off, and hit a 25-footer with two seconds left. The Cavs won despite shooting 28 percent from the field in the first half to trail 46-36. They won despite shooting 34 percent for the game, and despite Campy Russell shooting 1 for 11.

They won because Cleamons and Snyder forced Bullets guard Chenier and Bing into 17 of the team's 25 turnovers and because Smith connected when the Cavaliers needed it most.

THE AUTOPSY: Fitch: "That was the worst first half I've ever seen anyone play and yet we were down by only 10. I'm just glad we got this monkey off our backs."

Snyder: "I feel this thing will be a real slugfest. I'd really be surprised if there are any runaways."

Robinson: "We should have put them away like we did in Cleveland. They've got the momentum now. They are an emotional bunch of guys and that crowd in Cleveland will really have them pumped."

GAME 3: Much of the Cavaliers' success during the regular-season was due to a bench that included Foots Walker, Campy Russell, Nate Thurmond and Austin Carr. Another NBA playoff-record roaring crowd at the Coliseum—21,061—watched the star-crossed Carr score 17 points in an 88-76 victory. Carr, who survived a twice-broken right foot and a twice-operated-on right knee, scored 13 points in the second quarter when the Cavaliers took command of the game and a 2-1 series lead.

"That's the best I've moved to the basket all year," said Carr, 28.

The Bullets were stunned. After outscoring the Cavaliers, 37-19, and outrebounding them, 13-8, in the first period of Game 1, they had been completely dominated. In the 11 subsequent quarters, they were outscored 244-218 and outrebounded, 142-128.

THE AUTOPSY: Hayes: "We're making those guys look like superstars. They're coming at us and shooting it right in our faces from everywhere and anywhere. We're the ones who should be controlling the games, but they are. They're pushing us all over, doing whatever they want. We can talk about how good we are, but we'd better start playing some basketball."

Carr: "I never thought (the playoffs) could be like this — even after we got into the new building. When I first came here (1971), there was a lot of negativism and I started thinking that way. It changed my personality. That's what losing does, especially when you are used to winning."

GAME 4: Bullets coach K.C. Jones shook up his rotation. Starting for the first time all season was Nick Weatherspoon, a 6-7, 205-pounder who had been buried so far in Jones' doghouse that he appeared in just four of 19 games for a total of 41 minutes from mid-February to late March. Weatherspoon had 19 points and 8 rebounds, but it was six-year vet Clem Haskins (22 points) who was most responsible for the Bullets 109-98 victory at Capital Centre that tied the series, 2-2.

THE AUTOPSY: Fitch: "Their bench was the difference. If they had gotten anything like that from their bench last year against Golden State in the Finals, they would have won four straight, not lost four straight. Tonight, the Bullets found new life."

Bullets owner Abe Polin: "Those bastards aren't going to win another game."

GAME 5: Those bastards did—and on an airball. The appetizers, the first four games of the series, were done. The main course was unfolding. And, boy, did it unfold in front of the NBA's third-straight record crowd of 21,312 at the Coliseum in Richfield. How loud was this crowd? It was so loud that with time running down—10 seconds, nine seconds, eight seconds—and the Cavaliers trailing, 91-90, none of them were able to hear their coach, Bill Fitch. He was wildly yelling for them to foul someone, anyone. Campy Russell, catching Fitch from the corner of his eye, grabbed Elvin Hayes. Seven seconds remained. If Hayes made one shot, the Cavaliers would need two points to tie the game. Two shots and it's over. Hayes choked on both. Rebound, Brewer. Time out, Cavaliers.

Taking the inbounds pass after time out, Bingo Smith attempted to duplicate his Game 2 heroics—a 25-footer that beat the Bullets. This time, though, Smith unleashed an airball from 14 feet.

While eight others watched the flight of the ball and did nothing, Cavaliers guard Jimmy Cleamons did something. He grabbed the ball, put up a reverse layup, and watched it crawl through the basket for a 92-91 Cavaliers victory.

THE AUTOPSY: Smith: "I wish I could say I planned it that way. I didn't. It was the little things like that that used to go against us. The little things that seem to turn in your favor when you become a winner. I used to think the Celtics were lucky when they won so many games like this. It's not luck. Things like this happen to teams when they become winners. Things like this used to happen to us for years. We were never able to do them to other teams. Now, it's different. Now, we're winners."

Fitch: "That was option number two. Were we lucky? Granted, the percentages of a team scoring with six seconds left on the clock two times to win games are not good. But we gave ourselves the chance to win both times. We made some of our 'luck."

Cleamons: "I watched Bingo make the move, watched the flight of the ball and saw that it was short. It wound up in my hands and I put it up. I knew I had put it up in time. I didn't know if it would go in, though, because it was not an easy shot. To me, it was just two points that gave us a 3-2 edge in the series."

Bing: "I can't put into words what I'm feeling right now. My mind is a blank. I don't ever recall losing two games like this before."

Hayes: "The game wasn't lost there (two missed free throws), man. You can pick any two missed foul shots during the game and say that they cost us. Why don't you ask the coach why . . . ask the coach why we lost. Don't talk to me."

Jones: "One thing we all have learned about the Cavaliers this season—they will play you for 48 minutes."

GAME 6: Carr scored 27 points in 31 minutes off the bench, but the Cavaliers' starting backcourt—Cleamons and Snyder— shot a combined 4 of 27 from the field for a total of 14 points. The result? The Bullets, despite blowing a 17-point lead, won in overtime, 102-98, at Capital Centre. Washington's victory tied the series, 3-3. Hayes roughed up Chones and Thurmond for 28 points, 13 rebounds and eight blocked shots. Unseld had 18 rebounds and eight assists, Chenier 24 points in 49 minutes.

THE AUTOPSY: Snyder, one of the game's best pure shooters, tried to explain missing 8 of 9 shots from the field. He had an ice pack on his left shoulder. "I wish I could blame it on this," he said, pointing to the ice pack, "but I can't." He couldn't because he is right-handed.

Fitch, commenting on the series going down to one game, said: "There is enough pressure going into this last game without putting anymore on ourselves. We have no intention of losing this thing now, but if we do, the world is not going to end. I have told my guys that this will not be the last important game they will ever play. The thing I won't let my players do is feel that we've blown it all if we lose one game."

Jim Brewer: "I'm glad we're going back to Cleveland. The home court is going to mean a lot to us."

How close were these two teams? After six games, the overall point totals were Bullets 557, Cavaliers 551.

GAME 7: After six games, 47 minutes and 51 seconds, the series still had not yet been decided. With nine seconds remaining, it was a tie game, 85-85. All 21,564 fans at the Coliseum stood. Time out, Cavaliers.

Taking the inbounds pass, Dick Snyder eluded Wes Unseld. "I had my head buried in his chest and I couldn't see up the court," said Snyder. A fake inside opened things up. Snyder had an open lane to the basket. Twelve feet from the rim, he was confronted by Phil Chenier. Snyder threw up a high-arching shot, a shot that barely eluded Chenier's outstretched fingers. The ball bounced off the backboard and through the basket. Cavaliers 87, Bullets 85. Time out, Washington. Four seconds left.

"I could not be elated when I made that shot," said Snyder. "I had four more seconds of dealing with Phil Chenier."

The game and the series ended when Elvin Hayes could not get his hands on a midcourt pass. Chenier did, but missed an off-balance 10-footer on the baseline as time expired. "I could have used one more second," said Chenier, who hit 14 of 21 attempts for 31 points.

Mass hysteria took over when Chenier's shot missed. The fans stormed the court. "I have never experienced anything like that in my life," Carr said years later. "It was unreal. I remember looking over my shoulder and seeing people coming at me. They were coming from everywhere. They were frantic. It was like a flood, like something happened. I got weak in my knees. The noise, I'll never forget the noise."

THE AUTOPSY: Snyder: "This is my biggest thrill in basketball. I don't want to play these guys again."

Chenier: "What happened in this series just proves there is too much emphasis put on the experience factor. It doesn't take long—a few seconds, the first shot in the first game—and you've got your experience."

Thurmond: "People haven't seen the real Cavaliers in the playoffs yet."

The victory over the Bullets earned the Cavaliers a best-of-seven Eastern Conference Finals series against the 12-time NBA champion Boston Celtics.

These Celtics were a blend of aging veterans and youthful veterans. John Havlicek and Don Nelson were 36. Paul Silas was 33. The brilliant youth was in Charlie Scott, 25, Dave Cowens, 27, and Jo Jo White, 28. It was a fast-breaking team coached by Tommy Heinsohn, one that had the best record in the East at 54-28. "If the Celtics get running well," said Snyder, "there is no way we will beat them. I do think we have the rebounding to contain their break."

Not for long. On the evening of May 4, 1976, two nights before Game 1 against the Celtics, Chones suffered a break in the fifth metatarsal bone of the right foot.

"I remember it like it was yesterday," Chones said years later. "I went up to block a shot put up by Campy (Russell) and came down on someone else's foot. I heard it snap. I knew right away it was broken. There was a reporter there. Fitch asked me if I could try to walk normal to go downstairs to get it X-rayed." The X-rays were positive.

"The sad part about this," said Chones, "is that I was more sure of beating Boston than I was of beating Washington. I thought we could win it in six. We played Boston off their asses the previous time we played them (a 101-92 victory in Boston one month earlier). Foots (Walker) ate them up."

Without Chones, Fitch put up a brave front. "Really," he said, "the pressure is on the Celtics now. They are going to have to go around and say they got beat by the Cavaliers when they didn't have Jim Chones. As for Jim Chones, he would have played with a cast on his foot and with crutches if I told him he could. That's the kind of person he is."

Games 1 and 2 of the series were at Boston Garden. Chones was there on crutches. "Hell," said Fitch, "we'd miss all the noise on the team bus if he wasn't there. No one makes more noise than Jim Chones."

Thurmond more than held his own in Game 1, getting 16 points and nine rebounds in a team-high 39 minutes, but the Cavaliers were overpowered by Havlicek and Silas in a 111-99 loss. The Havlicek-Silas combo outscored Bobby (Bingo) Smith and Jim Brewer, 47-4. White added 20 points, Cowens 14 points and 12 rebounds.

Havlicek, six months older than Thurmond, was asked about the Cavaliers' backup center playing big minutes. "Thurmond can get himself accustomed again to playing 35 minutes," Havlicek said. "After all, he's younger than I am."

The Celtics took a 2-0 lead in the series with a 94-89 victory in Game 2. It was a game that got away when Thurmond fouled out on a disputed call with 7:36 left in the fourth quarter and the Cavaliers trailing, 75-73.

Cowens, coming across the middle, put up a shot that appeared to be blocked by Thurmond. Official Darrell Garretson saw it otherwise, whistling Thurmond for the foul that sent him to the bench. It left the Cavaliers with two journeymen— John Lambert and Luke Witte—to go up against Cowens. Thurmond was uncharacteristically livid. "A referee just doesn't guess on the sixth personal foul of a playoff game," he said. "There's a lot of money on the line. A lot of pride."

CBS-TV play-by-play announcer Brent Mussberger later told Thurmond replays showed that Thurmond did not foul Cowens. That infuriated Thurmond more.

"Dave Cowens is a good basketball player," said Thurmond, "but he isn't the best. He is not a Wilt (Chamberlain), a Russ (Bill Russell) or a Kareem (Abdul-Jabbar). He's just a good basketball player."

A Boston writer asked what the series would be like if Chones had been wearing a uniform instead of a cast. "If we had the real Cavaliers," Thurmond said, "Boston wouldn't be in this series. If they were lucky, they might have taken it to five games. They have five players and that's it. We're without our leading scorer, and if this game had been called right, the series would be 1-1, not 0-2."

Thurmond's fireworks were not all that followed Game 2. A simmering feud between Mileti and Fitch exploded when Mileti ripped Fitch while on United Air Lines flight No. 999 from Boston to Cleveland. Mileti claimed Fitch wanted out of his contract, which had two years remaining at $75,000 a season, to become the head coach of the Los Angeles Lakers. He said he was upset with Fitch continually saying he was underpaid, and labeled him as an ordinary coach.

In a wide-ranging interview with the *Cleveland Press*, Mileti said: "He (Fitch) said he wanted out of his contract, that he had a chance to go to Los Angeles and wanted to take the job. I was shocked. But, he miscalculated (Lakers owner) Jack Kent Cooke. Jack never contacted me. I carried Bill Fitch for all those years that he won 15, 20 games. Now, he wants to be a front-runner and feather his own nest. He wants to be a star.

"I am from the old school. A contract is like a coin. It has two sides. I honored his when we were going bad and I now expect mine to be honored. The average salary of an NBA coach today is $61,000. You can look it up. I tore up Bill Fitch's contract with one year to go on it last June and signed him for three years at $75,000 a year. With other benefits, he can make up to $100,000. Bill Fitch wanted a contract from Day One. He said he wanted the security. He got it. He threatened breach of contract and a lot of other things. If he followed up with some of his threats, he'd never get another job in the NBA.

"Some of the threats are so sophomoric and idiotic it's unbelievable. I told him, 'You know what? I've been threatened by the best. Good luck, Billy, you do it.' I told him to think about it. I told him two things his father would tell him. Number one, I don't think you want to be known in your profession as a front-runner. It is not in your best interest. Number two, it would not be in the best interest of the club. It would be very hard to say a contract has meaning to players if an exception was made here."

Mileti evaluated Fitch's job as general manager and coach. "As a general manager," he said, "he's done a hell of a job. As a coach, he's just ordinary. Did he ever ask to leave the club before? No, he was a loser. Bill Fitch has underestimated me. This is no game, this is a business. It is not easy making a $1 million payroll when your club is 15-67 and there is no attendance. He didn't have to make sure that was done. I did."

Mileti's attack stunned Fitch. "First of all," he said, "I am shocked. I am shocked that he would carry on this matter in the newspapers and especially at a time when we are in a championship series. I categorically deny I ever requested to leave to coach the Los Angeles Lakers or anyone else. That is all I will say."

Nearly 20 years later, Fitch again denied he wanted out to coach the Lakers.

The Mileti-Fitch blowup set the stage for Game 3, which the Cavaliers won, 83-78. With Thurmond anchoring the middle and playing 40 minutes —he had nine rebounds, six points, six assists, four blocked shots and three steals—the Cavaliers held the Celtics to 34 percent shooting from the field in cutting Boston's lead in the series to 2-1. The Celtics' 78 points matched their all-time playoff low since the 24-second shot clock was introduced 22 years earlier.

"I think Nate lied about his age when he was a kid," said Fitch. "I don't think he's really 34. We are adjusting better with

Nate the more we play. We're becoming more comfortable. We're not getting a lot of points, but we're not panicking, either."

Cowens and Silas combined for 41 rebounds, nearly outrebounding the Cavaliers, who had 44. Cleamons, playing 43 minutes, led the Cavaliers with 18 points. Doug Clarke wrote in the *Cleveland Press*: "If the air in the Celtics locker room seems vaguely fraught with concern over one Nate Thurmond, it's because he has already changed the shape of this playoff series."

Fitch was asked how many times Thurmond would be capable of playing 35 to 40 minutes a game. "Nate promised me he is not going to get tired until the cast comes off Jim Chones' foot," said Fitch.

Fitch added that when he wanted to take Thurmond out of a game, he had to send in two guys to do it. "One goes out to replace him," said Fitch, "and the other goes out to pull him off the floor."

An ailing foot sent Havlicek to the bench early in the first quarter of Game 4 at the Richfield Coliseum. It was all the Cavaliers needed. With Havlicek out, Bingo Smith hit 13 of 17 shots over Don Nelson and Steve Kuberski, scoring 27 points in a 106-87 Cleveland victory that tied the series at 2-2. Thurmond, playing 37 minutes, forced Cowens into missing 15 of 20 shots from the field.

Cowens was stunned. "I'm not talking," said Cowens. "I'm not being uncooperative, but I don't have a thing to say." Teammate Paul Silas did. "We are playing right into his (Thurmond's) hands," said Silas. "We're trying to force things inside and power is his game. We've got to make him work harder."

It was a tough game for Celtics coach Heinsohn. He and Cleamons nearly came to blows in the first quarter over some courtside comments Cleamons made. After the game, as the Celtics headed for their locker room, a fan dumped a beer on Heinsohn. "They hit me with the whole thing, the whole damn thing," said Heinsohn. "Beautiful Cleveland. 21,000 kids. Crazy."

Game 5 was back at Boston Garden. The Celtics won, 99-94, but it wasn't easy. They pulled out all the stops. Minutes before the tipoff, they sent Havlicek through the runway from the Celtics locker room and onto the court, a la Willis Reed in Game 7 of the Knicks-Lakers NBA Finals of 1970. Heinsohn got himself thrown out with two minutes left in the third quarter, and none other than Red Auerbach, who had not coached the Celtics in 10 years, left his seat in the stands for one next to the press table.

"What I will always remember about that," said long-time Cavaliers play-by-play voice Joe Tait, "is that as he is walking over, he pulls out a cigar and the place goes crazy. They run off a bunch of points and it is just about all over."

Amazingly, it wasn't just about over earlier. Obviously intent on getting Thurmond into foul trouble, the Celtics succeeded. He had four by the middle of the second quarter. Cowens went to work, getting a playoff-high 26 points, 11 rebounds and six assists. Yet, it took two free throws by Havlicek with 14 seconds left to ice the game. Bob August wrote in the *Cleveland Press*: "The Cavaliers go back into the Coliseum tomorrow night one game down, but with no reason to be dispirited. After all, the mighty (Washington) have fallen in the other playoff. This could be the year of the underdog."

It wasn't. With 21,564 wild and crazies believing there would be a Game 7 in Boston, the Celtics won Game 6 and ended the series at the Coliseum. The Celtics' poise won it. Cleamons, Russell and Snyder shot a combined 17 percent (6 of 35) from the field. Carr had 26 points, but it wasn't enough. Smith had 16 points, but it wasn't enough. Thurmond, playing 43 minutes, had 14 rebounds and 13 points. Yet, it wasn't enough. The Celtics, with White, Cowens and Scott scoring 29, 21 and 20 points, respectively, advanced to the NBA Finals against Phoenix by coming from two down—69-67—at the end of the third quarter to outscore the Cavaliers, 27-18, in the last 12 minutes.

The Cavaliers had run out of miracles. It was a bitter pill for them to swallow. With 17 seconds left, Smith fouled out. Taking a seat next to Fitch, he broke down and cried.

"A lot of things went through my mind there on the bench," said Smith. "They say that right before you die, your whole life passes before your eyes. Right then, all our mistakes—during the season and tonight—flashed through my mind."

In the locker room, Nate Thurmond sat on a stool and bowed his balding head. He wept openly, figuring his last shot at a championship ring was gone.

"I don't think experience had anything to do with this," said Thurmond. "I don't think the best team won either, but that is sour grapes. We had a lot of guys with a lot of heart and this is a tough thing to swallow. Time is running out for me. I've been this far before. Just one time, I want to go all the way."

Years later, several of the Cavaliers looked back at the Miracle of Richfield.

"I have been told that series against us is the only one in which Dave Cowens did not foul out of at least one game," said Chones. "He didn't have to foul Nate. Nate played brilliantly, but he played a lot of minutes and a lot of them were tired minutes. They got a lot of easy baskets. No one got easy baskets when Nate and I were out there. When we were out there, it was like going through the trees.

"I never realized how good we were until years later when I played with the Lakers and we won a championship. I remember the night we took the championship. I was sitting in my hotel room in Philadelphia afterwards and I was watching television. Everyone was outside cheering. I started crying and said to myself, 'Damn we had a championship team in Cleveland.'

"I'll never forget those crowds at the Coliseum. They will never be like that again. These players today have no idea what it is like to be cheered by a crowd that is totally in love with you. All they cared about is that you made the effort. They didn't care about missing layups, missing jump shots. They wanted to be a part of it all."

Jim Brewer talked about the noise. "The thing I remember was how loud it was before every game," Brewer said. "There was a policy then that the building could not be open until a certain time. When it was opened, the people stormed in. The building rocked. I had never heard anything like that before and I've never heard anything like that since."

Added Austin Carr: "Do you realize what it takes to make a concrete building like that vibrate? But they did it with all their screaming and stomping. That's what was most amazing to me."

Jimmy Cleamons perhaps said it best. He said the fans became an extension of the players.

"The fans needed something to latch on to and we were it," said Cleamons. "It was true joy and enthusiasm. We were the bums from nowhere. This is a team, though, that got respect. I like to tell a story about when I was a rookie playing with the Lakers. We had a big calendar of all the games in the locker room. Every time you came to Cleveland, there was already a 'W' put down. The Lakers just knew they would win any game against the Cavaliers. That changed. Our team in 1975-76 gained the respect of the league. I'm proud to have been a part of it."

CHAPTER FIVE

"The Voice"

A Cavaliers radio broadcast never has been and never will be a Cavaliers radio broadcast unless Joe Tait is doing the broadcasting.

Tait is a legend in Cleveland radio. He is to the Cavaliers what Chick Hearn is to the Los Angeles Lakers; what the late Johnny Most was to the Boston Celtics.

Tait has the knack of getting followers of a Cavaliers game to become emotionally involved. Jump into the car on a zero-degree winter night in Northern Ohio, run the radio dial and pick up Tait's voice. It takes just minutes to get an idea of how the Cavaliers are doing.

Tait's feelings cannot be hidden behind his voice, which always gives him away. There is a sense of urgency in his voice if the Cavaliers are in the midst of wiping out a sizable deficit. There is a sense of anxiety in his voice if they are in the midst of losing a sizable lead. There is a sense of "oh-boy-do-I-feel-good-about-myself" when the Cavaliers are pounding someone. There is a sense of nothingness when the Cavaliers are being pounded.

The Miracle of Richfield season was Tait's coming out. Fans taped his broadcasts of the playoff series against the Washington Bullets and Boston Celtics. A record was cut. Tait's voice became the official stamp on a Cavaliers game.

Tait, now 57, grew up on a farm in Evanston, Illinois. His athletic career began as a 5-foot-8, 185-pound, 10-year-old in Aurora, Illinois, when he was handed a football uniform.

"I put the helmet on sideways," he said. "I was looking through an ear hole and thought to myself that this must really be a tough game to play."

He played basketball for two years at Aurora High School. "I played basketball on the junior varsity reserves my sophomore and junior seasons," he said. Not much basketball, though. In two years, he took one shot.

"I remember it well," he said. "Our team was up something like 75-25 and the coach put me in. I always said that if I ever got into a game, I was going to try a halfcourt hook shot. I used to practice that shot. The coach told me that if I ever took it in a game, I'd be finished."

Not long after getting into the game, Tait was in the vicinity of halfcourt. He stopped, looked over at his coach and fired up a halfcourt hook shot. "There was a sub already coming onto the floor while the ball was still in the air," said Tait. The shot went in.

"Not too many guys end their basketball careers shooting 1.000," he said.

Tait used to play golf frequently, but cut that down to once a year in the mid-1970s when he regularly played in a Boy Scout outing. In three years of playing in that outing, he shot scores of 138, 142 and 144. "When I was playing regularly," he said, "like two or three times a week, I wasn't bad. I'd get my scores down to 110 or 115."

Tait attended Monmouth College, Monmouth, Illinois, and while in school there, got a job working at radio station WRAM. Included in the job was broadcasting Monmouth College football games. "The football team was horrible," said Tait. "I think it won something like six games in five years."

While doing Monmouth College football games, Tait became friends with an assistant football coach from Coe College, Cedar Rapids, Iowa. The assistant's name was Bill Fitch, who often scouted for the Coe College team.

"We saw a lot of each other," said Tait, "and we became friends. He was always kidding me. Monmouth would be losing something like 66-0, and he'd tell me I had it sounding exciting, like it was a 6-6 tie."

Fitch was Tait's first-ever interview. "He ragged on me all the time," said Tait. "I must have used him as my halftime guest six times a season." Tait bounced from radio station to radio station around the Midwest after he left Monmouth. Occasionally, he'd run into Fitch.

Not long after Fitch was named the Cavaliers' first coach in 1970, Tait sent a letter of congratulations. "I added a P.S.," said Tait. "I wrote that if he ever needed someone to do for the Cavaliers what I used to do for the Monmouth College Fighting Scots, just give me a call."

Cavaliers owner Nick Mileti had not named a full-time radio broadcaster when the Cavaliers opened their first season in October 1970. The first seven games were done by Bob Brown, a Mileti associate who worked for the organization.

Mileti talked to Fitch one day about the broadcasting job. He said he wanted someone doing the radio play-by-play who had never done pro basketball before. He wanted someone who could make a bad team sound fun and exciting.

Fitch smiled. "I know just the guy," he said. "I don't know where he is, but I'll track him down."

Tait was managing a radio station in Terre Haute, Indiana. "Basically," he said, "I was going nowhere in broadcasting. I had given up about getting an on-the-air (play-by-play) job." Fitch telephoned Tait. "He wanted me to come to Cleveland and do a tape," said Tait.

Here is what Tait's resume looked like when he applied for the Cavaliers job in October 1970:

Year	Station- City	Job description
1969-70	WBOW, Terre-Haute, IN	Station manager, disc jockey
1968-69	WIOK, Normal, IL	Sports, disc jockey
1966-68	WOVB, Athens, OH	Sports
1965-66	WREX-TV Rockford, IL	Sports director
1965-66	WLRL, Rockford, IL	News, sports, disc jockey
1964-65	WILO, Frankfort, IN	Sports, disc jockey
1964	WJRL, Rockford, IL	News, sports, disc jockey
1963-64	WDZ, Decatur, IL	Disc jockey, sports
1960-63	U.S. Army Security Agency	
1957-60	WRAM, Monmouth, IL	Sports, news, sales
1956-57	WFS Monmouth, IL	Campus radio station

The Cavaliers' first home game ever was played at the Cleveland Arena in October 1970. They lost, 110-99, to the San

Diego Rockets. As Bob Brown broadcasted the game live on the air, Tait did a tape of the game while sitting in the hockey press box. Afterward, he gave the tape to Brown and went back to his hotel.

The next morning, he got a call from Mileti, who wanted Tait to come over to the team's offices. "He asked me if I wanted the job," said Tait. "I told him that I guess I did."

Mileti said there was one problem. "Joe," he said, "I don't have any money to pay you. I can afford to pay you $100 a game. We'll be doing 72 games the rest of the year."

Tait was making, including salary and commission, about $14,000 a year in Terre Haute. "He (Mileti) was asking me to come to Cleveland to take a 50 percent paycut," said Tait, "and I did. I looked at it like this: At long last, after about 15 years, I was finally getting the shot I always wanted. I figured that it might never happen again and I might end up hating myself for the rest of my life if I didn't take it."

Tait returned to Terre Haute. "I told my wife at the time (Edith) that we were going to Cleveland," he said. "She wasn't too thrilled. When I said I had to take a 50 percent paycut to take the job, she really wasn't too thrilled."

While driving to Cleveland several days later, Tait tuned in the Cavaliers-Philadelphia game that was being played in Philadelphia. The Cavaliers were en route to being pounded, 141-87. The 54-point loss remains the worst in franchise history. "You can just imagine what I thought listening to that game," said Tait. "I'll never forget it. Andy Musser was doing the play-by-play, Sonny Hill was doing the color commentary.

"After the first five minutes, they began ripping the Cavaliers unmercifully. They said it was the worst team they had ever seen. They said it had no talent. They questioned how anyone in Cleveland would spend so much as a dime to see this team play. They said the franchise would fold by the All-Star Game. If not by then, certainly after one year. That would be it. Expansion might work in Portland and Buffalo, but it was never going to work in Cleveland. They just kept chopping and chopping and chopping.

"By the end of the broadcast, it did not seem to all concerned that I had made a wise decision."

Tait's first NBA broadcast was a Cavaliers game in Buffalo. "I was all set to accompany the team on the trip to Buffalo," said

Tait. "A secretary in the office had given me a wrong time for the team's departure, though. I missed the flight by more than two hours. It was a Saturday and there were no other flights there. As I was paying for my parking at the airport, I asked the attendant how far it was to Buffalo.

"He told me it was about 200 miles. He told me to get on (Interstate) 90 East. I did, and that's how I got to my first game." To supplement his income during that season, Tait worked on daily and weekend newscasts for two Cleveland radio stations. He also was the voice for two area auto speedways. "Nick Mileti told me the day I took the job," said Tait, "that he'd make up for it some day." Mileti did. The day an ownership group he headed bought the Cleveland Indians two years later, Mileti called Tait and offered him the job to broadcast their games.

During the first four years he worked for the Cavaliers, Tait was relatively unknown around the league. The team was so bad, not many people listened, not many people cared. It did not mean, though, he did not make some memorable calls.

The Cavaliers were 0 for the franchise at 0-15 when they arrived in Portland for a game against the Trail Blazers in November 1970. With the skull Fitch had purchased at a curio shop propped up near the bench, the Cavaliers hung on for their first-ever victory, 105-103. "Winning that game," said Tait, "was even tougher than it looked. With the game clock headed for triple zeroes, I was yelling like crazy that the Cavaliers were winners for the first time. I kept saying it was over, it was over, it was over.

"One problem. The final buzzer never sounded. All I could say was that, well, maybe it's not over. The officials met near the official scorer for what seemed like hours. They broke up, finally ruling that, yes, it was over."

Fitch constantly pulled tricks on Tait. Tait, a hefty fellow who loves to eat and eat fast, sat down with Fitch one night after a game on the West Coast. Fitch was drinking a cup of coffee. Tait ordered a Hyatt Riot, the largest sundae made by the Hyatt hotels. The sundae was placed in front of Tait. Fitch watched it disappear.

While Tait was wiping his mouth, Fitch pulled out a stop watch. "New record," said Fitch.

"What are you talking about?," asked Tait.

"You've just set a new record for eating a Hyatt Riot," said Fitch. "One minute, 20 seconds."

Tait regularly took on-the-air shots at the league's officiating crews. At one of the team's weekly downtown luncheons where numerous league topics were discussed, Fitch mentioned that Atlanta broadcaster Skip Carey had been fined $2,000 for detrimental remarks aimed at the officials. Moments later, Fitch looked at Tait and said, "Joe I hate to inform you of this, but not long ago we got this wire from the league. I thought you should have it. Read it, but not aloud."

Fitch handed the wire to Tait, whose eyes immediately got large.

"Come on, Joe, read it," said someone in the audience. Reluctantly, Tait did.

"Due to your constant harassment of the officials," the wire read, "and comments that were made that are not in the best interest of the NBA, I hereby fine you $2,000 for your conduct on the air." It was signed by league commissioner J. Walter Kennedy.

"I got sick while reading this," said Tait. "All I could think was, 'My God, where am I going to get $2,000 to pay this fine?' Near the end of the hour-long luncheon, Fitch turned to Tait and said, 'By the way, Joe, the wire was a fake.'

"For nearly one hour," said Tait, "I was dying."

Tait emceed these luncheons, which were attended by the downtown businessmen. Oftentimes, players were the guests. One of the guest players was Barry Clemens. Clemens was an intelligent player who survived in the NBA because he had a good outside shot. He also stuttered.

Tait called Clemens up to say a few words. Clemens did. "I'dddddd liiiiiike tttttto tttteeeeelll yooooooou guuuuuuuys abbbbbbbout mmmmmmmmmy caaaaaareeeeer, bbbbbbbut IIIIII knnnnnnnnow yooooooooou haaaaaave tooooo geeeet baaaaack tooooooo woooooork iiiiiiiiin annnnnnnnnn hooooour," he said, smiling.

The audience broke up in laughter.

Clemens also said he'd like to get into coaching some day, but said that by the time he got the pre-game speech out of the way, it would be halftime.

Fitch was notorious for watching game films. He watched them day and night. Years later, he picked up a nickname: Captain Video. While on the road, Tait often killed time by watching the tapes with Fitch.

"It got to the point," said Tait, "where I knew the offense better than the players did. In fact, it began screwing up my play-by-play. I'd see one of the guards come down the court and signal what play was about to be run. I would anticipate the play before it was actually run. When it wasn't run right, I was the one looking like a fool."

Tait was present for a film session Fitch was holding with Mike Mitchell, then a rookie, in 1978. "Fitch kept trying to get Mike to understand a certain play," said Tait. "He kept going over it again and again with him. Mike could not understand it. Finally, Fitch paused, looked over at me and asked if I could understand what he was trying to get across. I said I did.

"Fitch looked at Mike and said, 'Come on now, Mike, this guy broadcasts our games. If he can get it, you've got to be able to get it.' "

Tait befriended many of the players. On one Thanksgiving, he invited Dwight Davis, Cornell Warner and Warner's brother to his home for dinner. Davis brought his fianceé.

"At the time," said Tait, "I had two shepherd dogs. Not long after Dwight got out of the car, one of the shepherds came off the back porch, jumped over the railing and headed for the car as everyone was getting out. Dwight looked up and not only saw the first shepherd, but the second one coming right after the first." Davis, not knowing where else to go and scared to death of dogs, jumped on top of the car. "Cornell was still in the car," said Tait. "He was laughing so hard, he was crying. His brother kept saying that he should get out and help Dwight. Cornell kept saying that there was no way he was getting out of that car."

Tait said that only one Cavaliers player ever refused an interview. It was in the early 1970s and the player was Greg (Stretch) Howard, a 6-9, 215-pounder who usually walked around with a scowl on his face. "Our first exhibition game that season was in Cincinnati," said Tait. "I walked into the locker room and approached Stretch to ask for a pre-game interview."

"I don't want to talk to you," Howard said.

"I said OK and told him I was sorry I asked," said Tait, who turned around and left the room.

Moments later, with Tait gone, Rick Roberson, a 6-9, 235-pound center with a scowl that could match anyone's, walked over to Howard. Pointing his finger in Howard's face, Roberson said, "Hey, that's the only guy who has good things to say about us. You talk to him. Don't ever give him that kind of shit again."

Howard got up and walked out the door. "Hey, buddy," he said, calling for Tait. "About that interview. I'll do it."

"He gave me a good interview," said Tait. "The funny thing about Stretch is that I had heard on several occasions that he just didn't like white people. Yet, I can remember one day when we were in New Mexico to play an exhibition game, I saw him walk out of the hotel and give a friendly greeting to the nicest white couple you'd want to see."

Tait is not the only media member with memories of Howard, who played 48 games of one season (1971-72) for the Cavaliers. "He got very upset with me once after I wrote that he and Luther Rackley were vying for the center spot," said Bill Nichols, who covered the Cavaliers 11 seasons for the *Cleveland Plain Dealer*. "I was talking to him one day during training camp. We were standing in front of his locker. He opened it up. Out fell a gun. I looked up. He had several others in there. I stayed away from writing any confrontational stuff about him after that."

Tait always marveled at the reaction of the general public to seeing a group of black guys who stood anywhere from 6-5 to 7-foot traveling around the country. "I got on an elevator once with Jim Brewer, Bob Rule and Fred Foster at the Dell Webb Townhouse in Arizona," said Tait. "We go up a couple of floors and this little guy, a casper milquetoast sort, steps on. He pushes the button for the eighth floor and looks around to see four of the biggest, blackest, not-very-friendly-looking guys he'd ever want to see. No one is smiling.

"The elevator stops at the sixth floor. He excuses himself and says he must have pushed the button for the wrong floor. With that Fred informs him that he's punched eight and that's where he is going to get off. We get to the eighth floor, the door opens and the guy leaps out. The doors close and everyone is going berserk."

Tait often served as a buffer between the club and the public. While the public might not necessarily believe Fitch or

Mileti, they seemed to believe Tait and his down-home style of handling potentially touchy situations.

Like during the days in the early 1970s when the Cavaliers announced they were leaving the Cleveland Arena for a new facility 25 miles to the south in rural Richfield. "The attitude was negative from everywhere," said Tait. "People in Cleveland and near Cleveland were upset that the team was leaving the city and they would have to drive 20 or 25 miles to see the games. People in the area were upset because they did not want their pristine lifestyle upset."

One day, while the Coliseum in Richfield was under construction, Mileti took Tait for a tour. "So," asked Mileti, "what do you think?"

"I think," said Tait, "that one day this will be the largest corn crib in Summit County."

Tait recalled a time when Mileti was scheduled to speak to the Richfield PTA. "He chickened out," said Tait. "He sent me, instead. I had to go out there and face those people who had everything but a rope, tar and feathers. They were mad. It was like throwing a lamb to the wolves. Somehow, though, I staggered through it."

Years later, after it was announced that the Cavaliers were moving from the Coliseum to a new downtown arena, Tait recalled speaking at a father-son banquet at the United Church of Christ in Richfield. It was located across the street from the Richfield elementary school he spoke in 20 years earlier. "Now," said Tait, "they were mad about the Cavaliers moving away and back to Cleveland. They were mad about the money the businesses in the area would be losing and about the monies they would be losing in taxes."

Tait looked out into the audience that day and said, "I am sure that some of you people in the audience today were here in 1974. You don't know how funny it is to hear you moaning and groaning about the fact that the Cavaliers are leaving. You people wanted to burn that place (the Coliseum) down 20 years ago."

Tait could broadcast Cavaliers basketball for the next 25 years, but he will always be linked to the Miracle of Richfield season — 1975-76. Particularly the seven-game playoff series against the Washington Bullets. Bobby (Bingo) Smith hitting the buzzer-beating 22-footer over Leonard (Truck) Robinson to win Game 2 in Washington, 80-79; Jimmy Cleamons putting back a Smith airball to beat the buzzer and the Bullets, 92-91, to win Game 5 at the Coliseum; Dick Snyder hitting an off-balance running one-hander to beat the Bullets, 87-85, to win Game 7 and the series at the Coliseum.

No player on that team was more admired by Tait than Nate Thurmond, the 34-year-old warhorse who parlayed professionalism with a hellish 17 minutes on the court to become the final piece that had as much to do with the Miracle of Richfield as anyone.

Before Thurmond was acquired by the Cavaliers in the deal that sent Steve Patterson to Chicago in late November 1975, the Cavaliers were 6-11. After Thurmond, they went 43-22 over the next 65 regular-season games to win the Central Division title with a 49-33 record. Tait, like many people, didn't give much thought to the trade at the time it was made.

"No one, including me," said Tait, "thought he had anything left. The general opinion seemed to be that maybe some folks would come from Akron to see the team play because Nate was from Akron. That was it."

That wasn't it. "Nate came with an unbelievable presence," said Tait. "Fitch was smart enough to know how to use him and not to hassle him. Nate, in turn, became a coach on the floor."

Tait recalled an incident not long after Thurmond arrived. It gave a hint to what Thurmond's value would be. "We had played a game in Milwaukee," said Tait, "and the next morning we couldn't get out because there was so much fog in the area. We had a game scheduled that night against New Orleans at the Coliseum, so we boarded a bus for Chicago and O'Hare Airport. We get to O'Hare and find out we have no reservations on the plane scheduled to fly to Cleveland.

"Well, Fitch goes nuts at hearing that. He's ready to go over the counter after this guy and I am holding him back. He's steamed. Eventually, he calms down and we are taken over to Butler Aviation, where arrangements are made to get a plane to fly us back to Cleveland. We spent the whole day at Butler Aviation. The players began grumbling. What I remember the most is Nate walking around to each of them, trying to calm them down. He explained to them that these things happen in the NBA. He told them that they should not let this sort of thing bother them. Get some sleep, he said. He kept them cool."

The Cavaliers did not reach Cleveland until 9:40 p.m. The game, played in front of 6,149 fans at the Coliseum, did not tip off until 10:45 p.m. The Cavaliers won, 112-90.

"Nate Thurmond had as much to do with that victory as anyone," said Tait. "He brought class to the team. Hell, the level of dress even went up. These guys were used to walking around wearing jeans with holes in them. Some guys still wore the jeans, but at least they were without the holes. It took a month or so to realize what he was doing for the club, but after that, it became apparent."

The playoffs of 1976 lasted for five weeks. They began with a 100-95 upset loss to the Washington Bullets on April 13 and ended with a 94-87 Eastern Conference Finals loss to Boston at the Coliseum on May 19. The frenzy generated by the basketball team over those 37 days is not likely to be duplicated.

Tait says he knows why.

"The timing for something like that to happen was perfect," he said. "The Indians were dead meat, the Browns were not doing much, and hockey had died. The Cavaliers were a team of overachievers. Ten guys were playing and ten guys had a part in the team's success. I have a theory on why people still talk about that team today.

"Even after we win a world championship some day, people who are old enough will remember that Miracle year. It was like the first girl you ever fall in love with. You may end up 10 years later finding somebody else, loving her more and marrying her and having a great life together. But you will never forget the one you loved first and the emotion that went with that first love. This was really a first love affair — the fans, the team. It was an easy team to love because there were no superstars on it.

"There is no doubt in my mind that they would have won it all had Jim Chones not broken his foot between the Washington and Boston series. In my mind, that was a no-doubter."

Three years after the Miracle of Richfield season, the Tait-Fitch twosome that began with a telephone call to Terre Haute, Indiana, in October 1970 ended. Fitch announced his retirement after the Cavaliers completed the 1978-79 season with a 30-52 record.

"Fitch ran out of gas," said Tait. "It was the same thing as Lenny (Wilkens) in 1993. Fitch once told me that you know you are through when they know what you're going to do even before you do it. He developed a bunker mentality. He didn't want to talk anymore. I thought Bill Fitch was a hell of a coach — as long as you could put up with him. His style was like the gunfighter at the turn of the century. He lasted nine years in Cleveland, but it ran out."

CHAPTER SIX

"No More Miracles"

After the` Miracle of Richfield season, the beat writers from the *Cleveland Plain Dealer* and *Cleveland Press* picked the Cavaliers to win the NBA championship in 1976-77.

And, why not? Everyone was back on a team that captured the hearts and souls of Northeastern Ohio. The writers looked like geniuses when the Cavaliers won their first eight games and 16 of 20 in 1976-77. Fitch, though, could see trouble when the Cavaliers lost five of their next 10 games. They were 21-14, sitting atop the Central Division, but Fitch was concerned. "A great deal of our effectiveness in the previous season," he said, "was because of our depth, and our depth was greater than that of three-quarters of the teams. This season we are just another team."

They were just another team because injuries cut into the effectiveness of four keys to the Miracle Season— Chones, Cleamons, Russell and Walker. "That was a team to the nth degree," said Fitch. "It was put together where you needed all the working parts. If you were to lose a Foots (Walker) or an (Austin) Carr, you were in trouble."

Another thing was beginning to take its toll on the Cavaliers —the influx of American Basketball Association players into the NBA.

The ABA folded after the 1975-76 season, and ABA stars such as Moses Malone, Artis Gilmore and Maurice Lucas went up for grabs in the dispersal draft. The Cavaliers got no one. They became a victim of their own success in 1975-76.

"The ABA was a seven-year farm system," said Fitch, "and the players over there were first-round, second-round draft choices. With the merger, it was like you were starting all over again. The merger was good in that it kept teams like Cleveland who needed the money alive, but we were not as good a basketball team because of it. I suppose if I had known all the numbers the way Nick (Mileti) knew all the numbers, I would have cut my throat.

"The only numbers I knew, were what our record was and that what we had to give our players was not enough."

The euphoria over the Miracle of Richfield took its biggest hit on a February night in Houston. Thurmond, chasing down a loose ball, tore cartilage in his left knee. He went down in a heap, was helped off the floor by Chones and John Lambert, and left the Summit on crutches. "That's it for the year," he said. "I know from experience that it will have to be operated on. I don't know, if at my age (35), that I can come back from another operation. I'm not trying to be overly dramatic, but that's the way I feel."

One thing bothered Thurmond, a proud man, about the way he left the court in Houston. He was carried off the floor.

"I did not want to go out being carried off the floor," he said. "I wanted to go out walking off the floor. I have dreamed of ending my career that way . . . walking off the floor. Right now, I feel terrible. I have been playing a long time and if this is the last one, well . . . It's tough. That's all I can say."

The Cavaliers were 27-23 at the time Thurmond went down.

They finished the season splitting their next 32 games and were ousted by the Bullets in the first round of the playoffs. Thurmond played one minute in Game 2 against the Bullets, getting a rebound and a blocked shot in the Cavaliers' lone victory, 91-83. Then he was gone. It took just 114 games over two seasons—the Cavaliers won 71 of them — for Thurmond to etch himself forever into franchise history.

"Just about anything that can be said good about a person can be said about Nate Thurmond," said Fitch.

With Thurmond gone, the center play fell to Chones and Elmore Smith, who was acquired in a January 1977 trade with Milwaukee. Nearly twenty years later, Chones said the injury to Thurmond might have been avoided.

"I remember very well when he got hurt," said Chones. "I was upset. Fitch had been giving me less time. I told him that he can't play Nate that much. Nate was the kind of guy who let it all hang out all the time. He was such a tremendous player for us. Out of all the players I've ever played with, I respected Nate and (Earvin) Magic (Johnson) as much as anyone.

"I don't think the fans really understood the magnitude of what he meant to us. We've never had that kind of dominating big man in Cleveland since. He could shut off the lane against guys who used to walk in there in the fourth quarter. He wasn't fast, but he could slide and get there to help. He'd show on picks. He could step all the way to the top of the key and get back to the basket to block a shot or get a rebound. I know that sounds simple, but it is not easy to do.

"Injuries hurt us the year after the miracle season. At some point, the body can't take it anymore and you have injuries. You're either practicing too hard or playing too hard. You can't stay up there at that physical and emotional level forever. That's what happened to us. Nate gave so much of himself in the playoffs. At the halftime of those games, he looked like he had just run a marathon. You see players tired, but he shouldn't have been that tired. He was old, though. They asked a lot of him. I could see in training camp that he was a little slower. He was a little more irritable. And, they were asking him to play more. You just can't do that."

Players around the league could see that the Cavaliers were no longer the same team without Thurmond. "Losing Nate Thurmond really hurt them," said Bullets forward Elvin Hayes. "He was a big key to that ballclub. He was their plugger on defense. Jim Chones and Elmore Smith were good centers, but they played alike. Where they were weak is where Nate was strong. Their year was the year before. They had everything going for them."

Fitch's last two seasons in Cleveland—1977-78, 1978-79—were often turmoil-filled. In October 1977, the Cavaliers got Walt Frazier from the New York Knicks as compensation for the Knicks signing veteran free agent Jimmy Cleamons.

Yes, Walt Frazier in Cleveland. Well, not actually Cleveland. Walt Frazier in Richfield. He was 32, he was a seven-time All-Star, he drove a Rolls, he wore wide-brimmed hats, fur coats and he practiced yoga. He was coming from New York City to Richfield, Ohio, and he was not happy. He was viewed by teammates as being sullen and aloof—as though he looked at playing for the Cavaliers as playing in the CBA after playing in New York. He also was accused by the team's front office of faking foot injuries that limited him to 51 games in 1977-78. He was ripped in the media for not sitting on the team's bench during games.

At one point, Fitch said, "I never misjudged anyone (as badly) as I did Walt Frazier." Years later, Fitch discussed Frazier at length. "Don't believe everything you read about him," Fitch said.

"We gave up nothing for him, really. Jimmy (Cleamons) was going. Walt was making big dollars ($450,000), but New York paid his salary. I thought that Walt, had he stayed healthy, would have been excellent for us. One of the two greatest practices that I've ever been a part of in all the years I coached involved Walt Frazier (the other involved Dave Cowens in Boston).

"It was the first practice we had after I brought him to Cleveland. He put on a clinic. It was something people would have paid to see, the way he orchestrated things and what he did for our team. He played 18 straight games for us and when he did, we were among the cream of the crop (13-5) in the league.

"He got hurt, though, and Walt was one of those players who could not play hurt. That's where all the commotion came from. He had some health problems that I don't think we were even aware of. And, he had woman problems. All of that fell on him when he was injured. He was not done when we got him. Everyone reacts to injuries differently. With a guy like (Dave) Cowens, you'd wrap whatever it was that hurt and he'd go out and play. Walt had a low pain threshold. Was he faking it? The press in New York said he faked it because he was unhappy in Cleveland. I knew he was hurt. Our medical guys were as good as any in the league. It was a shame what happened with him. I feel that if he had stayed healthy, he might have led us down the path further than Lenny (Wilkens) did."

Fitch said there was one thing Frazier told him that he could not get used to about living in Aurora, a quiet suburb of Cleveland. "He said he could not get used to going out to dinner and not having people recognize him," said Fitch.

Frazier had one great game while with Cleveland. It was high drama in Madison Square Garden. The last two years of Frazier's 10 in New York were not good ones. The New York media thought Frazier was showing wear that comes from too many high-intensity games in front of the league's most severe critics. Frazier was hearing boos in the Garden.

In an October 1977 game at the Garden, though, Frazier turned back the clock to those nights in the early 1970s. One of those nights when he was Cool Clyde Frazier, running a show with a cast of characters that included Willis Reed, Dave DeBusschere, Earl Monroe and Bill Bradley. On that October night in 1977, Frazier had 28 points, eight rebounds, five steals and four assists.

With 17 seconds left and the 117-112 overtime victory assured after his fifth steal, Frazier was at midcourt. He was dribbling the ball with his left hand and he was throwing his right fist high in the air. He was smiling. Once more, he owned New York. The Garden rocked.

Talking about those final seconds, Frazier said, "I guess I really blew my cool out there. I was a real ham. This game gave me the same satisfaction I had when we won two titles and when I played for Southern Illinois and we won the NIT."

Frazier averaged 16.2 points in 51 games of his first season in Cleveland. The last two years were a disaster. He appeared in 15 games before finally being released in October 1979. In the end, Frazier felt that much of the adverse publicity he got playing slightly over two seasons in Cleveland was unfair.

"I was hurt," he said. "It was frustrating for me. I wanted to play. I wanted to contribute. For some reason, though, I was criticized and questioned. No one, for example, questioned Greg Pruitt of the Browns for being out, and he shouldn't be questioned. No one will question Elmore Smith for being out, and he shouldn't be questioned. When Walt Frazier goes down, though, he is questioned. And when the team goes 5-0 then, it is because I am not playing. The same thing happened a couple of years ago in New York. I had an injured back. I couldn't play. It was as simple as that."

Frazier talked about not sitting on the bench. "It was erroneously reported that I did not come to the games," he said.

"I did. I watched them on closed circuit television in the locker room. There was no way I could help sitting on the bench. I couldn't coach. Actually, I was better off in the locker room because I was receiving therapy while I was watching the games.

"It's funny. If I had been on the bench during those games, people would have said all Walt Frazier wants to do is get dressed up, go down to the games and sit on the bench. I couldn't win no matter what I did."

The most tragic figure to ever play for the Cavaliers—Terry Furlow—played during Fitch's last two seasons. Furlow was 23 when he came to the Cavaliers from the Philadelphia 76ers in October 1977. He possessed an uncanny jump shot and a volatile personality.

"I liked him a lot," said Chones, "but he was a druggie. He was intelligent, he had a good sense of humor, but he was in the twilight zone a lot."

A Cleveland writer discovered this after a game at the Richfield Coliseum. With just about everyone cleared out of the team's locker room, the writer approached Furlow for some post-game quotes. While the two talked, the writer noticed something on the floor between them. It was a marijuana cigarette. Furlow looked at the writer as if to say he had no idea where the joint came from. The writer picked it up and put it in his pocket.

"Terry Furlow was one of the tragedies of our time," said Fitch. "The drugs affected his personality. He could be nasty and rude. In those days, we didn't know too much about how drugs affected personalities. I had to deal with his personality changes on a day-to-day basis. There were days when he'd be real ugly; days when he'd be happy (and would) be the best kid on the block. His moods were up and down. It was a tragedy. When he was right and in a mood that was the real Terry Furlow, he was a great kid. When he was in a bad, foul mood, he just couldn't control his emotions. I had a suspicion that he wasn't the way he was by accident. At the time, we thought it might have been a chemical imbalance. In those days, we didn't know exactly what was going on. He was the first to come along."

Furlow died on May 23, 1980. He was 26. He was killed when the Mercedes-Benz he was driving hit a bridge abutment on a freeway in the Cleveland area. Seven different substances were found in his bloodstream.

The Cavaliers won nine of their last 10 games in 1977-78 to make the playoffs, where they lost a best-of-three series in two straight games to the New York Knicks. There were several tight games down the stretch of the regular season. In the 81st game, at Atlanta, Foots Walker banked a 17-foot shot off the backboard as time expired. The Cavaliers won, 111-109. Walker was mobbed by his teammates, who pulled him down to the floor in exuberance.

"Then," said Walker, "I looked up to see this white guy kissing me all over the face."

It was Fitch.

"I was wondering what the hell was happening," said Walker. "I didn't know who it was on top of me at first. When I found out, I began having second thoughts about making the shot."

John Lambert, observing the scene, said, "I knew you guys had something going on all along."

The 1978-79 season was Fitch's last in Cleveland. At the start of the season, it did not look like it would be his last. The Cavaliers had chosen Mike Mitchell, a promising 6-8 forward, with the 15th pick in the draft. They began the season with a 4-0 record.

"One thing I remember about Mike Mitchell," said Fitch, "is a call I got from (Philadelphia general manager) Pat Williams. Pat tried to convince me that I should not take Mike ... that he was a chain-smoker. A lot of guys tried things like that so you wouldn't draft certain players. They wanted to scare you off."

In the first week of training camp, Fitch wondered if Williams knew something he didn't know.

"Mitchell played like a dog," said Fitch. "He kept saying he was listless for some reason. He couldn't get up and down the court. He couldn't get back on defense. You'd sit and talk to him and he was the nicest kid you'd ever want to meet. I couldn't see any dog in him. I asked him about the smoking. He swore he didn't smoke."

Fitch went to Dr. Nick Sekerak. "Doc said he wanted to bring him into the (Cleveland) Clinic," Fitch said. "Doc saw him one morning. Mike came back for our evening practice that night. I didn't believe what I saw. He played like someone had stuck a firecracker up his ass. He went like hell. He ran like a deer.

"The next morning, we had practice again. He went like hell again. Finally, I talked to Doc Sekerak. It turns out all the kid needed was some tranquilizers. He was uptight, just the opposite of what we thought. Doc put him on Valium and he was fine. That was the key. What I really liked about Mike Mitchell was that he had great legs. He could jump over you without a dribble."

The Cavaliers' 4-0 start in Fitch's final season was an illusion. Mitchell ultimately became one of the few bright spots averaging 10.7 points, 4.1 rebounds and shooting 51 percent from the field in 20 minutes a game as a rookie. Two years later he was an All-Star.

The Cavaliers took their 4-0 record into the Silverdome against the Pistons. Coaching the Pistons was 38-year-old Dick Vitale. With 1:25 left in the third quarter of what was about to become Cleveland's first loss (110-105), Vitale went haywire over a call against the Pistons. It took two assistant coaches, one trainer and a 350-pound Burns security guard to physically remove the kicking and screaming Vitale from the court. This is the same guy who missed three of Detroit's first six games that season because of stomach problems and what was termed "mental strain."

The Cavaliers who knew Vitale were not impressed. "The whole thing is an act," said Furlow, who grew up in nearby Flint and knew Vitale for about eight years.

Afterward that night in the Silverdome, Vitale told reporters: "You guys better hope I'm successful, because I'm a hell of a talker." How prophetic. Yes, he is.

Injuries to Frazier, Bingo Smith and Elmore Smith triggered a slide in Fitch's last season. The 4-0 start was followed by 14 losses in 15 games. After dropping to 4-4, the Cavaliers were about to begin a seven-game, 13-day trip.

"I'm not going to panic," said Fitch. "My dad raised only half an idiot . . . that's the half coaching."

The strain of losing was getting to Fitch and getting to the players. With 1:03 left in a game at Denver, Fitch got into an argument with official Richie Powers. They jawed in front of the scorer's table. The crowd of 15,211 at McNichols yelled for play to continue when Fitch spotted the ball resting on the floor at midcourt.

He took off after it. Racing him to the ball was the other

official, Roger McCann. Fitch got there first and kicked the ball—right into McCann. Then Fitch got the boot.

Asked how this losing compared to that of the first season, Fitch said, "There is no way of saying how bad death is. I feel terrible about this. I can't enjoy a game. I can't enjoy a steak. I can't enjoy a good book. No one likes you. You don't even like yourself. The whole thing just eats away at you.

"I can hear the cheap remarks from the stands. These are the guys who squawk about your coaching, about your players. Would they ever confront me on the street? Hell, no. Because they know I'd take a pop at them if they did. This team has been a winner. It may not have won a championship, but it has been in the ring of opportunity. There was no reason why I would change the faces of a team that had the fifth-best record in the league over the last three seasons. What I need is someone's center.

"I haven't had the chance to turn down Bob Lanier or Kareem Abdul-Jabbar, though. This league is funny. No one calls and says, 'Look, I'll give you Leon Douglas until Elmore Smith comes back.' My problem is that I'm not smart enough to predict things like the injury to Elmore Smith. Nine years ago, defeat came immediately after the jump ball. Here, we are pecking away and still in a lot of games right down to the end. And, if we lost a guy nine seasons ago, all it meant was there was one less body in the food line."

Fitch said he was doing one thing he did nine years ago. "I'm like O.J. Simpson," he said. "I run through airports. I don't want to be seen by people. It's different when you're winning. When you're winning, you walk through airports."

The post-Miracle crowds at the Coliseum began to dwindle. There were 4,459 at the Coliseum in early January 1979 when Fitch and veteran official Earl Strom went at it. After a 116-113 loss to the Bucks, Fitch was asked to comment on Strom, who had dealt out four technical fouls.

"The only parts of Earl Strom's body not ready for retirement are his ears," said Fitch. "No one, if they are mad or drunk, can show good judgment. He got emotionally involved in this game. He just about broke his back to spin around and see Jim Chones jumping up and down. He wanted to make sure he got the technical. Earl Strom is the kind of guy who is buddy-buddy to everyone when you see him in airports and places like that.

"I get along with him fine, off the floor. I don't want those kinds of friends in the league anymore, though."

During one stretch of nine losses in 10 games, the players exploded on Fitch in a newspaper story. One player said, "There is one way to do things. His way. It's strictly a one-way street. We're afraid to go to him."

Their 101-point scoring average was the worst in the league.

"We're running too many patterns and all we're showing for them is the same 15-footer we could be getting off the break," said Foots Walker. "And, off the break, we'd have a better chance at rebounding because everyone is scattered all over and not set defensively."

"We're like robots," said another player. "We are too predictable. We come down the floor, run a play and there are always two or three guys waiting for you. When Campy (Russell) goes to the basket now, it seems like he's driving through eight guys. It's taken away any inside game we had."

They wanted to run more, rather than set up halfcourt stuff. "Basketball in the NBA as it's now played," said another player, "is geared to running. We lay back too much. We're too cautious. Sure, we'll get buried once in a while if we run, but everyone does. Yes, we have few turnovers, but so what? In Boston's heyday, the Celtics averaged about 25 turnovers a game.

"There is more bickering going on than I've ever seen here. Guys are yelling at each other right on the court. No one helps each other out at the defensive end anymore. If your man gets by you, no one is going to help because he doesn't want to leave his man and risk being yelled at. I can remember when guys used to cry after a loss. Now, no one seems to care."

Fitch took his own shots at the players. After a 120-103 loss to Portland, Fitch ripped the entire team— with the exception of Bingo Smith.

"I was satisfied with the way Bingo Smith performed in the second half," said Fitch.

Why? Because Smith was benched in the second half. Campy Russell was one of few players who chose not to hide behind an anonymous quote. "I've lost a lot of my creativity simply because of the way he (Fitch) wants me to play," said Russell. "He wanted me to tone down my game."

Russell was bitter because Fitch did not play him much early in his career with the Cavaliers. "My first year was really frustrating," said Russell. "I felt I had what it took to play here. I felt I was just as good as the guys playing ahead of me. But, it was the situation. Fitch just didn't want to play me. He never gave me any reason why."

Frazier said he and Fitch nearly came to blows before a game in Portland. Fitch, Frazier said, became upset when he said he could not play in a game against the Trail Blazers. "He (Fitch) told me to step outside into the hallway," said Frazier. "He said he would punch me. I told him to go ahead. We didn't fight, but we came close. The problem that I had with Bill was that he would sit down and talk to me, tell me one thing, and then go to the newspapers and say something entirely different. It was like he was lying to my face. I lost all respect for him.

"I don't think it was just Walt Frazier. Bill just didn't hit it off with anyone. He wasn't prejudiced against me. I think he would have done the same against any player."

The final weeks of the 1978-79 season were tough on Fitch. The team continued losing, finishing with a 30-52 record. Also, he and his wife, Margaret, were divorced.

"And," said longtime friend and Cavs radio play-by-play voice Joe Tait, "he had become burned out coaching in Cleveland, just like so many coaches become burned out."

Fitch's last season in Cleveland ended with four straight losses, the last in San Antonio. He sounded disenchanted.

"I have the same excitement," he insisted. "I no longer try being liked. Players will use writers, their lawyers and fans to get to you. Certain generals enjoyed wars. I don't know about fun. I don't enjoy coaching the players as much. But, I relish the challenge."

He talked about Cleveland, saying, "I studied psychology in school, and if I wasn't a coach, I'd hang out my shingle here, treating writers and coaches and managers. I'd be a millionaire. This town has so many hangups, it's a gold mine for a shrink."

Fitch resigned from the Cavaliers in a press conference on May 21, 1979. At one point in the press conference, he put on dark glasses so no one would see the tears. He praised Mileti, the owner who publicly ripped him three years earlier. He called coaching in Cleveland the best nine years of his life.

"You guys," he said, "have heard every one-liner I have to tell."

Rather than ending his stay in Cleveland with a one-liner, he ended it with a story.

"There was this 98-year-old man and a 97-year-old woman appearing before the judge asking for a divorce," he said. "The judge wondered why now, after 80 years of marriage.

"The husband paused. 'We thought we'd wait until all the children died,' he said."

Two days later, Fitch was named coach of the Boston Celtics. More than 15 years later, Fitch talked about his last season in Cleveland. "At the end of the year," he said, "I was thinking about getting back into college coaching and ended up in Boston. Nick (Mileti) and I couldn't have had a better relationship at the end. We became good friends and still are. Nick Mileti was one of a kind. He was a good man through good times and bad times. He knew how to lose. If you don't know how to lose, you shouldn't be in the NBA. Nick Mileti was not a good loser, but he knew how to lose. He was street-wise.

"In my case, it was time for a change. You burn out. I did."

CHAPTER SEVEN

"Prelude to Trouble"

With Fitch, the dominant figure for nearly a decade, departed from the organization, an entire front-office shakeup was in order for the Cavaliers. Mileti orchestrated the restructuring, appointing Stan Albeck the coach and also naming Ron Hrovat general manager and long-time Fitch assistant coach Jimmy Rodgers director of player personnel.

The new group wasted little time asserting itself. In September, guard Randy Smith was acquired from the San Diego Clippers in exchange for the Cavs' No. 1 pick in the 1980 draft and cash. Shortly thereafter, Albeck opened his first training camp. Some of the veteran players, particularly Chones and Frazier, were not impressed with Albeck's methods. In their opinion, Albeck often acted almost as if he were a condescending professor teaching a course on hoops and they were his somewhat slow students.

"When they named Albeck coach, I heard he was a screamer and crier. I didn't like criers," Chones said. "His thing was that if you scored so many layups, you'd win. He'd use charts and illustrations to try and get points like that across to us. It was a joke. We used to sit there and laugh at this guy."

Chones didn't laugh at him for very long.

Perhaps reading correctly that Chones had very little professional respect for him, Albeck orchestrated a trade of one more remaining link to the Miracle of Richfield season.

"Stupid Stan tried to let his wife coach the team," Chones said years later. "I played (in camp) for about a month. I thought he didn't know what in the hell was going on."

One day Chones and Frazier were sitting around in Chones' hotel room near Calvin College in Michigan, where the team was preparing to play an exhibition game. Frazier was busting Chones' chops.

"Sweets," said Frazier, "I heard they're going to start John Lambert ahead of you."

"Damn," said Chones, "he's not a center or a forward. He's strictly a role player. Oh, this is great."

To be truthful, Chones didn't know what to think. He had been haggling with management all summer. He didn't like Albeck. He was beginning to wonder if he had any kind of future with the organization.

"I wasn't in their plans," he said. "I had tried all summer to get more money. I was underpaid, making $175,000. I'm doing all the work — rebounding, blocking shots. If I'm doing all that, I told them, pay me more. But Jimmy Rodgers was player personnel director. He didn't know what in the hell was going on, either."

That same day that Chones and Frazier joked with each other at Calvin College, Chones found out what in the hell was going on.

"Stan came to me and said, 'We traded you to the Lakers.'" Chones recalled. "I almost laughed in his face. But instead, I said, 'Oh man, Stan, is that right?' He said, 'Yeah, we've decided to go with John Lambert.' I said, 'You know what? John will do a good job for you. He can rebound. He can run. It could be good for the both of us.'

"But I know what is going on. I know they can't win without me. Stan told me, 'You don't have to play tonight. We'll just say you're injured. You can go back to your room if you want.'"

So Chones went back to his room, where Frazier remained.

"Walt, you ain't going to believe what just happened," Chones said. "They traded me to the Lakers. They really are going to go with Lambert at center."

Frazier looked at Chones. Chones looked at Frazier.

Then they both broke out laughing.

Shortly thereafter, Chones received a phone call from Lakers GM Bill Sharman.

"We only want you if you want to come," Sharman told Chones.

"I'll be there tomorrow if you want," Chones replied.

So Chones left Cleveland after five years and 400 games as a Cavalier. The closest he came to a championship was during the Miracle of Richfield season, when he broke his foot just before the Eastern Conference Finals vs. Boston and effectively ended the Cavs' magical run. In Los Angeles, though, Chones would finally get his ring. The Lakers had a rookie that year named Earvin (Magic) Johnson who would inspire Chones and the rest of the team to the greatest of basketball heights.

"The Lakers were so professional," Chones said. "The organization was so tight. Everything was right, and, of course, that was Magic's rookie year. It was a great time to go to that team.

"I fit in out there, too. After my first couple of practices with the Lakers, Kareem (Abdul-Jabbar) came up to me and said, 'Damn, how could they let you go? What are they doing in Cleveland?' But Stupid Stan didn't think the way I played would help them win, and I didn't suck up to him like a lot of other guys did."

The timing on the decision to trade Chones to the Lakers for Dave Robisch and Los Angeles' third-round pick in the 1980 draft could not have been worse. Three days later, Elmore Smith underwent the first of three knee operations that would shelve him the entire season. Smith was supposed to team with Lambert at center.

Three games into the season, Frazier was waived — thus ending a brilliant career that included two NBA championships and seven All-Star appearances. Unfortunately, all of that happened for Frazier before he came to Cleveland. He was with the Cavs for parts of three seasons, yet appeared in a total of only 66 games. His career NBA scoring average was 18.9; it was just 14.5 with the Cavs.

Later in the same month, another Miracle player was dealt away when Bingo Smith, the club's second-leading scorer to that point behind Austin Carr, was traded to San Diego for the mere price of a third-round draft pick in 1980 and future considerations.

Struggling to adjust to all the new faces and the new coach, the team lurched off to a 2-7 start. It rallied to pull within one game of .500 at 19-20 on December 29, but that was as close to a winning record the Cavs would get the rest of the rather nondescript 1979-80 season.

Yet play-by-play man Joe Tait does remember a couple of incidents from, as he called it, "the Stan Albeck file."

"We were struggling, about 11 or 15 games under .500, and we went to San Diego to play against the Clippers," Tait said. "A lot of Stan's friends and neighbors came down to see the game. And we had an 11-point lead at halftime, blew it, and lost by about 11 or 12. It was an embarrassing performance."

After the game, Albeck flew back to Los Angeles while the Cavs flew on to Kansas City for their next game.

"Albeck was to meet us at the airport to go on into the city on the team bus with us," Tait said. "Now, Stan up to that point had been the happy-go-lucky, slap-you-on-the-back, everybody's buddy type of coach. But he gets on that team bus in Kansas City — and I'll never forget this — he says something to (trainer Charlie) Strasser, and Strasser says, 'Yeah, it's all set up.' "

With that, Albeck stood up and walked toward the back of the bus where the players were sitting. He glared at them.

"When we get to the hotel," said Albeck, "you guys have 45 minutes to get into that hotel, get to your rooms, into your practice uniforms, get taped and get back on this bus! We're going to Kemper (Arena) for practice."

Said Tait: "Now this announcement came at about 7 o'clock at night. Most of the guys were figuring on getting in, maybe catching a little dinner, and calling it a night. But we rolled up to that hotel, the boys go in, they come back out — and I figure I'm going to tag along just to see what in the hell is going to happen."

What happened was brutal.

"Three hours of hand-to-hand combat," Tait said. "There were fights breaking out all over the place. He had 'em runnin', draggin', smashin'. I mean they'd have a scrimmage and then he'd have 'em run gassers. This went on for three solid hours."

John Lambert's back went out on him during this circus. The sweat-drenched Lambert came over and took a seat next to

Tait. "He's trying to kill us all!" Lambert gasped. When the marathon practice season finally concluded, Albeck gathered the players around him.

"I have never been so embarrassed in my life than at what I saw last night in San Diego," Albeck told them. "And I want you to know that we have 12 games left in this season, and I'm going to hold one of these (practices) every time we play like we did last night in San Diego. So if you guys want to do this another dozen times, keep it up."

The Cavs, 27-43 when Albeck called the killer practice, beat Kansas City the next night and ripped off eight straight victories to suddenly claw within striking distance of the playoffs. They won 10 of their last 12 overall, failing to qualify for the playoffs by two games. "But the guys played their asses off down the stretch," said Tait.

The Albeck-coached Cavs of 1979-80 also fashioned one of the most memorable moments in franchise history one night when Chones and the vaunted Lakers came to town on their way to that championship. For one night, anyway, the Cavs played like champions. They beat the Lakers in four overtimes at the Coliseum, 154-153. Tait, who has broadcast more than 2,000 Cavs' games over the years, still calls it "the greatest single game I've ever broadcast. Absolutely. Absolutely."

The Cavs entered the game with a 23-31 record. The Lakers were on their way to a 60-22 season. But with Mike Mitchell having one of those nights where he was hitting everything, the underdog Cavs kept rallying to tie the score at the end of first regulation and then one overtime . . . two overtimes . . . three overtimes.

By the end of the third overtime, several Cavs had fouled out — most of them trying in vain to stop Lakers center Kareem Abdul-Jabbar, who scored 42 points. In the fourth overtime, journeyman Bill "Poodles" Willoughby was assigned the task of slowing Abdul-Jabbar. He slowed him enough to permit the Cavs to win behind Mitchell's 34 points before a crowd of 13,820.

"When it was over," said Tait, "I turned to (WWWE-radio talk-show host) Pete Franklin sitting next to me and said, 'Pete, you can either be a guest on the post-game show or you can go home. Because I'm going to midnight,' which is when Pete normally went until (with his post-game call-in show). I told him it was going to take me until midnight to unwind. My heart was just going bang-bang-bang! I remember I interviewed anybody that moved after that game, I was so pumped. I even interviewed (Indians manager) Dave Garcia."

Years later, Tait reflected on why it was such a special game to broadcast.

"Well, for one thing, the Lakers were a hell of a team — and we weren't," Tait said. "And we had three or four guys foul out. Without a doubt, it was the single most emotional game I ever broadcast. We kept coming back. In each of the four overtimes, we were down like four, six and just kept coming back and tying it up right at the end. We had to make a run at them at the end of regulation to even get it into overtime."

Albeck remembered the game well, too.

"We kicked their ass," he said, smiling years later. "Seriously, it was a great game. I don't know if I can say it was the greatest single game I was ever involved in, but it was one of the most memorable."

So memorable that Albeck to this day still keeps cassette tapes of Tait's broadcasts in the glove compartment of his automobile.

"Whenever my wife and I are on a long drive somewhere, we might pull them out and listen to them. I've probably listened to the tapes of that game a hundred times," Albeck said. "The funny thing is that the game went so long that it took several cassettes to get the whole game on there."

Meanwhile, life off the court for the franchise was not going too well. Mileti was beginning to encounter money problems reminiscent of the early years, as attendance waned in the post-Miracle years. Average attendance went from a high of 12,738 in 1976-77 — the season after the Miracle year — to 9,000 in Fitch's last season and 8,730 in Albeck's first.

Mileti wanted out. He also wanted to make some money on getting out. In a series of rather swift stock transactions that left investor Lou Mitchell out several hundred thousand dollars, Mileti first sold his interest in the club to Mitchell, who stayed in the business only long enough to get a better look at the books, which appeared to have been doctored a bit to get him to invest in the first place. When Mitchell wanted out, another investor named Joe Zingale suddenly appeared. He happened to be Mileti's cousin.

Mitchell sold out to Zingale at a significant loss after owning the club only a few weeks.

"I came into the office one day in the summer and saw this big guy with his shirt open down to his navel and all these gold chains flapping around," Albeck said. "(Assistant coach) Mo McHone asked me who it was, and I jokingly told him, 'Hell, I don't know. He's probably our latest owner.' Later on I found out that I was right, that the guy I had seen was Joe Zingale."

Zingale didn't own the club for long. He never intended to. After buying Mitchell's interest at a bargain price, he looked for someone willing to pay a higher price just to get in on the action of a major sports franchise.

Mileti knew just the guy. His name was Theodore J. "Ted" Stepien.

"I worked for four different owners in a span of a couple months," said Cavs public relations director Bill Needle, who now is a talk-show host at WKNR in Cleveland. "It was an easy league to get into, and franchises always appreciated. But at the time, I think the team changed hands that frequently because it was the art of the deal. People were making paper money on the sale of the franchise. It was an easy league to get into and you could make a quick hit on selling the team because there was always someone waiting to buy in.

"Because as bad as the league might have been at the time, it was still pro sports . . . . But it got bad there for awhile because you rarely knew who owned the team week to week. As much as I tried, I didn't know who to suck up to."

Mileti knew Stepien from their involvement in ownership of the Indians, when at one time each had owned a piece of the team. The rest of Cleveland knew Stepien from the ill-fated Great Softball Throw from atop Terminal Tower in that summer of 1980.

Stepien owned the Cleveland Competitors, a professional softball team managed by a friend who later would play a pivotal role in his years as owner of the Cavaliers, Don Delaney. In June of 1980, someone came up with the idea of dropping softballs off the top of Terminal Tower and having members of the Competitors attempt to catch them 700 feet below. It was estimated beforehand that the balls would reach the ground in about 6.6 seconds and would be moving at 144 miles per hour.

Offering a clue as to how he loved to be in the middle of the action, Stepien himself insisted on climbing to the 52nd floor and out onto the small ledge where he figured he could best send the balls on their downward flight. But confusion reigned at the historic moment. Walkie-talkies that were supposed to communicate to the folks below when the balls were coming malfunctioned. As a crowd of about 5,000 who amazingly had nothing better to do that day waited anxiously in the southwest quadrant of Public Square, Stepien decided to forge ahead anyway.

With reporter Ron Kovach of the *Cleveland Press* actually holding Stepien's legs while he leaned out over the ledge, Stepien muttered: "This is bad. I'm really going to hurt somebody. I was a bombardier in World War II, but it wasn't like this."

No, it wasn't. But he was right about hurting somebody.

Stepien's first toss hit the hood of a car stopped at a red light on Superior Ave. The next one hit spectator Russel Murphy, 66, on the left shoulder. "I didn't even see it coming. It just hit me. I'll be sore, I can tell you that," the retired foundry worker told the *Press* before heading to the hospital.

Still, the balls kept coming — with no warning and in direct line with the mid-day sun, making them impossible to spot until the very last of the 6.6 seconds they were in the air.

The third ball hit another spectator who wasn't as fortunate as Murphy. Or was she? She later sued Stepien and came away with a sizable amount of cash. Gayle Falinski, 24, apparently had been holding her arms aloft to shade her eyes when a softball drilled her right wrist, breaking it instantly.

The fourth ball drilled the pavement out of the players' reach as police began making a move to stop the madness and the restless crowd began to boo. But the walkie-talkies still weren't working. Finally, the fifth ball was caught by Competitor Mike Zarefoss.

Fifty-two floors up, Stepien let out a cheer. "He caught it! He caught it! Yay! Yay!" the *Press* quoted him as saying.

Years later, an employee of Stepien's reflected on that day, finding it impossible not to hold back the laughter. "What I didn't know until afterward," said the employee, "was that they wanted him to throw them off the observation tower. But he wanted to go higher. So they actually had to hold his legs and he's almost out on this flagpole.

"It ended up costing him something like $150,000 in lawsuits. He hit some guy in a car waiting for a stoplight on Superior Ave. I mean, can you imagine that? A guy sitting in his car in the middle of the day, waiting on a stoplight, and this softball just smashes into the hood of his car? They told Ted he was supposed to just drop these balls off (so the wind wouldn't catch them), but he said, 'No, if I'm gonna throw 'em off, I gotta be loose and free to throw these things.' . . . They had a big crowd down there, and he throws 'em out way the hell over their heads. I just chuckle every time I think of that guy waiting for the stoplight on Superior Ave."

Stepien bought 37 percent of the Cavaliers from Joe Zingale that summer for $2 million. He eventually would own 82 percent of the team. Shortly before buying the team, he drove out to Lakeland Community College in Mentor, where the Competitors were practicing under the watchful eyes of Don Delaney.

"I'm going to buy the Cavaliers," Stepien told Delaney. "Are you with me?"

Delaney, who actually was quite an accomplished small-college basketball coach, was stunned.

"Oh, shit. Yeah, of course I'm with you," Delaney replied.

The Cavs used to train at Lakeland, and Delaney had previously gotten to know Bill Fitch and Jimmy Rodgers. "I went on a couple of trips with Jimmy Rodgers, scouting and stuff like that," Delaney said. "I got to know those guys pretty well. We used to go out after they were done with practice (during training camps at Lakeland) and drink beer, stuff like that.

"So when Ted said that, I thought it would be a good way to learn, a good way to get my foot in the door and learn the business."

He had to learn fast. Stepien didn't start him in the mail room. He told Delaney he wanted him to be the Cavaliers' new general manager.

Albeck, meanwhile, did not like all the sudden changes in ownership. When Stepien also announced that he was bringing on Bill Musselman as the new player personnel director, Albeck got even more nervous.

"(Indians president) Gabe Paul and (Indians manager) Dave Garcia told me, 'If Stepien buys the team, get the hell out of town as fast as you can. He's nutso,' " Albeck said. "In my first conversation with the man, he said he wanted to fire me. Sure, that made me a little nervous."

Stepien denies this. He also denied bringing in Musselman to force Albeck out. "I wanted Stan Albeck to be our coach the next season. In fact, he had a contract to coach the team. I was not going to let him out of it," Stepien said.

One problem. In his deal to buy into the team, Stepien unwisely had allowed Mileti to remain as president and call most of the shots. It was in the contract he had signed. There was little he could do without Mileti's consent.

On the day of the draft in June 1980, the situation was in turmoil. Albeck was the coach but he wasn't. According to most eyewitnesses, he reportedly chose the team's first-round draft pick — guard Chad Kinch out of the University of North Carolina-Charlotte — and then left the premises. Albeck denies this.

"I stayed until the end of the draft. And yes, I drafted Kinch. I drafted Chad Kinch because I thought he could play," Albeck said.

He couldn't. His NBA career would last a total of 41 games over parts of two seasons with Cleveland and Dallas.

Earlier, prior to the draft, Albeck claims Stepien told him to draft (Cleveland) Euclid High product Rich Yonaker from North Carolina "because he knew his Dad." Albeck said Stepien wanted him to select Yonaker high in the draft, with a first- or second-round pick.

"Look, Ted, he's not good enough to be a No. 1 pick. Maybe Dean Smith can find him a good job in another field or something," Albeck said he told Stepien.

"Who's Dean Smith?" was Stepien's reply, according to Albeck.

"I knew we were in trouble then," Albeck said.

For the record, Stepien said he told Albeck to draft Yonaker — but with a later pick. "Seventh, eighth round, I didn't care. I just wanted to give the kid a look because I knew his family," Stepien said.

Regardless, it was obvious these two men could not work together. By the middle of the 1980 draft, it also became obvious to public relations director Bill Needle and several reporters that no one was left in the room to work the draft. They were forced to make the Cavaliers' remaining three or four selections in the 10-round draft amongst themselves.

"By the ninth round, I'm there by myself," Needle said. "So this is it. My first time (drafting), and I'm thinking, 'This is cool. I'm going to find a guy who is going to make the team out of the ninth round. The story will be known. I am going to get out of this PR statistic shit and I am going to get into personnel, I just know it.'

"So we get to the ninth round, and the Marty Blake (NBA scouting) book is sitting there on the table. I start flipping through it. By this point, there is no one left available that you've ever heard of. So when I went to school at Ohio Northern, we played Central State every year and Central State was always good. And I see in the book that Melvin Crafter, a 6-5 guard, was the leading scorer at Central State. I'm thinking, 'A 6-5 guard, not bad. He plays the 'two spot,' he probably can handle the ball, do what you need to do.' Cleveland's turn to pick comes and I take Melvin Crafter out of Central State University. And I'm thinking, 'This is a helluva pick.'"

Cut to rookie camp later that summer. Needle was still feeling pretty good about his selection, and couldn't wait to see him in person.

"I was still thinking, 'This is going to be the greatest low-round pick in the history of the NBA. Better than Mo Cheeks. Better than Andrew Toney. Randy Smith? Forget Randy Smith. This guy is going to be great,' " Needle said.

So Needle walked up to Crafter and introduced himself.

"I'd like to welcome you to the Cavaliers," said Needle, "and I also want to let you know that I was pretty instrumental in you being drafted by the Cavs."

Crafter looked Needle right in the eye.

"Oh yeah, how come so late?" he said, still staring hard.

Melvin Crafter, who thought he should have gone much, much earlier in the draft, never made it out of rookie camp before getting cut.

Albeck didn't do the cutting, however. One day after the draft, he split for San Antonio to coach the Spurs. Stepien protested his defection to the league, but the league produced a letter signed by Mileti that claimed the Cavs had given Albeck permission to leave and sign with another team. Stepien was furious with Mileti, and later would accuse him of "leaving behind a mountain of unpaid bills" after the original Cavs' owner finally split the scene for good and headed to Hollywood to make movies.

A footnote to the Albeck-Stepien feud: One of San Antonio's two third-round draft picks that season was Rich Yonaker from Euclid High and North Carolina.

Stepien attempted to make friends fast in the media. He simply went about it in the wrong way. After the news conference announcing the latest new owner, reporter Sheldon Ocker approached Stepien and introduced himself for the first time.

"I cover the team for the *Akron Beacon-Journal*, and we'd like to do a long magazine story on you," Ocker said. "Would it be possible to come out to your house and spend some time with you?"

"Oh, that would be great," Stepien replied. "Come on over Sunday after church. We'll sit around the pool and watch porno films."

Ocker was stunned. "All I could think of was that at least this guy was going to go to church before he planned to sit around the pool and watch porno films," Ocker later said.

The film session thankfully never came off. Ocker got lost trying to find Stepien's house, and Ted was nowhere to be found when Ocker finally arrived at the Gates Mills residence.

The reporter tracked him down later that same day at the Cosmopolitan Club in Willoughby, where Stepien was wasting no time getting after what he considered to be important Cavalier team business. He was conducting auditions for cheerleaders, who soon would be named the Teddi Bears after Stepien's youngest daughter, whose nickname was Teddi.

Ocker's bizarre introduction to Stepien continued when he arrived at the Cosmopolitan Club and witnessed what was taking place. All members of the Cavaliers' front office were required to attend and submit questions to Stepien, who was supposed to then forward the queries to the aspiring Teddi Bears.

"But Ted wasn't asking any of their questions. He was asking his own," Ocker said. "He would ask things like, 'What's your favorite color?' And then move on to something like, 'If you were on vacation, would you go to a nude beach?' "

Afterward, Stepien implored Ocker to return to his house and conduct the long-delayed magazine interview. When Ocker arrived, Stepien was sitting with Shirley and Dave Morgenstern, whom Stepien had hired to "choreograph" the Teddi Bears. They were sifting through index cards, going over notes made on each of the candidates they had "interviewed" that afternoon.

"Stepien would say things like, 'No, she's a dog. She's out.' And then he would fling the index card over his head, behind him. Then he would look at another one and say something like, 'I gave her a 10. She has big tits. She's in.' " Ocker said.

The whole time, Ocker sat there amazed, fearing what might lie ahead.

CHAPTER EIGHT

"Terrible Ted and Mr. Bill"

As Stepien took control of the team, one local writer suggested this would put an end to "a farce of four ownerships in a period of months." Little did anyone know what a farce Stepien's ownership would become. It wasn't as if the team was in great shape when he assumed the reins, having ranked next-to-last in the NBA in attendance the previous season. But Stepien, who drove a Mercedes with his initials "TJS" engraved on the vanity license plates, quickly offered evidence that he would take the team to a new low.

In August, he embarked on an unprecedented preseason road tour designed to drum up support for the club. Traveling with no coach, no players — only himself, Delaney and a few front-office staffers — Stepien motored as far east as Erie, Pennsylvania, to sell his team to the public. Of course, it was the middle of baseball season, and with the basketball season nearly three months away, no one paid him much attention. It was the first sign that Stepien meant well, but had no idea about how to market his team.

He plowed on anyway. He passed out countless season-ticket brochures with — you guessed it — Ted Stepien's smiling face on the cover. He expressed the utmost confidence in Bill Musselman as his coach, repeatedly pointing out that Musselman had been recommended to him by none other than then-Oakland

A's Manager Billy Martin. It meant little to Stepien that many fans were outraged over his selection of Musselman as coach, having never forgiven Musselman for his permissive role as coach of the University of Minnesota years earlier when the Gophers incited an ugly brawl with beloved Ohio State University.

Most Cavs' fans were also Ohio State fans. Most Cavs' fans, in fact, were far more loyal to Ohio State at the time than the Cavs. Totally underestimating the underlying bitterness that still remained from Musselman's role in the 1972 Big Ten brouhaha, Stepien instead appeared to treat it too lightly. He proclaimed that he wanted to set up a meeting between Musselman and former Cav Luke Witte, who had played center for Ohio State and suffered a terrible beating during the incident, "to bury the hatchet." Never mind that Musselman himself had revealed the dark side of a complex personality that day by watching contentedly as several of his Minnesota players nearly buried their feet into the side of Witte's head via repeated kicks.

One Minnesota player, Corky Taylor, seemingly had offered a hand that day to help the bleeding Witte up off the floor. But when Witte grasped the hand, Taylor grabbed it and promptly kicked Witte with sickening force in the groin. Several years later, Witte received a hand-written letter, several pages long, from Taylor. In it, Taylor expressed sorrow for what had happened and laid all blame for the incident on Musselman, whom he said had whipped the Minnesota players into a frenzy with a week of practices and a pre-game speech that all ended with them chanting, "Kill! Kill! Kill!" Another Minnesota player involved in the brawl was Dave Winfield, who later would go on to gain baseball fame.

Stepien wanted all forgotten and forgiven. His plan was to have Musselman and Witte, who played briefly for the Cavs in the mid-70s, to stand at opposite ends of the court just before player introductions on opening night at the Coliseum. Then the lights would be doused, and a single spotlight would be shone on each man as they walked toward center court, where they were to shake hands.

"They would walk to center floor and shake hands, and then the lights would come on in the arena. That's how Ted wanted to start the season," Joe Tait said. "And Luke told him to pound salt."

Stepien and Tait were destined to have problems themselves. Shortly after taking over the team, Stepien summoned Tait to the Competitors Club in the basement of the downtown Statler Hilton.

"You know," said Stepien, "I really don't want you to be play-by-play announcer for the Cavaliers."

"Why not?" asked a stunned Tait.

"Well," replied Stepien, "I firmly believe that the play-by-play announcer should be an arm of the PR department, and at all times put the best interests of the team forward in the broadcasts. And you don't do that. You criticize, and I don't believe that's right."

"If you feel that way, Ted, why don't you just pay me off?" Tait asked. Like many others who had been employed under Mileti, Tait knew he had just signed a three-year guaranteed contract. It was worth more than $125,000.

"I can't do that," Stepien replied. "That's too much money. But I'm going to be on you. I'm going to be listening to you."

Tait, however, is not a man to be intimidated. When Stepien next moved on to small talk and asked Tait what he thought of the team being fielded for the upcoming season, the veteran broadcaster was blunt.

"You're not going to win 30 games," Tait said. "First of all, you picked the worst possible guy to coach in Bill Musselman."

"I always thought that was a hell of a thing for our announcer — who was supposed to be building us up as a team — to say to me, the owner, the first time we met," Stepien later said.

This laid the foundation for a feud that would culminate in Tait leaving the organization at the end of the season. And once again, Stepien totally underestimated the loyalty with which Clevelanders embraced Tait.

"Joe is Mr. Cavalier. But that didn't matter to Ted," said Rich Rollins, one of the first men hired by Stepien in 1980. Then director of ticket sales, Rollins continued to work for the Cavs as director of community relations until 1993.

"Ted just did things without thinking. One day he said, 'I want to hire a new broadcaster.' Then he might say, 'I want a new PA guy.' . . . One day he called me up and said, 'Rich, we're getting a new team dentist, and I don't want the old dentist to get any more free tickets.' This guy had been here taking care of the team since Day One. But there was just no explaining that to him. I think that's how he made a lot of his enemies.

"Sometimes a guy would show up for a game and say, 'Where are my tickets?' And that was when he would find out, 'Well, you don't have a job here any more.' "

Stepien further enraged Clevelanders by announcing in an interview published in the *Cleveland Press* his intentions to eventually rename his team the "Ohio Cavaliers," adding that the plan would include scheduling several home games in other cities. Ironically, two of the three cities he mentioned as possible alternate "home game" sites — Buffalo and Pittsburgh (with Columbus being the other) — weren't located in Ohio at all.

Other early marketing tools employed by Stepien included the hiring of team mascots George Schauer and Don Buttrey. Schauer, a native of the Cleveland suburb of Wickliffe, was billed as "Crazy George, the World's Greatest Ballhandler." His act included oversized balls, hula hoops and a flourishing finish during which he shaved a woman's leg while spinning a basketball on the end of a razor. Buttrey's act was less subtle. Billed as "The Amazing Boot," his only apparent talents were crunching empty beer cans with his teeth, blowing up firecrackers inside his mouth, and devouring raw eggs and whole powdered donuts.

Schauer, incidentally, was being reunited with Musselman, his former coach at first Ashland College and then the University of Minnesota. "I guess astrology has a lot to do with it. Both Musselman and I were born on August 13," said Schauer, whose explanation of his presence seemed to make as much sense as anything else.

The scantily-clad dancing Teddi Bears, of course, were another marketing tool that judging by today's NBA standards simply appeared to be ahead of its time. Of allowing his daughter, Nancy, to be a Teddi Bear, Stepien said: "I happen to like good-looking girls, and I see nothing wrong with them at the games, as long as everything is in good taste."

This from a guy who several times was heard to introduce Nancy with the line, "This is my daughter, Nancy. Doesn't she have great tits?"

And sometimes, when the Teddi Bears weren't at the games, everything wasn't always in the best of taste. Stepien often served as a master of ceremonies at the downtown luncheons where the Teddis wore even less clothes than usual, modeling lingerie. Stepien, a widower since the death of his wife, Ann, in 1979, also opened himself to criticism by openly dating young women around the same age as some of his daughters.

"Looking back now," said Bill Needle recently, "I am less harsh on Ted than I was. There were some things that he did that the league later ended up adopting — like the concept of continuous entertainment. The problem with Ted Stepien was that he had no taste. When the league crushed him, I'm sure the league had no idea that they would eventually become, in a way, the Teddi Bears and the guy who eats beer cans.

"Ted was the same way with free-agent contracts. He gave some outrageous contracts to free agents. The actual concept of signing free agents was good, and one that a lot of other teams soon picked up on. But he had no taste. He picked free agents who couldn't play and paid them tons of money."

Alas, Stepien's marketing genius did not produce the desired results in 1980. And the team's dismal performances in the exhibition season did little to help.

After winning their first exhibition, during which Musselman went all-out for the victory by playing guard Randy Smith the entire 48 minutes in a triumph over Detroit, the Cavs fell 106-76 to Indiana in a game played in Youngstown. Sports Editor Darrell Lowe of the *Ashtabula Star-Beacon* wrote afterward: "Hey, this group of Cavaliers will get you on your feet — and right out the door."

After the Youngstown fiasco, Musselman admitted to reporters: "We need some help. That's no secret."

It was, in fact, the worst-kept secret in the NBA. That the Cavs needed help was a vast understatement. And Musselman had already set off murmuring around the league that the team's new ownership and staff didn't know what in the Sam Hill it was doing.

How could a coach play his best guard, Smith, the entire 48 minutes in the very first exhibition game? Preseason games traditionally were used to work players into shape slowly, especially veterans, and to take extended looks at younger, unproven players who might have a chance at fitting in. Musselman's decision to play Smith those 48 consecutive minutes sent out a dual signal: The new coach wanted to win badly, but had dangerous ideas about how to go about it over the long haul in the NBA.

"You never knew what in the hell Musselman was going to do," Delaney said. "We had a lot of cases where he would play a guy one minute one night and 48 minutes the next. There was no pattern to what in the hell he was thinking.

"Bill Musselman was a piss-poor coach. When Ted first named him coach, I'm thinking, 'This is a guy who has been around and had some success. This guy must really know basketball. I can learn from this guy.' . . . But right away, I found out that, hey, I couldn't learn anything from him. This guy would start practice late because he would be over in Brecksville playing racquetball. He would go up to the gym late, and then still be making out his practice schedule. I'll show you junior high coaches that are better prepared. I couldn't believe this guy operated like this."

Rollins used to spot Musselman's car at a racquetball club on his way into work in the morning. Once he arrived at the Coliseum, Rollins would poke his head into Delaney's office and tell the GM: "It'll be awhile before practice gets started today. The coach is playing racquetball again."

Meanwhile, the players would be suited up and getting more steamed by the minute. But it was not unusual for Musselman to postpone morning practices by an hour or more on a moment's notice, usually based on how his racquetball game went that day.

Musselman would turn on a player and orchestrate his exit from the team in similarly bizarre fashion. One day during training camp in 1980, the coach burst into Delaney's office and pounded his fist on the GM's desk.

"Today is the day I trade Campy Russell!" Musselman shouted. "Campy is going today!"

It was just before 10 a.m., with practice slated to start in a few minutes. Musselman dispatched assistant coach Gerald Oliver to the locker room and slammed the door to his office.

Oliver went down from the Cavs' offices on the second floor of the Coliseum to the locker room in the basement and wrote on the chalkboard: "Practice is postponed until 11 o'clock."

The players, who had arrived around 9 a.m. to get taped, were furious. Musselman was oblivious to their foul mood as he worked the phones upstairs, trying to complete a deal that would rid him of "cancerous" Campy Russell once and for all.

A few minutes before 11, Musselman sent Oliver to the locker room again. This time Oliver wrote: "Practice is postponed until noon."

At noon, the trade still hadn't gone down. Again Oliver went down to write on the board that practice was now postponed until 2 p.m.

"By then the players were livid," Delaney said. "They went upstairs to the practice gym and were kicking balls all over the place, knocking out ceiling tiles and everything else. These players, they're going like berserko. I mean, they're going nuts."

It would get worse. At 2, Oliver wrote that practice was off until 4. And at 4, Oliver finally wrote on the board: "Practice is canceled until tomorrow at 10 o'clock."

"Poor Gerald Oliver," Delaney said. "Musselman kept sending him down to write on the blackboard. He knew he couldn't do it himself; the players would've killed him. That was the day he traded Campy (to New York) for (Bill) Robinzine. But it took him all day to do it."

Of all places to open the regular season, the Cavs had to do it in venerable Boston Garden against Larry Bird and an old friend, Celtics coach Bill Fitch, who would not make the opener enjoyable for his former team. Fitch, in fact, must have thought at times that the clock had been turned back 10 years and he was watching that first hapless Cavs' team he coached. Not that he felt sorry for them. To the contrary, Fitch instructed his Celtics to apply full-court pressure the entire 48 minutes — and they continued to do so even after they had built a 36-point lead at 110-74 en route to a 130-103 rout.

"That was some baptism, wasn't it?" Stepien noted afterward.

As he boarded the team bus, Stepien was overheard saying: "I don't know how the Celtics can be so good. They don't even have cheerleaders."

"To me, that set the tone," said Needle, one of those who heard Stepien's incredible post-game comment. "This is after a summer of polkas, Teddi Bears and men who eat beer cans and set firecrackers off in their mouth. Just a fuckin' freak show. And he gets on the bus after this decimating and humiliating loss and says something like that."

Doug Clarke, Cavs beat writer for the *Cleveland Press*, wasted no time teeing off on the team. He wrote of the season opener: "Right away, one got the feeling this was not going to be a classical gas. The Cavs' team bus got caught in an hour-long traffic jam getting to the Garden and, en route, passed a local tavern named 'Teddy Bear Lounge.' The bear on the advertisement had one blackened eye. . . . As a baptism, it was like being led to a polluted river and having the minister holding the infant's head under water until it cried, 'Uncle.' "

Playing without holdout Foots Walker and the still-missing Mike Bratz, who had failed to show in Cleveland for awhile after being acquired from Dallas for a first-round draft pick, the Cavs had no chance against the veteran Celtics that ill-fated night on October 11, 1980. Worse yet, the Cavs continued to stink up arenas around the country — including their own — as the early stages of the season unfolded.

Stepien found himself bombarded, taking hits from fans and media alike over virtually everything he attempted to do. His mascots — Crazy George and The Amazing Boot — were ridiculed. His Teddi Bears were taunted. And his choice for a fight song, set to the dreaded polka music and hand-delivered to area radio stations along with a pound of kielbasa just prior to the season, lambasted. Even Tait, once the loyal company man, began to join in.

In a question-and-answer column Tait penned for the *Press*, he wrote of Stepien and the Cavs on October 21, 1980: "There is no doubt that Ted Stepien and his organization have been a primary target for the local media since their takeover of the team. I honestly feel that some of the rhetoric has gone beyond the realm of good taste, and the entire situation has been bordering on overkill. However, Ted and his troops have brought much of it on themselves.

"One thing that Stepien must learn is that you can't win a war with the media . . . Another thing to remember is that often times it's the little things that kill you. The ridiculous polka fight song is a classic case in point. Questionable trades, corny show-biz, and promises of on-court success that obviously can't be kept have turned off a lot of fans."

Stepien did not take kindly to the criticism, especially when it came from Tait — whom he considered to be part of the organization. Yet as Stepien's first season of ownership trudged on, Tait's criticism became more pointed and much more frequent. It also often came on-air, during broadcasts of the team's games.

Before long, Tait, whose salary actually was paid by radio station WWWE and not the Cavs, found himself barred from traveling on the team bus. Stepien issued an edict that anyone employed by the organization spotted with Tait away from the arena would be dismissed. Needle eventually lost his job because of it.

But when the owner tried to push the players on this issue, he realized he could only go so far with those who owned guaranteed contracts.

"When he made that announcement in the locker room, that no one was to associate with me, the next day we were leaving for the West Coast," Tait said. "And so Donnie Ford comes out of the locker room and says, 'What are you doing tomorrow night?' I said, 'Nothing that I know of.'

"And so what they did, at the Vacation Village where we stayed in San Diego, was book a table at the restaurant directly across the street. This restaurant had a huge bay window looking out toward where you came out of the hotel and came down to get a cab. And Donnie Ford called out there ahead and reserved that table for the entire team. All the ballplayers, every last one of them, were sitting with me at that table that night when Ted came out to get a cab and go somewhere with his little honey."

As Stepien began to step into his cab, Ford stood and banged on the huge bay window, loud enough for Stepien to hear. The owner turned to look — and saw Tait, along with all 12 of his players, waving to him.

After losing six of their first eight games in the regular season, rumors of dissension in the locker room had already begun to haunt Musselman. Players grumbled that their coach was playing some players too many minutes, others too few.

The starters sometimes would go the whole 48 minutes, a la Randy Smith in that first exhibition game. Others, like Bill Robinzine, wouldn't play at all as some nights Musselman distributed all the playing time amongst only seven players. Several players voiced their complaints at what was billed "a motivational meeting" conducted by Oliver, and Musselman responded by using his bench liberally in what became the team's first road win at New Jersey on October 25.

Even young Bill Laimbeer got into the act, hitting 7 of 10 shots for 15 points. Robinzine added 10 points in 18 minutes, his most action of the season.

The Cavs won their next game, too, handling Indiana at the Coliseum for a 118-100 victory that gave them a modest two-game win streak. All seemed rosy — but only for an instant. Musselman exploded when the Cavs lost their next game, 119-101, to star-studded Philadelphia at the Coliseum. It mattered little to him that the Sixers had Julius Erving, Bobby Jones, Darryl Dawkins and Caldwell Jones on their roster. Musselman felt the Cavs had been outhustled, and he vented his frustration to the media afterward.

"A couple of guys — where were they? It didn't look like they were even on the floor," Musselman raged. "You could tell the intensity of some players by their numbers on the (stat) sheet, or you could just look at their uniforms when they walked off the floor. I just didn't like that."

Replied Dave Robisch: "He better not have been talking about me. I've never loafed in a game in my life."

This marked the beginning of the end to a brief but bitter feud between Musselman and Robisch, who clearly was one of the team's better players but had been battling the coach since training camp. The previous season, Robisch had averaged 15.3 points and a team-high 8.0 rebounds, playing in all 82 games.

Despite this, Musselman did not like the way Robisch challenged his authority. He began telling Stepien that Robisch was "poison," and that he felt Robisch had to be removed from the team before the poison spread to the rest of the players and he had a mutiny on his hands. Delaney, realizing that Robisch was perhaps the team's top overall player, quietly cautioned Stepien against trading the 6-foot-10, 240-pound center.

At one game, however, as Delaney watched from the stands, he witnessed an exchange between coach and player that convinced Stepien in a flash that Musselman was right in thinking they had to move Robisch.

"A guard drives down the left side and breaks out, beating his man," Delaney said. "Robisch, who was guarding a guy on the right side, leaves his man and rotates over to help just like he is supposed to. Somebody else was supposed to rotate over and help him (by picking up the man Robisch left). The guard goes up for a shot, Robisch goes up . . . and he blocks it! Makes just a great play, and falls to the ground right there on the baseline.

"The ball hits the rim and falls off, right into the hands of Robisch's man. He just drops it in, and all of a sudden everybody's saying, 'Well, goddamn, Robisch won't guard anybody.' Well, hell, he made a great play. He did exactly what he was supposed to do."

Musselman obviously did not see it that way. As Robisch picked himself up off the floor and began to run upcourt, Musselman chastised his center.

Robisch, infuriated because he was certain he had done the right thing, turned toward the Cavs' bench and saluted his coach with a middle finger right in full view of the crowd.

"Fuck you, Bill!" Robisch added for good measure, loud enough for most in the sparse crowd to hear.

Musselman yanked Robisch from the game and told him he would never play again for the Cavaliers. The next day, the coach marched into Stepien's office and told him of Robisch's unforgivable transgression.

"This guy is poison," Musselman said. "We have to get rid of him."

"You're right. I can't believe he did that," said Stepien, who valued an employee's loyalty above all else.

Delaney could not change Stepien's mind on the matter, and Musselman, upon learning Stepien had been swayed by the incident, pressed even harder for a trade. He got hot on a skinny 6-11 center warming the bench for Denver named Kim Hughes.

"Yeah, Robisch told the Coach, 'Fuck you.' Like he's the first guy who ever did that in the history of the game," Delaney said. "For that, we're going to trade him. And Kim Hughes is available. No wonder. He's probably one of the biggest stiffs to ever play the game."

Nonetheless, Stepien insisted that Delaney be dispatched

to Denver to take a look at 6-11 Hughes. Delaney did as he was told.

Upon arrival in Denver, the son of the head of Stepien's Denver Nationwide office picked Delaney up at the airport and asked him which player the Nuggets had that interested the Cavs.

"Kim Hughes," replied Delaney.

"What? Kim Hughes? Are you crazy?" the young man asked again as he nearly lost control of the automobile.

"He almost ran off the road and into a telephone pole when I told him that," Delaney later recalled.

At the Nuggets' game that night, Delaney's worst fears were realized instantly.

"Here's Hughes, 6-feet-11, and he's playing. He gets the ball five feet from the basket, and he won't turn around and shoot it. He throws it back out," Delaney said. "He goes to the foul line, and he's lucky to hit the rim. I mean, in junior high he would be a lousy shooter.

"And the crowd is booing him. They're booing him that night in Denver. So I get back in the car after the game, and the kid who is now going to drive me back to the airport says to me, 'Well, what did I tell you?' And I said, 'Oh my God, you were right. What a stiff! I mean, this guy is terrible.' Plus he hurt his knee that night. He got a knee injury, and they had to carry him off the court."

What Delaney had discovered did not surprise him, for he feared Hughes was not a very good player. In his two previous seasons with Denver, Hughes had averaged 2.6 and 3.1 points, respectively. He possessed one of the worst touches from the free-throw line in league history, and eventually would retire with a .333 percentage on foul shots.

Word spread to the Nuggets that the Cavs were interested in Hughes. Denver management was thrilled. They hoped to rid themselves of Hughes, and were doubly pleased to learn that the Cavs were willing to part with a serviceable player like Robisch to get him.

"I go back to Cleveland to report," said Delaney, "and we have a meeting. I say, 'This guy is a stiff. No way we want him, Ted.' But that Musselman, he's smart. He says, 'Ted, I have a video I want you to look at.' We're sitting in (Musselman's) office and he's got it all ready to go. He pulls out this video and it shows Kim Hughes playing.

"Hughes is at the top of the post, he's got the ball, and he's making beautiful passes to guys for layups. Then it shows him making a hook shot — probably the only one he's ever made in his life — over Kareem Abdul-Jabbar. Honest to God. I couldn't believe it."

Stepien looked at Delaney in disbelief after viewing the videotape.

"What do you mean this guy's a stiff?" Stepien said to his GM. "Bill's got this tape of him and he looks pretty good to me. He's making hook shots over the best center in the game. Listen, we've got to get rid of Robisch. He's poison to the team. Bill's right. Let's make the deal."

So eleven games into the 1980-81 season, Robisch was dealt to Denver for Hughes and two future draft choices (a 1981 third-round pick and a 1982 second-rounder).

"We were hugging and kissing each other in the office the day we traded Robisch," Stepien insisted years later. "We didn't care if we got Shirley Temple in return. The idea was to get rid of Robisch and clear the way for Bill Laimbeer to start at center."

Hughes' career would last just 45 more games, but at least the Cavs never had to worry about how poor a free-throw shooter he was. Despite playing the center position at 6-11, he incredibly failed to draw a single shooting foul as a Cavalier and never made it to the free-throw line in a Cleveland uniform.

In a total of 331 minutes as a Cav, he didn't do much else, either, shooting .346 from the field and averaging 0.7 points.

Hughes' main claim to fame as a Cav came on St. Patrick's Day, 1980, when he painted his penis green. The next day he proudly showed this off in the locker room, telling his teammates that "the girls all loved it last night."

Robisch went on to play four more seasons with Denver, Sacramento and Kansas City before retiring, although he never again was as effective as his last full season with the Cavs.

The same day Robisch shuffled off to Denver, Robinzine, who had played very little since arriving from New York in the trade for the popular Campy Russell, was dispatched to Dallas along with two No. 1 draft choices. In exchange the Cavs received two more mediocre prospects in Richard Washington and Jerome Whitehead. Combined, they had averaged a whopping 7.9 points the previous season. Having already received Austin Carr in the expansion draft and a 1984 No. 1 pick for Mike Bratz from Stepien's gang, Mavs coach Dick Motta was delighted to deal with them once again. He would later say: "I was afraid to go to lunch for fear that I'd miss a call from Cleveland."

Now the expansion Mavericks owned the Cavs' first-round picks for 1983, 1984 and 1986. Later they would trade the infamous Geoff Huston, who would be arrested for allegedly exposing himself to a convenience store clerk in suburban Cleveland, and a third-round pick for the Cavs' 1985 first-rounder. That gave the Mavs a solid block of Cavs' No. 1 picks four years in a row, leaving, of course, the Cavs themselves with none.

It was unfathomable. In an incredibly short period of time, Stepien and his charges bartered away the team's future for a handful of veterans who would prove troublesome off the court and mediocre at best on it.

Robinzine was furious that the Cavs failed to inform him of his change of address until he arrived at Cleveland Hopkins Airport early Thursday morning for the team's flight to Los Angeles and the following night's game against the Lakers. His luggage made the trip; he didn't.

Later it was learned that the Cavs originally planned to trade Robinzine straight up for Washington. But Musselman previously had expressed interest in acquiring Whitehead, and Dallas management coyly asked the Cavs' coach if he still wanted him. Musselman said yes and eventually decided that Whitehead was worth two No. 1 draft choices.

Hughes, meanwhile, nearly didn't arrive in Cleveland at all. The knee injury Delaney witnessed that night on his scouting mission in Denver almost nixed the deal for Robisch, but Hughes eventually passed a physical. Amazingly, he then was placed on the injured list with a sprained knee immediately upon his arrival in Cleveland. It was an omen of things to come.

It was under this pall that the Cavs embarked on a long West Coast road swing that would take them through six cities.

With Robisch gone and Hughes already on the injured list, the Cavs were left with a new starting center the first night of that trip. His name was Bill Laimbeer, and he admitted to the *Akron*

Beacon-Journal's Ocker that he was more than a little nervous about making the first NBA start of his career against the Lakers' famed pivotman, 7-foot-2 Kareem Abdul-Jabbar.

"I was thinking that I might take a jump shot and he'd block it into the fifth row," Laimbeer said. "Before the game I was joking to some guys that I'd probably foul out in the first quarter, or (Abdul-) Jabbar would score 82 points. I just saw him on TV the other day and here I am starting for the first time — and maybe the last time — against him."

Laimbeer, however, did a decent job against the future Hall of Famer, holding Abdul-Jabbar, Ocker would later describe, "67 points short of 82." Laimbeer managed 16 points and 8 rebounds himself.

Despite Laimbeer representing a bright light for the future, the Cavs in the present continued to stumble. They lost in Portland and fell by 35 in Seattle. It was during the embarrassing 118-83 loss at Seattle that Whitehead finally made his first appearance as a Cav. As he bounded off the bench and tore off his warmup jacket en route to the scorer's table, the cloth swatch bearing Whitehead's name on the back of his jersey suddenly was hanging by only a few bare threads. Musselman, in a memorable moment, walked up behind him and ripped the swatch off before sending Whitehead anonymously into his first action as a Cavalier.

Two more losses at Golden State and Utah were followed by even more embarrassment, as NBA commissioner Larry O'Brien announced on November 6 that the league, in an unprecedented move, was putting a temporary halt to Stepien's trades.

In a memo distributed to all 23 NBA clubs, O'Brien said there would be no more trades permitted with Cleveland without the approval of Joe Axelson, the league's operations director.

Echoing league-wide concerns, one NBA executive said at the time: "The Cavs act as if draft picks are monopoly money, and they're getting two free players by landing on Community Chest."

Another NBA front-office type added: "The fear was that what Stepien was doing was having a harmful effect on the credibility of the league. It's not like a store, where if a guy bankrupts himself nobody else is affected. A league is a partnership. You're only as strong as your weakest team. If one brick is pulled out, the whole building can fall down."

Thus, O'Brien's edict came down despite — or perhaps because of — Stepien's earlier claim that "there will be no more trades unless it's a blockbuster." After meeting with O'Brien, Axelson and Deputy Commissioner Simon Gourdine in New York and being told of the league's intentions, the man now being referred to as Terrible Ted was furious.

"They told me to clear all trades with the league," Stepien told Bill Nichols of the *Plain Dealer*. "They were concerned about the Robisch-Hughes trade. I told them the trade was not for Hughes, but so we could start Bill Laimbeer at center. Also, Robisch, who is 31, had signed a four-year contract."

Stepien failed to mention that he was the one who had granted Robisch that contract, worth $1.2 million. He also conveniently forgot to point out that he had agreed to pay a portion of Robisch's salary to get the Nuggets to agree to the trade involving Hughes.

"If the league had stepped in when San Antonio took our coach (Stan Albeck), we probably would have made just one trade, the one for Campy Russell, who Albeck didn't like," Stepien continued. "I want Bill Musselman to get the players he thinks he can win with. I would have done that with Albeck, too. Axelson admitted he has not seen film of Laimbeer, or seen him play in person. I suggested he see him."

Again, Stepien failed to mention that Robinzine had been the fruit from the Russell trade, and that the decision to move Robinzine had been made by Musselman after only 11 games.

Clearly the league could no longer hide its deep concern over the frequency of questionable trades being made by Stepien. O'Brien and others did not like the fact that the team had but one No. 1 draft pick left until 1987 — and that one, the 1985 pick, would soon enough be gone in the NBA-approved Huston deal with Dallas later that season.

Stepien did not think the league should be meddling so much in his team's affairs. He also admitted he was concerned about all the shots he was taking from the media.

"I'm optimistic about the club, and I'm committed for 10 years," Stepien told Nichols. "But I don't like all the shots I get from the media."

Stepien was even more expansive in an interview with the *Cleveland Press*, during which he said: "I'm disgusted because those at the top of the league have never seen, live or on film, the players we traded for. My God, won't anybody give us a chance? Look at us at the end of the season and then tell us about it.... This action is a humiliation and undeserved.

"They are picking on the new kid on the block. If they want me to sell the club, I will. (But) it all comes down to winning. What if we make the playoffs? Then I will have the last laugh."

The more Stepien talked with reporters about the incident, the more he fumed. And the more he seemed to believe himself when he vowed to build a winner his way or no way.

"I deeply resent the Commissioner's conduct," Stepien added in the *Press*. "It is unprecedented. It is unfair. Nobody is more dedicated than myself to bringing Cleveland a winner. I've made mistakes, but I'll correct them. I'm putting out a ton of money and I'm footing the bills. The league should be so lucky to have somebody else like me around."

The league obviously did not see it the same way. And the local media was about to step up its attacks, both in frequency and venom.

In the most incredible move to date in what was rapidly developing into a most incredible ownership, the decision was made to waive Whitehead after only three appearances in a Cavs' uniform. This, remember, was the player for which Musselman had encouraged the club to surrender two No. 1 draft picks — only 17 days earlier! The decision also came just 11 days after Stepien's meeting with the commissioner in New York.

A headline in the *Akron Beacon-Journal* screamed: "Whitehead deal totals: No. 1 + No. 1 = 0."

Delaney remembers the day Whitehead was waived.

"Yeah, Musselman said he was a stiff. A stiff. And that he couldn't play," Delaney said. "And that was almost right after we traded for him."

Or rather, right after Musselman traded for him.

Most deals during the Stepien era were initiated in Musselman's head and executed by the man who amazingly later would go on to coach again in the NBA with the expansion Minnesota Timberwolves. Virtually all parties who worked for the team or observed closely during those tumultuous, dark days agree with that.

"It was 100 percent Bill Musselman. One hundred percent," Delaney said. "He would do anything, believe me. He would kill to win a game, but he didn't want anyone to oppose him. He was the most vicious human being I have ever met.

"Even the secretaries in the office hated him. Every secretary hated his guts. But you know what? He loved that, he wanted that. He fostered that in people."

Added Rich Rollins: "People say it was Stepien who screwed up the team, but it wasn't. It was Musselman."

"Bill Musselman told Ted everything he wanted to hear. And that was what Ted wanted, so then he put all his trust in the guy," Needle said.

And finally, from Ocker: "Musselman was a con artist. Ted's stupid, and you could really get caught in Musselman's web if you were a dumb ass."

Regardless, Stepien took most of the heat for the deals. And everywhere Stepien turned, he seemed to compound his growing personal nightmare. He took out a full-page advertisement in the *Plain Dealer*, headed by the caption: "Cavaliers Close-Up: Get acquainted with your 1980-81 Cavaliers." In it, in addition to small mug shots and capsules of information about each individual Cavs' player and a large mug shot of Stepien, was a brief letter addressed to the fans by Stepien himself. It read:

> "Dear Cavaliers' Fan,
>
> Everyone connected with the Cavaliers looks forward to your attendance at The Coliseum. Your presence at the games will demonstrate your support of the Cavs and of the entire professional sports scene in Northeast Ohio.
>
> It is important to all area residents that we keep Northeastern Ohio a top sports center in the nation.
>
> Support, patience, enthusiasm: It takes all three to make a new team, as the 1980-81 Cavs are, a winning team. Come see for yourself the Cavs in action. We have a good coach, a good team, and good halftime entertainment.
>
> Thanking you for your support,
> Ted J. Stepien, President"

Whitehead, incidentally, was pictured in the advertisement, which appeared nine days after he arrived — and eight days before he was waived. Stepien mistakenly thought the ad would show that he was reaching out to fans, that he was sincere about his pledge to build a winning ballclub. But if he wanted sympathy and understanding, he missed the mark. The advertisement idea brought only more ridicule.

Later in the season, Stepien's marketing people put together another ad promoting Denver's only Coliseum visit of the season. Two Nuggets were featured prominently as must-see attractions: All-NBA forward David Thompson and "former Cav star" Dave Robisch! The irony was amazing. Six weeks after dealing away the popular and competent Robisch, Stepien still was determined to use the player to sell some tickets.

The same advertisement pumped the halftime entertainment of "Crazy George and the Teddi Bears, 33 beautiful young ladies under the direction of Dave and Shirley Morgenstern." Despite such irresistible attractions, the crowds remained sparse at the Coliseum — down nearly 25 percent from the year before when the Cavs ranked among the worst in attendance in the NBA. As the losses mounted, reaching eight in a row at one point early that season, Stepien's support of Musselman wavered. He said he would evaluate his coach at the first of each month, and mandated that the team must start winning "two of every three at home. If we don't ...well, then we'll see."

CHAPTER NINE

"Mayhem at Richfield"

As shocked as Stepien and Musselman may have been at the torrent of league-wide criticism being directed at their operation, it was about to get decidedly worse. Acerbic WWWE-radio talk show host Pete Franklin, who drew vast numbers of listeners, was just getting warmed up — on the airwaves and in print. In a column published November 13, 1980 in "Sportsbeat," a local sports weekly, Franklin really cut loose.

He wrote: "When the owner of the team is a more than slightly out-of-whack character like Theodore J. Stepien, and he has hired a coach who keeps around him as a close associate an eggshell, beer can-chewing freak (i.e. "The Amazing Boot"), then you know that the head of the asylum is not only whacko, but his keeper is equally so.

"In private conversations with executives, coaches, scouts at an NBA level, I could get none of these people to get on the air and comment on the Cavaliers' most recent deals. Nobody could talk more than five minutes about them without gagging, giggling and genuinely going into a howl. It is expected after these marvelous transactions that the thing to do in the NBA is call the Cavs and make a trade. Whatever is left of the franchise can be culled for almost anything conceivable.

" . . . When something looks, walks, talks and smells like a duck, damn it's a duck. And in this case a man is so inept as to be an unfortunate caricature of a clown. I speak of the well-meaning owner of the Cavs, whose contribution to the desecration of a sports franchise has been monumental. In only a few months, he has completely and thoroughly shattered and demolished this team."

Franklin had a unique perspective on the Cavs. Love him or hate him on the air — and there seemed to be no in between for his legions of listeners — Franklin long ago had proven himself an astute observer of the Cleveland sports scene. He worked at it. He attended Cavs, Indians and Browns games whenever he could, and he asked questions afterward of players, coaches and front-office personnel as if he were a beat writer requiring insight for a game story the following day. That is why most sportswriters, even though some of them could not stand Franklin's egotistical on-air antics, still respected the man. He did not fake it like other talk-show hosts. He craved inside information, and he knew how to go about obtaining it like the best reporters.

In a short period of time, Franklin grew to despise everything Stepien stood for. His talk show became a one-man crusade to drum Stepien out of ownership. And many of his words, which came in the form of biting criticism, would later prove quite prophetic.

Consider how he concluded that "Sportsbeat" column in November, 1980: "I love the Cavs," Franklin wrote. "I always have. They were born on my show a decade ago. They were horrible in the beginning, but they were lovable.

"They became a sports giant in our community a few years ago. Cleveland demonstrated that it can and does and will support any big-time, major-league franchise . . . . Our one hope (for the Cavs) is that a new owner magically appears on the horizon. As much as a basketball franchise can be raped and plundered as this one has been, it can also be built again with just one or two transactions. First-round draft choices can be reacquired with astute negotiation.

"All of this will take the proper counsel of NBA people. It will take an owner without an enormous ego."

When the Cavs finally did win a game, such as when they held off Atlanta for a 114-111 victory at the Coliseum on November 13, 1980, the media still got its digs in. Wrote Doug Clarke in the *Cleveland Press*: "The Cavaliers, proving that the sun really does shine on some dog's head every day, won a game of basketball last night."

A few days later it was Ocker's turn, and in a Sunday column he mused: "It is no longer a question of whether the Cavaliers can reverse their course and turn the season into an artistic success. Picasso wouldn't touch this bunch with a 10-foot roller. Only owner Ted Stepien — who sees, hears and thinks what his ego permits — still has delusions of post-season play. Making the playoffs is no more within the scope of the Cavaliers' powers than making 20 consecutive free throws is within the capabilities of Kim Hughes.

"Though the season is but one-fourth complete, what we are talking about is survival. The goal of the Cavaliers must now be to endure as a Northeast Ohio institution in the face of Stepien's persistent, though inadvertent, efforts to destroy them."

Small, but embarrassing incidents involving the Cavs continued to pile up, and usually Stepien was in the middle of them. When the club returned from an early 0-6 road trip, Stepien met the plane at the airport, 33 Teddi Bears in tow, and promptly instructed the cheerleaders to begin chanting "Go, team, go."

Fuming and red-faced, the players for a short time refused to deplane. As Ocker noted: "All they wanted to do was sneak home, take the phone off the hook and fantasize [about] themselves wearing Celtic green."

On the court, an increasing number of players were beginning to defy Musselman. As one player exited the huddle during a familiar fourth-quarter fade, he was overheard saying of the coach: "I don't know what he wants us to do, but let's try and win anyway." Crowds at the Coliseum were dwindling, usually numbering no more than 3,000 or 4,000. And those were the announced figures. At times it seemed like the crowd was half that or less. Stepien's dream of owning a major sports franchise had disintegrated into an ongoing nightmare from which he had no idea how to emerge.

He tried battling the media. Enraged over a negative article written by Clarke of the *Press*, Stepien chose to confront him — in front of some 2,000 fans at the scorer's table during halftime of a home game. In addition to yelling at the top of his lungs, Stepien soon began poking Clarke in the chest with an index finger.

When Clarke stood to defend himself, a burly associate later described in news accounts as the owner's "driver-bodyguard" joined the fray and engaged in a jawing and shoving match with the journalist. This soon escalated to the point that Stepien, who had initiated the ordeal, suddenly felt compelled to play peacemaker. He stepped in between Clarke and the so-called bodyguard, lest a brawl break out right on press row.

Clarke's cynical reporting style did not sit well with Stepien from the outset. As the team's troubles mounted, Clarke's cynicism in print took on a harsher edge, and Clarke was not a man to be intimidated or to back down in a confrontational situation. Sometime after the halftime incident involving Stepien's bodyguard, Clarke arrived at a game with a bodyguard of his own.

"I thought a friend of mine by the name of Cortez Brown would fit that bill nicely," Clarke said. "Cortez played ball at Kent State. He was 6-foot, no taller. But if you wanted to take off his sports coat and shirt, this guy was built like a fucking battleship. He had a tight, small waist with a barrel chest and big arms. And let's say an interesting face. He was not the kind of guy you would go out of your way to fuck around with."

Stepien and his aging bodyguard didn't. At the end of the particular game attended by Mr. Brown, Clarke made it a point to walk directly in front of Stepien on his way to the locker room afterward.

"Ted's bodyguard was a fairly big guy who I'm sure could handle himself quite well. Having said that, let me also say that he had some mileage on him. He was graying in the temple area and well past his prime," Clarke said. "And here I come with my guy. The bodyguards looked at each other, and it was obvious that there was no match there. Cortez could eat this guy alive.

"Ted had this look on his face, sort of a simpleton look, like he was thinking, 'Holy shit! He's got a bodyguard, too, and he's bigger and stronger than my guy.' Like he could not believe A) That I have a bodyguard; and B) That it's a guy like Cortez."

Musselman, like his boss, made no secret of the fact that he did not care for Clarke's probing questions. After one game in which the recently activated John Lambert sat on the bench throughout a rare 130-122 victory over Denver at the Coliseum, Clarke asked Musselman why he hadn't responded to the chants of some 1,500 fans left at the end who clearly wanted to see Lambert play during garbage time.

Musselman exploded, kicking Clarke out of his office.

"I'm not worried about Lambert," Musselman exclaimed. "Who wants to know about Lambert? You? Your paper? Even when we win a game, you look for some dirt to write. Why don't you take a hike?"

Others, however, did wonder about Lambert, the last hold-over from the beloved Miracle of Richfield team. *Press* photographer Paul Tepley caught the popular player toward the end of the Denver game, sitting at the end of the bench, his hands out-stretched with shoulders shrugged and palms turned upward as if to say, "Hey, I don't know why I'm not playing, either."

Lambert was placed on waivers the very next day. Was it revenge for Lambert having discussed his lack of playing time with Clarke? For Tepley having photographed him? Musselman denied it, but others thought so.

The irreverent, irrepressible Clarke forged ahead, suggesting as much in his story the following day. The headline on that article read: "Cavs cut Lambert, bring in beer seller." It was in reference to aging guard Mack Calvin, a former ABA All-Star who, at age 32, had been working in Denver at a beer distributorship. Calvin took Lambert's place on the roster.

In Calvin's first game as a Cav, Musselman left himself open to more criticism by inserting him into a tight game at the Coliseum vs. the vaunted Lakers.

"(Calvin) didn't even have time to practice with the team," Delaney said. "And we're up a couple of points against the Lakers with maybe three or four minutes to go. That would have been a hell of a win for us. But Bill puts Mack in there, and, well, Mack obviously is about 20 pounds overweight.

"I mean, Christ, he's dribbling the ball off his foot and everything else. He's falling down. He's doing the best he can — but we end up losing the game. It was ludicrous, bringing in a guy who has not even practiced with the team, is out of shape, working in a brewery. When you saw stuff like that, you really had to start wondering what the hell was going on in Musselman's head."

Calvin, one of the sport's real gentlemen, eventually got himself in shape and tried to help the team. But he further incurred the wrath of the few fans the Cavs had left when inserted into another game about two weeks later at the Coliseum.

Unbeknownst to Calvin, any time the Cavs were able to hold their opponent to less than 90 points and win at home, all fans in attendance would be able to exchange their ticket stubs for a free sandwich at local Chick-Fil-A restaurants.

"So he gets in the game at the end," remembered Delaney, "and we're beating somebody. And the fans are all excited, because if we hold this team under 90, they're going to get a free chicken sandwich. They want us to slow the ball down, don't shoot, play defense.

"Well, Mack gets in and he's scooting all over the place, pushing the ball up court. He makes about three baskets real quick, and they're booing him. The fans are booing. He's running up and down the court like you normally would, trying hard. He thought, 'What the hell is wrong with these fans?' The other team did get over 90, too, and they got really pissed then."

That wasn't all they had to get upset about those days.

Clarke's ribbing aside, local media criticism was only part of Stepien's growing problem. By mid-November, publications from coast to coast were descending on the Cavs and picking apart their carcass like vultures. The *Boston Globe* dispatched reporter Bob Ryan to Cleveland for an in-depth feature that filled a full page and then some.

In it, Pete Franklin was quoted as saying of Stepien: "Charles O. Finley was a dirty SOB, but he was smart. This guy is a megalomaniac who's dumb . . . . I don't mind you quoting me on that because he's a schmuck, a dodohead."

Stepien's past simply had not prepared him for such attacks of a personal nature. The son of Polish immigrants, Stepien grew up in Pittsburgh, where he became a star athlete in football and basketball in high school. He settled in Cleveland after serving as a bombardier in the Air Force during World War II, only because he encountered the opportunity to enter the advertising business in the city.

A modest beginning in advertising eventually grew into the Nationwide Advertising Co., which by 1980 was generating $80 million per year in business and clearly gave Stepien the financial wherewithal to dabble in professional sports as he saw fit. Prior to buying the Cavs, he also had owned and operated the pro softball team from which he gleaned Delaney, his first Cavs' general manager. Plus he had owned a small piece of the Indians.

"I lived in Cleveland for 30 years and no one knew who I was," Stepien said at the time. "Then I bought the Cavaliers, and suddenly everyone knows who I am. You suddenly become very visible when you are a sports franchise owner."

He seemed, at first, to revel in that. Then he recoiled from the public scrutiny as his critics multiplied and their remarks became more pointed. He began to view all media as the enemy — and he engaged in a series of battles that comprised a war he could not win.

"Nothing in my life prepared me for the kinds of attacks guys like Pete Franklin laid on me. Nothing," Stepien said years later. "I had been successful all my life in every phase of my life. I was a star athlete in high school. I had a good service record. I built up a multimillion-dollar business from nothing. I had always had a great relationship with the media in my business with Nationwide, and I assumed I would continue to have a great relationship with the media."

He was wrong. Oh, was he wrong.

Several times early on in his first year of ownership, Joe Tait advised Stepien either in private or in public via his own newspaper column to abandon the confrontational style and make peace with the press. Stepien, who very quickly had come to view the veteran broadcaster as one of the enemy rather than a potentially powerful ally, ignored him.

Rich Rollins, a personal friend of Franklin's, offered Stepien the same advice on numerous occasions. Again and again, Stepien simply refused to listen.

By mid-December in 1980, Stepien had begun countering the waves of negativism by making vague threats to move the team out of Cleveland. This marked the beginning of a pattern that would continue throughout the remainder of Stepien's ownership, as he alternately would proclaim himself "savior of the franchise" for the city of Cleveland and then would threaten to move it to Toronto or Pittsburgh or Louisville or Cincinnati or Minneapolis.

Stepien told columnist Phil Musick of the *Pittsburgh Post-Gazette*: "I may be forced to move . . . . I was watching the Rocky

Bleier movie (on TV) with some people and I told them, 'Hey, Art Rooney didn't win for what, 39 years? And he was beloved. Me, they won't even give me a year.' I didn't inherit the Lakers or the Celtics; I inherited a bad team . . . . It's like you go into a bar and get sucker punched, and 90 percent of the wind is knocked out of you. I don't know if we (as a franchise) can come back."

As usual, Stepien thought he could solve most problems through some sort of public relations gimmick. One fan showed up for a game hoisting a sign that screamed, "Stepien must go . . . now!" The owner responded by demanding that Roy Jones, director of operations at the Coliseum, remove the fan and the sign. As an employee of the Coliseum management group and not Stepien himself, Jones refused, explaining that the fan had purchased a ticket to the game and had the right to express himself, as long as his message was not obscene.

An infuriated Stepien then instructed his brother Steve, who was visiting from Pittsburgh that particular night, to go into the stands and physically separate the sign from the fan.

The kicker to the sign story? At the Cavs' very next home game, the Coliseum was filled with almost as many signs as paying customers. Most of them were on the same type of cardboard with identical penmanship. As Ocker wrote: "The slogans on them seemed to be the product of a single mind, too, and not (that of) Woody Allen or Arthur Miller." The signs, of course, had been ordered put in place by Stepien himself and were all of a positive nature.

Again, Stepien did not understand why the local media took him to task for planting the bevy of sophomoric signs that read, "Ford is our future, Roger is a dodger, Randy is a dandy," and "Go Musselman's musclemen."

It was comical, but Stepien failed to see the humor in it. To him, this was a great marketing coup that did not deserve ridicule. Most of the signs had been handed out to children, who confessed to inquisitive reporters that they had been promised free tickets by "strangers who told them to wave the signs each time the Cavs scored a basket."

Typically, Stepien blamed everyone but himself for the Cavs' demise — yet he stepped forward to take the lion's share of credit when things began going better. And things did, believe it or not, begin to go better during the 1980-81 season. Through

December and January, it helped soothe Stepien's bruised psyche that the team began playing more competitively. After beginning the season 4-14, the Cavs split their next 36 games, going 18-18 to raise their overall record to 22-32 by the end of January.

When the team's record stood at 16-28, Stepien passed out "newsletters" to all the coaches and players as they sat on the team bus outside the Boston Garden following a game. It was a week-by-week prediction of which games he thought the team should win and lose for the remainder of the season. Stepien predicted a 24-14 finish for an overall record of 40-42 that he figured would be just good enough to qualify for the playoffs.

There also was a rare moment of a positive nature to remember on January 3, 1981, when the Cavs retired Austin Carr's number at the Coliseum. Carr, lost via the expansion draft to Dallas prior to the season, was by then finishing up his career with Washington. As he stood at midcourt prior to a game attended by a couple of thousand fans announced to number 3,902, Carr broke down and cried.

"I tried to stand there like a man," said Carr, "but I couldn't. There were too many good memories that came back to me."

Memories of when the building was filled, the Cavs were winning, and Carr was piling up the points. Those were far removed from reality by January, 1981. But Stepien was nonetheless beginning to feel good about himself again.

The league had reinstated the club's right to trade, although potential deals still had to be pre-approved by Joe Axelson. The team appeared to be improving. It was a perfect setting for Terrible Ted to strut his stuff in front of the entire nation at the 1981 NBA All-Star Game, which would be held at Richfield Coliseum itself.

Mike Mitchell was a late addition to the Eastern Conference team, replacing Atlanta's injured forward, Dan Roundfield. The Cavs had won six of seven games entering the three-day All-Star break, and plenty of luminaries from around the league and the entertainment industry, in addition to the NBA's finest players, were set to visit Cleveland.

There was nothing Stepien enjoyed more than yukking it up with celebrities. He wasn't even deterred when comedian Bob Hope inadvertently referred to him as "Ted Septian" during a banquet the night before the big game. He did, however, make one mistake prior to the All-Star Game that cut into his fun a little bit: He invited NBA Commissioner Larry O'Brien into town for a party.

Shortly thereafter, the Cavs were in New York for a game. And Tait received a call at his hotel from the NBA commissioner's office.

"Commissioner Larry O'Brien wants to see you in his office at 2 o'clock this afternoon. He will explain when you get here," the somber voice at the other end of the phone said.

Tait hustled over to the commissioner's office for the first time in all the years he had been broadcasting the Cavs. As Tait entered O'Brien's office, the commissioner told his secretary to hold all calls.

"I thought, 'My God, what have I done? What is he gonna do to me?' " said Tait, who feared he was going to be reprimanded for derogatory on-air remarks he had made about NBA officiating.

Then the commissioner pulled up a chair, sat right next to Tait, and asked: "Joe, what in the hell is going on in Cleveland?

"People tell me I can rely on you to give me honest answers. And very few people out there in that organization have been giving me straight answers lately. So I want to hear it from you."

O'Brien then related to Tait his tale of terror when he attended the luncheon sponsored by Stepien at the Competitors Club.

"I went out there for that party, that luncheon they had to announce that the All-Star Game was coming to Cleveland," said the commissioner. "I go to the door of this hall, and there are all these scantily-clad girls chanting, 'Larry, Larry, we love you Larry!'

"I run this gauntlet into the hall, I get in there and look up, and the next thing I see is a very big, fat, unshaven man standing behind the podium. And as I approach the podium, he takes a beer can and rips the top off in his teeth, spits it out, pops an egg into the mouth, and then takes a powdered donut and eats it — shoves it in round-wise!

"You know, it's funny, but the thing that stuck in my mind after that was that there was this little cloud of powdered sugar hanging in the air in front of his mouth after he chomped on that donut."

Then, after a pause, O'Brien leaned closer to Tait and got right to the point.

"Listen, we're taking the very best thing we have to offer, the NBA All-Star Game, to Cleveland. And I'm scared to death it's going to be turned into a freak show, a carnival. So talk to me. What in the hell is going on there?"

So Tait talked . . . and talked and talked and talked. Shortly after he was done, the NBA called to say they were taking over most of the All-Star preparations and that weekend's operations. Stepien and his men were largely removed from the whole deal.

Stepien also was bothered by a couple of other matters.

Incensed by a speech Tait had delivered to a small group of Jaycees in New Philadelphia on January 21, and further enraged by the continuing verbal bombardment laid on him nightly by Pete Franklin, Stepien and the Cavaliers filed a $10 million lawsuit against radio station WWWE in Cuyahoga County Common Pleas Court shortly after the All-Star Game. The suit sought not only the $10 million in damages, but also termination of the team's three-year play-by-play contract with WWWE.

Tait's latest crimes? Telling the Jaycees crowd of about 30 people that he felt "right at home" because "this looks like a typical Cavalier crowd." In a newspaper account of Tait's speech the following morning in the *Dover/New Philadelphia Times-Reporter*, Tait also referred to Musselman's coaching style as "stupid" and called Stepien "a sadist and masochist" for hiring Musselman in the first place. When someone in the small gathering pointed out Musselman's distinguished collegiate coaching record, Tait retorted: "That's right. He set an all-time NCAA recruiting violations record at Minnesota."

And when those comments prompted another questioner to wonder if Tait was worried about future employment with the Cavs, Tait laughed and replied: "No, I am not under Stepien's thumb. Thank God. It would be terrible to have your fate in the hands of an idiot."

Stepien responded by telling anyone who asked — and more than a few who didn't — that he could perform Tait's job as well as the venerable Tait could. Then Stepien invariably would launch into an impromptu bit of play-by-play, once doing so in the middle of a television interview with Gib Shanley of Channel 5.

Yet Tait was not the real target of the suit against WWWE. That was Pete Franklin. Cavs attorney Kent Schneider contended that Franklin's constant beratement of Stepien and the team over the airwaves contributed to economic losses for the club.

Translation: Stepien blamed Franklin's on-air criticism, and to a lesser degree Tait's, for all the empty seats at the Coliseum. He also wanted to force WWWE's hand to relinquish broadcasting rights — unaware that WWWE, assuming it could get a refund on $188,000 it paid up front for those rights, was willing and ready to bail out on the Cavs, a losing proposition with its advertisers.

Basically, Stepien wanted to silence Tait and Franklin. He figured he could force Tait out, and often spoke dreamily — and unrealistically, as usual — of hiring former Ohio State star and NBA legend John Havlicek to take Tait's place. Why would Havlicek want to become a play-by-play announcer for Stepien's Cavs? Good question. Stepien seemed to believe all it would take was a well-placed phone call and a little extra out of petty cash.

Reaction to Stepien's filing of the lawsuit was widespread and uniform. He was ridiculed again, taken to task for putting himself and a court action in the headlines when action on the court with the team had finally begun to look up.

The dispute eventually was settled out of court, with all parties essentially getting what they wanted. Stepien dropped the $10 million portion of the suit in exchange for WWWE canceling the final two years of a contract the station no longer wanted anyway. It also meant a pending change of address for Tait, whose contract was with WWWE — and by season's end, that thrilled both owner and announcer.

"I went through Ted Stepien and a very bad divorce at the same time," said Tait, "and I enjoyed the divorce more. It was a good time for me to get the hell out of town."

Ironically, though, the agreement meant Franklin would pick up additional on-air hours with which to torment Stepien. With no Cavs' games on WWWE, Franklin's Sportsline show would run, on average, two hours more per night when the game normally would have been on in its place. And Franklin's voice would continue to boom out over a 50,000-watt station, while

Stepien began negotiations to have tiny 5,000-watt WBBG acquire the Cavs' rights.

Meanwhile, the Cavs were at it again in the trading game. They parted with yet another first-round draft pick and little-used guard Chad Kinch, who had upset Musselman months earlier following an exhibition game when he persuaded the team bus driver to stop at a restaurant on the way back from the arena. And the recipient of that 1985 first-rounder and Kinch? Why, Dallas, of course. The NBA's Axelson even approved the deal, even though he admitted to being "obviously disturbed at Cleveland relinquishing another future first-round draft choice."

The arrival of Geoff Huston further deteriorated Musselman's relationship with guard Randy Smith. After making critical remarks about Musselman in the *Akron Beacon-Journal* in late December, Smith, the man who played all 48 minutes in the exhibition opener, suddenly found himself out of the starting lineup and his minutes cut considerably. Then his name began surfacing in trade rumors. All the while Smith, 32, continued to add to his ironman streak of consecutive NBA games played, which by midseason in 1981 had reached 743.

Musselman, of course, was not concerned with Smith's impressive streak. In fact, he seemed determined to end it — despite the fact that Smith appeared to be the team's second-best overall player behind only the explosive Mitchell.

"Musselhead and Randy Smith had a real problem," said Tait, "and Musselhead started really cutting his minutes back. I mean, to the point where he would get like 10 minutes a night, eight minutes a night.

"Late in the season, it was late in one game with about two minutes to go, and there was a mandatory timeout. Smith hadn't yet been in the game."

Musselman did not care. He had no intention of putting Smith in to extend his consecutive games played streak.

Then the rest of the team took a stand, right in the timeout huddle.

"They came over and said, 'We are not going back on the floor unless Randy Smith comes with us,' " Tait said. "And they were serious. They said, 'Either Randy goes in, or we're not going back out.' So Musselman put Smith in to keep the streak alive."

By mid-February, with the team losing regularly again and home crowds almost nonexistent, Stepien flip-flopped for the umpteenth time on the issue of whether he planned to keep the Cavs in Cleveland indefinitely. In an Associated Press story dated February 20, he said he stood to lose $3 million for the 1981-82 season and that he could "only give Cleveland next year to support us." If it did not happen, Stepien added, he would move the team to "Pittsburgh, Minneapolis, Louisville or Cincinnati. I've already told the (NBA) board of governors."

This statement was made precisely six days after Stepien had proposed a new downtown arena for the Cavs and told a luncheon group at the Cleveland City Club, "I'm here to stay .... I could sell the Cavaliers right now for $12 million. It's an ego situation. Somebody's always willing to buy a franchise."

Incredibly, Stepien also told that gathering: "I really have a nice relationship with the media." And when asked of reports that he might move the team to another city, he added: "Some of that is media talk."

Twisting the truth seemed to have become routine for Stepien and Musselman by the middle of their first tumultuous year. Musselman, in particular, was caught in several gaffes, but seemed not to notice nor to care. One time he told reporters on a team bus that during a game vs. Milwaukee the previous evening, one official, "a long-time personal friend," had knowingly given the Cavs benefit of several calls strictly because of his relationship with the coach. There was one problem with Musselman's tall tale. He had been spotted the previous evening approaching the scorer's table to get the names of the two officials, because he had not recognized them.

There also was the matter of Smith. Early in the season Musselman had touted Smith as a great defensive guard, while noting that Roger Phegley "couldn't cut it on defense." By midseason Smith was on the bench because, according to Musselman, he played poor defense and Phegley was the team's designated defensive stopper.

Beacon Journal reporter Sheldon Ocker once asked Stepien if he believed everything Musselman told him. Stepien said he did, and went on to add: "I didn't get to be the owner of a $90 million advertising business by being a bad judge of people. I can tell when somebody's handing me a line.

"You guys seem to think I'm not very smart because my English isn't always so good and I grew up poor in Pittsburgh. But I learned in the streets."

Musselman continued to tell Stepien what the owner wanted to hear, probably because he somehow believed it himself.

"With the (addition of the) one right man," Musselman told Bob Sudyk of the *Cleveland Press* in mid-February, "we have the nucleus to not only make the playoffs, but challenge for it all."

Musselman also continued to ridicule the NBA for insisting that Cavs' trades be approved before becoming official.

"The real reason why that happened wasn't written," Musselman said. "The league was upset about Dallas gaining so many No. 1 picks. It was stupid of the NBA to embarrass us. It was only embarrassing itself.

"We are members of a corporation. You don't put your own product up to ridicule. As businessmen, the NBA couldn't run a shoeshine stand."

Perhaps, but Musselman's continuing refusal to play Randy Smith more than a few nominal minutes a night left his ability to run a team as coach in severe question. After a stop in San Diego to play the Clippers in March, news stories appeared in several papers quoting an anonymous Cav as wondering if the decision to sit Smith, who was black, in favor of Phegley, who was white, wasn't racially motivated.

Musselman vehemently denied the charge — but two nights later, after having played Smith a total of 71 minutes in the previous eight games, he suspiciously called on the guard for a 37-minute stint. Smith responded with 21 points, even though he could not prevent yet another defeat, 118-100 at Milwaukee.

Alas, the season was slipping away. Only Stepien failed to see it.

Finally, little by little, Stepien began to realize that his first season was destined to be judged a massive failure. As the club's record slid to 25-46 — 3-15 since the end of January — he looked elsewhere to shift the blame. He had stood behind Musselman, or so it seemed. Shortly after the All-Star break in February, he began repeatedly telling reporters that Musselman would return as coach for a second season.

"It's in the hands of the lawyers. The agreement has been made," Stepien said.

Musselman continued to say he was not worried about coming back, that he had "a verbal agreement" with Stepien to return as coach. He often responded angrily to reporters who questioned him about it. "Are you doubting Ted's integrity? I suggest you guys study contract law," he responded testily on March 11.

Two days later, the man without a signed contract, but with a vast knowledge of contract law, was no longer the team's coach. After much persuasion (and a promise, written this time, of a raise) by Stepien, Musselman agreed to step aside as coach immediately and essentially become the team's director of player personnel, even though Stepien announced Musselman's new title as "vice president and assistant to the president."

Don Delaney, a man whose highest level of previous coaching experience came at Lakeland Community College and Dyke College, would replace Musselman as coach.

Upon assuming his new duties, a somber Musselman somehow kept a straight face when he told reporters at a news conference: "Right now the important thing is to get ready for the college draft."

Thanks mostly to trades engineered by Musselman in what had deteriorated into a disastrous year, the Cavs did not own a first-round draft pick until 1987, which was more than six years away.

CHAPTER TEN

"93 Days of Daly . . .
and More Mr. Bill"

As the conclusion of Stepien's first year of tumultuous ownership approached, the team was in shambles. Public relations director Bill Needle had been fired for associating with radio broadcaster Tait on the road against Stepien's explicit orders. Musselman, reduced from coach to scout who doubled as Stepien's personal spy, had spotted Needle conversing with Tait prior to a game at Indiana, and immediately darted to a pay phone to report the incident to the embattled, increasingly embittered owner. Stepien fired Needle immediately.

The collapse of the team's radio deal with WWWE also meant the end of Tait's 11-year love affair with the club. The voice of the Cavs would head elsewhere at season's end. Unbeknownst to Tait, however, he was about to go out in style. Picking up on an idea spawned by Doug Clarke, the *Press* beat writer who especially enjoyed yanking Stepien's chain, the radio station and virtually every media outlet in town soon began promoting the Cavs' last home game of the 1980-81 season as Joe Tait Night.

The team, of course, was once again reeling by this time. Delaney had done well initially after taking over for Musselman, with the team winning three in a row at one point and the suddenly popular new coach even earning "Star of the Game" honors from the usually cynical media after a home win over Atlanta.

Alas, the good times did not last. The three consecutive victories were followed by seven straight defeats. The final home game, on March 27, 1981, came on the heels of a 137-109 blowout loss at Milwaukee and, under normal circumstances, would not have been paid much attention. As with everything else during the Stepien era, though, these were not normal circumstances.

"We flew home from Milwaukee to Cleveland," said Tait, "and the porters (baggage handlers) were all saying, 'Hey, good luck on your big night. Have a great night.' And I didn't know what in the hell they were talking about."

He soon found out. The Coliseum that night was packed for the first time in years. The biggest crowd since a March 2, 1979 game vs. Seattle — 20,175 — showed up to honor Tait and heap abuse on the Cavs' now-despised owner. It would be the only sellout crowd during Stepien's three seasons of ownership, and he had little to do with it, other than the fact that the angry mob wanted to use the occasion not only to show support for the broadcaster he was running out of town, but also to voice their discontent over the fact that Stepien was staying behind to continue running the team.

The crowd arrived early and stayed late, rocking the building in a way reminiscent of the Miracle of Richfield playoff wars.

"We want Joe!" the crowd chanted.

Then it changed to, "Stepien must go! We hate Ted!"

"It really sounded ugly," Tait said. "But nobody was leaving this place. Philadelphia had us down by 35, but everybody was staying and chanting.

"Philly TV kept sending this guy with a hand-held camera down there where I was, and I kept seeing the little red light go on. I knew every time that light came on, they were talking about me. And I kept thinking, 'What do I do?' And all the while the crowd keeps chanting and chanting and getting louder and louder.

"I didn't know what to do. I figured I was not going to acknowledge them before the game is over, because I might stir them up even more. I thought, 'Well, if I stand up and acknowledge this crowd in some way, they might come right down and kill the guy.' Well, Stepien got up and left with about three minutes to go — and when he got to the runway (leading to underneath the stands and a quick exit), they showered him with beer, popcorn, hot dogs . . . you name it. They threw everything they could get their hands on at him as he walked out."

Then and only then did Tait dare stand and acknowledge the crowd.

The next season began with Tait off in New Jersey broadcasting Nets' games, with Delaney back as coach, and with Musselman predictably lurking in the background waiting to pounce on someone and get his old job back.

At first, Delaney was a hit as coach. The players, who despised Musselman, embraced him. The press loved him. And Stepien went around telling everyone that this was the coach he wanted to hire in the first place, "but I knew the media would crucify me, because no one knew who Don was. I knew all along that this guy really could coach basketball."

The Cavs also beefed up their roster by signing free agents James Edwards, Scott Wedman and Bobby Wilkerson in the offseason. So despite a relatively tough opening schedule, the team started out 3-2 under Delaney in 1981-82. They won at Dallas in a blowout, at Houston in a tight game, then edged Chicago by a single point at home.

"You can feel the difference," forward Mike Mitchell told Clarke of the switch from Musselman to Delaney. "You feel it sitting around hotel lobbies . . . on the bus . . . at practice . . . just everywhere."

The pleasant feeling was doomed to wither. And quickly.

After the decent start, the Cavs dropped four in a row. A 98-96 loss at Milwaukee — during which a Delaney-designed play did not come off at the end because Bill Laimbeer threw the ball away — brought the wrath of Ted down upon his good friend, the one he always knew could coach.

Delaney returned to his hotel room that night dejected over the loss, but proud that his players had competed. Then the phone rang. It was Stepien.

"The coaching staff lost the game tonight," Stepien said.

"What did you say?" an infuriated Delaney asked.

"The coaching staff lost the game," Stepien repeated.

"Who said that?" Delaney demanded.

"I was talking to Bill (Musselman) about it, and that's what he said. I think he's right," Stepien replied.

"Fuck you!" Delaney screamed into the phone, slamming it down.

Minutes later, the phone rang again. It was an apologetic Stepien, who could not stand to have good friends mad at him.

"Ted," said Delaney, "how could you listen to that asshole? We're playing the fourth- or fifth-best team in basketball, on the road, in Milwaukee, and we played them to the wire before losing. We should be happy. We know if we get them at home, we should beat them."

For the moment, Stepien was satisfied. But at every turn, Musselman attempted to undermine the new coach. He sat next to Stepien at home games near the bench, and often openly questioned strategies employed by Delaney. Feeling the pressure to win immediately, if not sooner, Delaney took the team to Atlanta and made a huge mistake.

"We've played some of the best teams in basketball, and we're playing these teams to the wire," Delaney told his players. "We're playing Atlanta now. We've got to beat these guys."

They didn't, losing in overtime to continue a losing streak that would grow to eight games and outlast the coach.

"I was devastated," Delaney said. "This was the team we had to beat, a game we had to have. That's what I had told them. What do you tell a team after they lose a game you said they had to have?"

So Delaney was left with little to say to his players — and it was still very early in the season. The coach met with Stepien at the Holiday Inn in Wickliffe after a seventh consecutive loss.

"We've got to do something," said Stepien, who nonetheless was reluctant to fire his long-time friend.

Suddenly, Stepien had an idea.

"Look, I don't want to fire you," he told Delaney. "Let's get rid of all your assistants. I'll fire all your assistant coaches and you can hire new ones."

"Ted, come on. That's not going to change anything," Delaney said. "Do what you have to do. If there is something I can do to help the team get better, fine. Just do what you think you have to do."

Stepien already had a coaching replacement in mind, planted there, surprisingly, by Musselman. The replacement was a little-known NBA assistant coach in Philadelphia. His name was Chuck Daly.

Daly, 52, may have been relatively unknown to the average fan — but NBA insiders knew who he was. Two years earlier, three teams had approached him about possibly becoming their head coach. He interviewed in Detroit and San Antonio, and turned down the opportunity in Dallas because he was so confident one of the other two would work out.

When neither did because of contractual disagreements that could not be ironed out, Daly found himself back on the bench as an assistant in Philly at the start of the next season. It was then that he made a decision.

"I was at such an age that I found myself thinking, 'The next job that comes along, I'm going to take it,' " Daly said.

The next job that came along, however, was in Atlanta and went to Kevin Loughery. That heightened Daly's resolve to land a head coaching position.

"The next job that comes open, I'm going to take it," he repeated to himself. "If I don't, I may never get to be a head coach in this league."

The next job that came open was in Cleveland, where the Cavs had started out the season with a 4-13 record after finishing 28-54 the previous season. Daly knew the team had problems. He knew the reputation of its owner.

But he aggressively pursued the job anyway. He had run into Musselman on a scouting assignment while Delaney was still coach, and Musselman quizzed him extensively about his coaching philosophies, his present situation, "and where my thought process was," according to Daly.

When the job came open, the Cavs quickly narrowed the search down to Daly and long-time NBA coaching veteran Hubie Brown. The Sixers were in Boston when Brown phoned and told Daly's wife he was removing himself from consideration, leaving Chuck as the frontrunner.

"I didn't know a lot about Ted," Daly said. "I knew things there were a little unstable, but I also was intrigued by the fact that it sounded like they wanted to try to do the right thing. They had gone out and looked to sign some free agents. I liked their building; I felt that at that time it was one of the nicest buildings in the NBA. I didn't know much about Cleveland, but I had grown up in western Pennsylvania, and I knew it was a great sports town. I knew it was going to take some time (to attempt building a winner), but in I went."

Daly finally had his first NBA head coaching position. But the situation he entered was more than a little unstable, as he soon discovered.

Upon his arrival, Daly encountered chaos. He could not find all his players, for one thing.

Two nights earlier in New Jersey, guard Bobby Wilkerson was driving to the basket when his legs got cut out from under him.

"He landed on his head and back," Delaney said. "We took him right to the hospital to make sure everything was OK. They said nothing was broken and he was going to be fine, but they wanted to keep him in the hospital overnight for observation."

The team, meanwhile, flew on to Washington for Daly's first game as coach. Wilkerson stayed behind in New Jersey, with plans to fly to Cleveland the next day for a follow-up examination at Lutheran Medical. Those were the team's plans for Wilkerson, anyway.

Wilkerson checked himself out of the hospital in Jersey early, and called Stepien from Hopkins Airport upon his return to Cleveland.

"Ted, this is Bobby Wilkerson. I'm at the airport and I'm OK, but my grandmother has died. I'd like to go to the funeral," he said.

"Fine, go ahead," a sympathetic Stepien said.

Following a 94-87 loss to the Bullets in Daly's debut, the Cavs returned to Cleveland. The new coach expected to find Wilkerson, who by now had been gone three days.

"Where did his grandmother live? Where was the funeral?" Delaney, who had been returned to the nominal title of general manager, asked Stepien.

"Hell, I don't know," Stepien responded.

"Don," said Daly, "someone's got to go and find this guy and bring him back. We need him."

So Delaney went off via a small commuter plane and rental car to Anderson, Indiana, Wilkerson's hometown. A few days earlier, he had been an NBA head coach; now Delaney was an errand boy flying through the Midwest during a December snowstorm in hopes of tracking down a missing player. In Anderson, he talked to aunts, uncles, brothers, sisters and cousins of Wilkerson. Strangely, none of them knew of the grandmother's demise. They also knew nothing of the where-abouts of Bobby.

"Sorry, I couldn't find him," Delaney said upon his return.

Finally, about one week later, Wilkerson resurfaced.

"He couldn't understand what the big deal was," Delaney said. "He just kept saying, 'Well, I got permission to go.' "

This was the situation into which Daly walked. And it immediately prompted him to make another decision. He would live out of the Holiday Inn in Richfield while coaching the Cavaliers. The situation was too uncertain for him to consider looking for a house, despite the fact he had signed a contract that included two guaranteed years, plus an option on a third.

One of the players who intrigued Daly when he arrived was big Bill Laimbeer. But at 6-foot-11 and around 265 pounds, Daly thought Laimbeer was overweight and, at first, played him little.

"I sensed we had something," Daly said. "He gave us rebounding and an unbelievable shot, even though he was overweight. And toughness."

Daly's arrival was heralded by Stepien, but did little to immediately inspire the players, who had grown numb. A number of the players wanted to be anywhere but Cleveland, including Laimbeer.

Hence, a disturbing pattern began developing. The Cavs would click for two or three quarters at a time, often building leads of 10, 12 or even 15 or 20 points. Then they would fall apart, blowing the lead and the game. It happened time and time again as Daly lost 17 of the first 19 games he coached, and 20 of the first 23.

It didn't take long for the phone calls to start coming from Stepien, usually at around 7 a.m. Sometimes Daly would answer them, and sometimes he would not.

"He would call me every morning," Daly said. "He was an early riser, and I'm one of those guys who doesn't get to bed until 3 a.m. But he would call every morning to talk about this, that and everything. And I would usually take the call."

Their talks usually centered around what could be done to make the team better. The day before Christmas, after Daly had been on board for only 20 days, Musselman decided the Cavs should move Mitchell, their All-Star from the previous season and leading scorer. Daly agreed to the deal — Mitchell and Roger Phegley to San Antonio for Reggie Johnson and Ron Brewer.

"We needed a 'two guard,' and we had (Kenny) Carr, Mitchell and Wedman to play forward," Daly said. "Brewer (a shooting guard) had been playing very well for them . . . . We were trying to shore up another position. Mitchell was a good player, though. At the time, maybe it was a mistake.

"But it was another one of those rushed deals, trying to improve our club too quick. I don't think it was any one guy's fault. I have to take as much responsibility as anybody."

It would not be the last deal — or the last mistake. Just before the trading deadline in 1982, Daly met with Stepien, Musselman and Delaney to discuss options on how they could improve the team. Their somewhat reluctant consensus: Trade Bill Laimbeer.

Only a few weeks earlier, Daly and Stepien had been riding together in Stepien's car to a team function.

"You know, I see the Laimbeer-Edwards thing here — and if you keep these two guys, I sense one could be a great high-post guy and the other, Edwards, can really score in the low post," Daly told the owner. "If we keep these two guys, I like the center spot. And then maybe if we make a deal for one or two other guys, we can solve this problem here and start winning a lot of games."

Stepien apparently did not listen. And Daly did not follow through on his gut instincts with conviction.

When the team's braintrust met just prior to the trading deadline, the prevailing feeling was that something needed to be done to not only obtain a couple of players, but also to secure a future No. 1 draft choice.

Daly was still wavering when he left the office that night for a speaking engagement on the east side of Cleveland.

"I took one speaking engagement that year. Only one, and it happened to be that night," Daly said. "One of the guys from the office drove me over there, and when I left the office I thought we pretty much agreed nothing was going to happen. But I sensed that Ted was getting terrific pressure from these people and the media about getting a No. 1 (draft pick). They really wanted a No. 1."

Somewhere around the Marriott in Beachwood, Daly ordered his driver to stop the car. He suddenly felt an overwhelming urge to call back to the office.

Musselman answered the phone at the Coliseum.

"Look," Musselman told the coach, "Ted's set. He wants to do something. We're going to make a trade of some kind. We've gotta do something."

"Hold off," Daly begged. "At least wait 'til I get back to discuss this."

To Musselman's credit, he did wait for Daly to return from the speaking engagement. Then they ran through all the trade offers they had for Laimbeer.

"We ultimately agreed on the Detroit offer because he pretty much — and I sensed this from Bill, because Ted wasn't there (at the final meeting) — had given an ultimatum that a trade had to be made. But I don't know if that's true," Daly said.

In reality, Musselman wanted the trade more than anyone. He and Stepien, to their credit, had discovered Laimbeer and been the first ones convinced he could play in the NBA. But now Musselman wanted to use Laimbeer to cover up past mistakes.

Laimbeer was the one player held in high enough regard around the league to bring them players plus a draft choice. And the team needed draft choices, because Musselman previously had traded all the other ones away.

Laimbeer and Carr were traded to Detroit for Paul Mokeski, Phil Hubbard and first- and second-round picks in the 1982 draft. On the same day, in a separate deal, Johnson was shipped off to Kansas City in exchange for Cliff Robinson.

And the revolving door to the Cavs' locker room kept on turning.

In continuing to trade at such a furious pace, the Cavs robbed themselves of the one thing successful sports franchises must have — stability. The overwhelming desire to win immediately at all costs was shortsighted and stupid, considering the shape the team was in. One minute the Cavs wanted to build with veterans; the next those veterans were shipped out in exchange for youth and a new, but hardly solid commitment to build through the draft.

The deal with Detroit wasn't a total disaster. In Hubbard, the Cavs acquired a player who would become one of the most popular in franchise history, a man willing to do all the little things, the dirty work, to help the team eventually develop into a winner. They would use the No. 1 draft choice obtained to select point guard John Bagley, who was, for a time, a decent enough player.

But Laimbeer went on to play in four All-Star Games and — ironically, with Daly as his coach — help the Pistons win two championships. The key for the Pistons during their back-to-back championship run? Stability.

"Going back and trying to reassess it now," said Daly, "I think Ted had the right idea. He was trying to do the right thing. I just think he's like a lot of people who buy teams.

"They think they can run it like any other business. They are very successful in their other businesses, but they don't realize that in basketball, the only assets you have are those 12 players under contract — and that's a whole new thing. You can't just go up to them and say, 'You aren't doing the job. You're fired.' It's a whole different assessment. And I think Ted was listening to a lot of different people because he wasn't a basketball guy. We kept getting different kinds of advice on making changes."

Eventually, one of the changes that would be suggested involved the man sitting in the coach's hot seat. Daly lasted only 93 days. He never moved out of the Holiday Inn at Richfield.

"By the time I left there, I knew every way in and out of that building," Daly said. "I didn't want anyone knowing when I was coming and going. They might ask me something about the team, and I didn't want to — or couldn't — try to explain what was happening."

Daly did strike up a friendship with Rich Rollins, director of ticket sales. He spent hours at Rollins' nearby home, where he stored part of his wardrobe.

"Chuck used to come over to my house all the time," Rollins said. "I was one of the few people around who had cable at the time, and he would come over to watch the (other NBA) games on cable. I stored his wardrobe at my house for three weeks one time. Boy, what a wardrobe he's got."

"The closet space at the Holiday Inn was a little cramped," Daly explained.

Daly saw the end coming before it actually went down. It wasn't hard to catch the signals. One day, Stepien invited him to the Competitors Club downtown for one of the lingerie shows the owner liked to officiate.

"I went down there thinking, truly, that this could be it — because at this point I was ready for it," Daly said.

Stepien kept the coach waiting while he presided as the master of ceremonies at the lingerie show. Then he pulled Daly aside.

"Why don't you quit?" Stepien said.

"No," replied Daly, "I don't want to quit. Why don't you fire me?

"No," said Stepien, "Why don't you quit?"

This childish exchange went on for several minutes. Finally, Stepien decided Daly could remain coach for the time being. He bought Daly a drink and told him, "You know, this is a little like Patton."

Daly wasn't sure what that meant at the time, but later figured it was in reference to the movie about the famous general, which included a scene when the general was asked to step down from his post but refused.

Nonetheless, Daly did not last much longer. One day, he showed up at practice and assistant coaches Bob Kloppenburg and Gerald Oliver were nowhere to be found. They were in the Cavs' Coliseum offices meeting with Musselman and Stepien, trying to decide who was going to tell Daly it was over, that Ted wanted to buy out his contract and send him on his way.

"Apparently they couldn't decide who was going to tell me and who was going to take over (as coach)," Daly said. "So I went ahead with practice. I fined the missing coaches each $500, just like a player who missed, and went on with practice. I didn't know what else to do, and I couldn't act like nothing had happened in front of the players."

The next day, Daly was surprised to still find himself the coach as the club departed for a long West Coast trip. Stepien himself flew out to Oakland, where the team lost to Golden State the next night, and told Daly it was over. Daly agreed to step aside if Ted would pay the remainder of that year's salary, plus $125,000 over the next year.

"I have no animosity," Daly said years later. "I felt good about the fact that he gave me the opportunity to become a head coach in this league. As it turned out, I could have been damaged goods and had trouble finding work again. But I got lucky and got another job, so it worked out."

Daly's departure left Musselman with the opening he had longed for since the day Stepien persuaded him to give up coaching and move into the front office. He seized the moment.

"The players were like, 'Oh shit, here he comes again,' " Delaney said.

The first day Musselman took over for Daly, he gathered the players around him.

"Starting today," said Musselman, "we're going upstairs and we're all running two miles before we even start practice. And I'm going to lead you."

Delaney remembers watching that first two-mile run.

"Twenty games left in the season or whatever, and Bill, of course, has been jogging every day. That's all he does, plus play racquetball. But basketball is a different kind of running. Plus it's toward the end of the season for the players and they're all tired, beat up, and they don't want to put up with this. So some of them are walking, some of them are barely making it.

"And, of course, that gives Musselman more ammunition. He's now saying, 'Goddamn, look, I was right. These guys can't even run two miles. Daly didn't do the job. They're not in condition.' Well, you take half the teams in the NBA and try to get them to run two miles before practice with 20 games left in the season, and they wouldn't be able to do it. It's a different kind of conditioning."

By all accounts, Musselman seemed to be losing touch with reality.

With the team floundering and the season's end rapidly approaching, there was little he could do — and he tried to do a whole lot. It only served to further alienate him from the players. By then Musselman had few friends in the front office besides Stepien, so he had nowhere to turn for support.

He had threatened to fire several secretaries, or actually had gone through with having Stepien fire them. At one point, some of the secretaries confided in Delaney and others that they believed Musselman was behind obscene phone calls they were receiving at the office.

Over the summer of 1982, it was noted that Musselman began a habit of rarely using the phone in his own office anymore, electing instead to use various payphones located throughout the Coliseum building to conduct whatever shadowy business he was pursuing. "We couldn't figure out what the hell he was doing," Delaney said. "We were thinking maybe we should have the phones tapped or something to find out."

More than once, Musselman had been caught spying on someone, usually on the road. One night in Houston a year earlier, trainer Paul Spicuzza opted to catch a late dinner with *Plain Dealer* reporter Bill Nichols and Joe Tait, who was still broadcaster at that time. As they walked down the street, they noticed the bushes by the sidewalk rustling. Finally, they spotted Musselman eyeing them from the shrubbery.

Spicuzza eventually was fired for associating with Tait against Stepien's orders, and other perceived indiscretions.

"Musselman was always jumping out of bushes and stuff like that. It was really strange," *Akron Beacon-Journal* writer Sheldon Ocker said.

Still, Musselman had some kind of a strange hold over Stepien. Even the players were aware of it.

"As a basketball man," said Phil Hubbard, "Ted took too much bad advice . . . . It had to be mainly Musselman. There may have been others, but Musselman had to be the main guy. That was who Ted listened to the most."

The players most certainly did not listen to Musselman at the end of that season or the beginning of the next one. Musselman rode Hubbard so hard the next fall in training camp that Hubbard began to wonder if he would make the team — even though he had a guaranteed contract. The team had drafted point guard John Bagley and small forward David Magley, and Stepien thought it would be neat to promote the team as "The Bagley & Magley Show" because the two draft picks had last names that rhymed.

"It was just crazy. They were pumping that up so much. Musselman was on me so bad, I didn't think it mattered that I had guaranteed money coming," Hubbard said. "I was the leading scorer in most of the scrimmages, and I still didn't think I was going to make the team.

"We had one play. One. Musselman carried a big briefcase with him, and we only had one play called 'Red.' Even that was kind of an open-type situation for Bags to drive in and break down the defense. I swear to you we only had the one play. I don't know what else was in that big briefcase he carried around with him all the time."

Stepien, meanwhile, outdid himself one day late in the 1981-82 season. A huge headline in the *Plain Dealer* again proclaimed the owner's professed intentions of keeping the team in town, reading something to the effect of "Stepien says Cavs aren't going anywhere." Yet as Dave Dombrowski, producer of Pete Franklin's show on WWWE, prepared to go on air that very night, he received an unusual call from a regular listener who happened to reside in Canada.

"I also listen to a sports talk show out of Toronto," said the listener, "and I can't believe what I'm hearing. Ted Stepien came up here today and held a press conference to announce he plans to move the team here. He's on the air now talking about it."

After a little checking around, Dombrowski learned that Stepien indeed had shuffled up to Toronto the day after proclaiming the Cavs were in Cleveland to stay. At an afternoon news conference there, he even unveiled a logo for "the Toronto Towers," with the initials "TS" very prominently displayed within the framework of the logo.

When Dombrowski took this information to Franklin, the passionate sports gabber was incensed. Dombrowski arranged to have Franklin call the talk show in Toronto immediately, while Stepien was still on live.

"Pete wants to go on as a normal caller. He doesn't want Ted to know he's coming on," Dombrowski told the other show's producer.

Knowing good radio when he heard the opportunity, the producer readily agreed. Franklin called in. Disguising his voice so he sort of sounded like a small boy, Franklin asked for Stepien.

"Am I talking to the dumbest man in professional sports?" Franklin asked.

After a pause, Stepien stammered, "I don't know what would make you say that."

Franklin then boomed over the on-air line in his real voice. For several minutes he laid into Stepien nonstop, calling him "a two-faced liar," among other things.

It was yet another example of Stepien's naivete regarding the media. How in the world he expected news of his Toronto press conference not to filter back to Cleveland, no one could understand. To do this on the same day in which headlines in the *Plain Dealer* trumpeted his intentions to keep the team in Cleveland seemed, to Cavalier fans everywhere, a thoroughly treasonous act for which there was no excuse and could be no forgiveness.

Later, Dombrowski and Franklin began ridiculing Stepien on weekly segments during Franklin's show. Called "As the Ball Bounces," the segments dealt in fictional characters — but it was very clear who narrator "Uncle Petey" was satiring. The main character in the soap opera was a professional basketball team owner named "TS," which Uncle Petey kept reminding everyone stood for "Too Stupid." The team owned by TS was coached by a character called "Musclehead." And the team's fictional GM was "Don DeLame Duck."

"The beauty of it," said Dombrowski, "is that all we had to do was play off stuff that actually happened. We didn't have to make anything up."

True enough. They gained more ammunition on the last day of the '81-82 season, which ended with a club record 19 consecutive losses and a 15-67 record that was the same as the Cavaliers had in their very first year of operation in 1970-71. Despite the atrocious finish, Stepien called public relations director Joe Steranka and shocked him by saying, "I'm going to have champagne in the locker room for the guys the last game."

"We're not really going to do this, are we?" was Steranka's initial response.

They did. On Stepien's orders, there were several bottles on ice when the Cavs came off the floor after losing No. 19 in a row, 116-113 to Detroit in overtime.

"The players, they were all embarrassed," Delaney said. "They took the champagne and shoved it into their bags. No way were they going to pop it open and drink it there. They did take it home, though. Poor Ted. He was just trying to do something nice."

Fortunately, someone else was beginning to assess the situation swirling out of control around Musselman and Stepien. Someone a little more sane than the average Cavs' employee about this time. His name was Harry Weltman, and he would play a key role in sending Musselman on his way and guiding the franchise down the path toward a return to respectability.

Using his own ingenuity, but mostly other people's money, Nick Mileti founded the Cavaliers and fulfilled his version of the American Dream.

No, Bill Fitch is not cleaning house. Upset with a call, he displays fine Bobby Knight-like form hurling a chair in the direction of official Bob Rakel during an early 1970s game at the Cleveland Arena.

Yes, that is Cavaliers forward Dwight Davis in the stands. He's not checking tickets. He's jawing with an abusive fan (the guy holding a beer), who had been heckling Davis throughout a game at the Coliseum.

Walt Wesley (44) throws his hands up in disbelief after John Warren (11) scores on a driving layup. The reason for Wesley's disbelief? Warren, taking a nifty bounce pass from Bobby Lewis (5), put the ball in the wrong basket to start the second half of a Year One game against Portland at the Cleveland Arena.

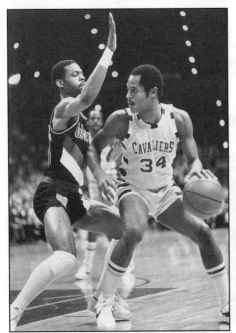

A great college career became a good, but not great, professional career when injuries thwarted Austin Carr (34). He did, though, become one of only two Cavaliers to score more than 10,000 career points.

Bobby "Bingo" Smith, guarded by Celtics Hall of Famer John Havlicek, put aside the knife and fork long enough to become one of the franchise's best-ever perimeter shooters.

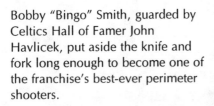

Lenny Wilkens made the 1973 NBA All-Star team as a player with the Cavaliers.

The Cavaliers landed their first legitimate center when former Marquette University star Jim Chones was acquired from the Los Angeles Lakers in May 1974.

Bill Fitch coaching on the sidelines during the Miracle of Richfield season.

In what has been labeled the greatest single shot in franchise history, Dick Snyder banked a running jumper over Phil Chenier to decide Game 7 of the Cavaliers-Washington Bullets' stirring playoff series in April 1976.

Fans celebrated the Game 7 triumph over the Bullets in 1976 as if the Cavaliers had captured their first championship, not their first playoff series. It would be 15 years before they witnessed another.

Nate Thurmond, as responsible for the Miracle of Richfield season as anyone, is a picture of dejection and exhaustion after playoff elimination by the Boston Celtics in 1976.

Yoga aficionado Walt Frazier was on the downside of a brilliant NBA career when he joined the Cavaliers in 1977 after 10 seasons with the New York Knicks.

All out of miracles: One year after the miraculous '75-76 season, not even divine intervention could salvage aging and injured Nate Thurmond's career.

His many critics contend that Bill Musselman was most responsible for nearly ruining the franchise during the tumultuous Ted Stepien years.

Ted Stepien found life as owner of the Cavaliers one huge headache.

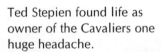

Don Delaney stepped from the softball field straight into the Cavaliers' front office—and later became the team's coach for a brief spell.

Joe Tait has seen it all as voice of the Cavaliers—and lived to tell the rest of us about it. His penchant for honesty led to banishment from the team by owner Ted Stepien.

The only Coliseum sellout during Ted Stepien's troubled ownership came on Joe Tait Night, when a packed house showed up to protest Stepien's termination of Tait's employment as Cavs radio broadcaster.

Chuck Daly is a Hall of Famer with two NBA championships to his credit, but he lasted only 93 days as coach of the Cavaliers under Ted Stepien.

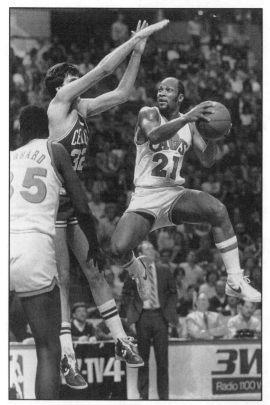

World B. Free usually found a way to get his shots off, even when guys like 6-foot-11 Kevin McHale of the Celtics blocked his path. Many credit the flamboyant Free with reviving interest in the team after the Stepien years.

George Karl (left) was General Manager Harry Weltman's hand-picked coach in 1984. Eighteen months later, a communication breakdown between the two men led to both of their firings.

Harry Weltman's legacy as GM was marked by more misses (Keith Lee over Karl Malone, left, in the 1985 draft) than hits (John "Hot Rod" Williams, right, in the second round in '85).

George Gund, left, and brother Gordon bought the Cavs from Ted Stepien in 1983. Though blind, Gordon remains to this day the driving force in the organization.

With Wayne Embry, left, as general manager and Lenny Wilkens as coach, happier times prevailed for the Cavaliers. But they, too, would eventually part ways after seven seasons as one of the most successful black GM-coach tandems in all of pro sports.

Under Lenny Wilkens' coaching, the Cavaliers twice won a club-record 57 regular-season games. But they never found a way to get past Michael Jordan and the Chicago Bulls in the playoffs.

Ron Harper could fly like Dominique Wilkins and the rest of the NBA best on the court, but management didn't care for who he ran with off it.

Mark Price: The best second-round bargain in the history of the NBA?

The Cavaliers hoped Danny Ferry would be a star when they traded Ron Harper and a pair of first-round draft choices for his rights in November 1989. Instead, players like the Bulls' Michael Jordan made him look over-matched.

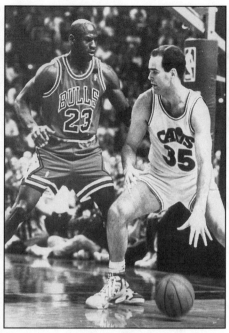

Brad Daugherty has his critics who contend he's no Patrick Ewing in the pivot, but he's made five All-Star teams. He also ranks as the all-time franchise leader in scoring and rebounding.

Celtics' great Larry Bird could only stay out of the way as Larry Nance threw this one down during the 1992 playoffs.

Mike Fratello was hired as coach in June, 1993 to bring fire to what had become a listless team.

This year, their 25th in the NBA, the Cavaliers moved into new state-of-the-art downtown digs at Gund Arena.

CHAPTER ELEVEN

"Saviors Step In"

Stepien did do a few things right during his ownership of the Cavs. Unfortunately for him and the city of Cleveland, these rare acts of intelligence and somewhat frequent fits of compassion came much too late or meant too little to earn Stepien the respect he so desperately craved.

Interestingly, there was a side to Stepien few people knew existed. He was generous to a fault, and not only with his team's future draft picks.

"He did some crazy things, but he also had some good points no one ever knew about. He helped a lot of people when he owned the club," Rich Rollins said.

One day, Rollins received a letter from St. Joseph High School requesting a donation from Stepien to put toward a bus the school was hoping to purchase.

"What do you want to do with this?" Rollins asked Stepien.

"Buy them the bus," Stepien said.

And so Stepien bought St. Joseph High a school bus. Estimated cost: $60,000.

According to Rollins, this was not unusual. Stepien rarely said no to someone who came asking for a charity donation to a worthy cause. Delaney recalled another time when he and Stepien were downtown and a street bum approached asking for spare change.

"What are you going to do with it?" Stepien, the recovering alcoholic, demanded of the bum. "If you're just going to buy a bottle of cheap wine, I'm not going to give you anything."

Then Stepien took the man by the arm and led him to a nearby restaurant.

"Give this man whatever he wants to eat off the menu," Stepien told the waiter. "But no alcohol."

This is the same man who could not say no very often to charity cases who wanted a job with the Cavaliers. Countless times Stepien would call Rollins, director of ticket sales, with the news that he had hired some hotshot who was going to single-handedly revive interest in the team's sagging season-ticket base.

One time a supposed friend of Musselman's was hired — and astonished Rollins by selling 17 season tickets during his very first day on the job. Only later did Rollins learn the sales were secured only because the salesman slashed prices by more than half without authorization, and offered to throw in such perks as tickets to upcoming Rolling Stones concerts at the Coliseum. Every single sale eventually failed to go through.

Another time, Delaney was sitting in his office when one of the latest Stepien-directed hires came in and closed the door behind him.

"Don," said the new salesman, "I've got to talk to you."

"What's the matter?" asked Delaney, noting the troubled look on the man's face.

"Don, I almost shot myself last night. I had the gun to my head, I had the gun cocked, and I was going to shoot myself. My life's over. My wife has left me, my kids hate me, and I'm not selling any season tickets."

Delaney, who had been immersed in some mundane paperwork, was stunned. "Wait a minute. Wait a minute here. Things aren't that bad," he stammered.

At times under Stepien, though, things were pretty bad. Rollins recalls one Christmas morning when the phone rang at 7 a.m. as he was preparing to spend the holiday relaxing at home with his wife and children.

It was Stepien. "Hey Rich, what time you got that sales force coming out in the morning?"

"Ted, the building is closed. It's Christmas morning," Rollins replied.

Stepien then launched into a tirade about how he was paying all this money to own and operate an NBA franchise, and now he couldn't even get into the building to sell tickets.

"I want you to get into that building," Stepien finally said. "And I want you to get on the phone to everyone in the sales force. I want their asses out there in two hours."

"Ted, I'm not calling them," Rollins said. "I'll go out there myself. I'll handle all the calls myself."

So Rollins headed out to the Coliseum, where he spent Christmas Day that year with a couple of security guards. The phones never disturbed them.

By the beginning of the 1982-83 season, Stepien had lost somewhere between $8 million and $10 million during his ownership and operation of the Cavs. Business was down at Nationwide Advertising, which Stepien had always counted on in the past to cover whatever losses he incurred in running the team.

On October 15, 1982, Stepien named Cleveland native Harry Weltman the club's executive vice president of operations. This was not like his other botched hires. Weltman was a smart, shrewd businessman with a strong background built in basketball and cable television. He formerly served as president and general manager of the St. Louis Spirits in the old ABA, and had been working for Warner Amex Cable in New York when Stepien came calling with an offer Weltman ultimately figured he could not refuse.

Stepien had recently come up with the idea of making the Cavaliers the focus of a regional sports network called "The Sports Exchange." In essence, it was the forerunner to the SportsChannel of today. But it had problems — as in Stepien had secured on-air talent and equipment, plus built a makeshift studio inside the Coliseum, before he actually had any cable subscribers lined up for his network. Stepien also had been boasting to friends that the Indians were going to join the Cavs on the new network, but he never actually secured the rights to Indians' telecasts.

Among the on-air talents hired by Stepien were two of his daughters, who served as anchors on sports-news shows that, again, were the forerunner to ESPN's popular SportsCenter segments (and of much, much poorer quality). Weltman essentially was hired to bring the cable TV operation together, but Stepien also promised him a hand in the basketball operations.

"When you are somewhat distant from something like that," said Weltman, "you seem to think you can fix anything. It was a period where they had very few draft choices. But aside from that, there was the challenge of building a really successful sports channel."

Among the people Weltman consulted before taking the job was David Stern, then an underling in the NBA commissioner's office. Stern, who later would go on to become the most successful and highly respected commissioner in the league's history, advised Weltman not to take the job.

"David Stern thought I was a little nuts for doing it," said Weltman, "and he may have been right."

Upon arriving in Cleveland, Weltman found the cable operation nowhere near ready to get up and running in a real sense. Stepien had been producing some shows, but only a handful of viewers were seeing them. A few hundred subscribers in the Kent area could get The Sports Exchange on their cable system, and no one else. More importantly, Stepien was running low on cash — and the cable operation essentially was put on hold because of it.

Weltman therefore found himself thrown more heavily into the basketball end of it right from the start, which was fine with him. Since the Spirits had folded when the ABA merged with the NBA in 1976, Weltman had longed to return to the front office of a professional basketball franchise. This was his chance.

With Stepien becoming increasingly more involved in trying to bolster revenue at Nationwide Advertising, he began distancing himself from the Cavaliers. Weltman quickly became the club's most visible figure, and his first major decision involved Musselman.

"I saw a few of the exhibition games, and it was obvious we were a terrible team," Weltman said. "And that's when the decision was made to change coaches."

Keep in mind that the season opener was only two weeks away at this point.

"It was my decision," said Weltman, who made it only six days after coming on board himself. "There were a lot of people who wanted Bill out. And Bill, I guess, was having his problems. He had a contract at that point, but I personally believe his heart wasn't in it. He went through a tough period of time here.

"I was the last person to make up my mind, because I wasn't listening to other people. I wanted to make up my own mind. But I could sense it was falling away from Bill, that he had been under a tremendous amount of pressure."

Officially, Musselman resigned. But he did so against his will. Amazingly, years later, Stepien said he regretted not sticking with Musselman longer. "That was the biggest mistake I made. He was a proven coach," Stepien insisted.

Weltman nonetheless named Tom Nissalke the coach, based in part on a recommendation from Delaney, whom Weltman knew from his days of playing ball at Glenville High School and in pickup games at Navy Park after Weltman had been discharged from the Army and returned to the area. Delaney became one of Nissalke's assistant coaches, relieved to be back in coaching, away from the tumultuous front office in general, and Bill Musselman in particular.

"Bill was like Adolf Hitler," Delaney said with disgust, years later. "I mean, the guy is paranoid. He is a paranoid person. Something is wrong with him. He's a schizophrenic or something."

So with two weeks remaining before the season opener in 1982-83, the Cavaliers had a new coach.

"We started two-a-days all over again," Phil Hubbard said. "Ten days to go before the season, and we're just getting into our second round of two-a-days."

The players accepted it, though, because they figured Nissalke was a vast improvement over Musselman.

"Tom saved most of his yelling for the younger guys. Us veterans liked that," Hubbard said. "Tom was OK, straight to the point . . . . I thought he was a good coach because he let you know where you stood and let you just play basketball. But we still were not a good team."

But they were better, improving from 15 wins the previous season to 23 under Nissalke. Even though Nissalke would not have been Weltman's first choice as coach, the decision to make a move with only two weeks prior to the season had left him with few available coaches from which to choose.

"The main thing is that I wanted to stop the laughing — because we were the laughingstocks of pro basketball, and probably all of pro sports. No question," Weltman said. "We were probably the worst franchise in the history of the league up to that point. So we had our work cut out for us.

"Nissalke did a good job because he was there, really, to instill some discipline and bring more organization to the team than there had been in the past . . . . While we certainly weren't a terrific basketball team, Tom did what he had to do. He slowed the game to a walk, we tried to stay close, and then we tried to steal a few games in the fourth quarter. I think a lot of people around the league began to accept the fact that we were becoming more professional, but also that we still had a long way to go."

Stepien, meanwhile, was just about finished. Despite the improvement in the team, negative publicity continued to consume him and keep fans away from the Coliseum. Average attendance in 1982-83 was 6,200, lowest since the club had moved from tiny downtown Cleveland Arena to spacious Richfield Coliseum in 1974.

At first, Stepien had no intention of selling the team. He planned to attract a major investor, or a group of investors, who could provide an instant infusion of cash to help cover his losses, by now estimated at more than $15 million. His plan was to offer 49 percent of the team to the new investors, and retain 51 percent, plus majority control, for himself.

Watching all this from a unique perspective were George and Gordon Gund, who had purchased the Coliseum in 1981. The Cavs were their primary tenants, so they did not like the idea of them moving to another city as Stepien often had threatened to do.

"You could just look at the fans and the attendance levels at their games, and you knew what the situation was as early as 1981," Gordon Gund said. "But we really didn't have an interest in purchasing the team until the salary cap was introduced in the NBA (in 1983). We felt total free agency was insanity. We felt we couldn't make any sense out of that."

They couldn't make much sense of what Stepien was attempting, either. "Clearly," said Gund, "the franchise was in shambles."

At about the same point in time that the NBA instituted its salary cap, the Gunds were approached with the idea that they buy the Cavs, while another group from New York would purchase Nationwide Advertising from Stepien.

The Gund brothers, powerful and rich, took a peek at Nationwide's books as well. Their accountants were impressed. So they went to the cash-poor Stepien with an offer.

"We'll bail you out and buy the Cavs," said the Gunds, "but only if you throw in Nationwide, too."

The deal was this: Twenty million dollars, with $2.5 million paid up front and the rest — $17.5 million plus interest — doled out in increments of roughly $2 million a year for 10 years. The Gunds financed all but the $2.5 million through bank loans and a note from Stepien.

Kent Schneider, Stepien's attorney, balked. He wanted four season tickets for life to Cavs' home games thrown in, plus use of a luxury automobile for Stepien for five years. The Gunds agreed.

Deal done. Almost.

One more detail remained before the Gunds' takeover could become official. They met with the NBA and demanded that some of the draft picks traded away so foolishly by Stepien and Musselman be returned to the team. Weltman assisted with the negotiations, using his relationship with Stern in an attempt to get the Gunds what they wanted and, in turn, keep his own job.

Stern, then the NBA's general counsel and executive vice president, would not become commissioner until a year later. But he was the one who convinced the league's other owners to permit the Gunds to acquire bonus first-round draft picks from 1983 through 1986. In return, the Gunds would make cash payments to the league.

"If the NBA owners had not been generous, the Cleveland franchise would have been out of business after the '82-83 season," Stern said in an interview in April of 1985. "The negotiations were hard on both sides. Harry and Gordon wanted to make sure the team would be represented in the near future. The owners didn't want to be in the position of bailing out a failing franchise.

"I had a feeling it (the eventual agreement) was a success when the Gunds complained that they hadn't been given enough, and the other NBA owners complained that they had given too much."

Added Gund: "If he says I was tough, you can see he was tougher — because David talked me into accepting what he wanted. I wanted more, to ensure that we had every opportunity to make this thing work."

Today the Cavaliers alone are worth an estimated $110 million to $125 million. Nationwide Advertising's revenues have climbed from about $60 million in 1983 when the Gunds took over to nearly $250 million a decade later.

That gives you an idea of George and Gordon Gund's business acumen. In 1993, *Sports Illustrated* magazine ranked professional sports' 93 team owners by net worth, "from the biggest billionaires to the merest of millionaires." The Gunds ranked fifth, with a combined estimated net worth of $1.5 billion.

Gordon Gund is the brother most involved with operation of the Cavaliers. George, a bit more eccentric and intensely private, is more involved with the NHL's San Jose Sharks.

The Gunds, whose father George II amassed the family wealth through a number of shrewd business investments and passed it on to his sons, were not unknown to Cleveland-area sports fans, and hardly beloved. The Cleveland natives had presided over the demise of the Cleveland Barons, an NHL team that merged with the Minnesota North Stars and spelled the end of professional hockey in Cleveland five years earlier. Gordon Gund to this day calls that experience "terribly painful."

He also is quick to add: "But I don't think owners should subsidize a sports franchise in a philanthropic sense. Sports franchises are businesses.

"People forget that the Barons first came to Cleveland because of George's influence with the then-majority owner. The team had been playing as the California Golden Seals, and (the majority owner) wanted to fold up shop. George convinced him to come to Cleveland and give it a try before throwing in the towel.

"We're native Clevelanders. We had a lot invested in Northeastern Ohio at the time, and obviously still do. We tried to make it work with the Barons. But after three years, we decided we couldn't continue to have the flow of red ink."

Gordon, the more personable of the Gund brothers, is a no-nonsense businessman who never has tolerated much flow of red ink. Much was learned about the pair when they met in 1978 with the NHL Board of Governors and a group of reporters in Montreal, where the merger of the Barons and North Stars was announced. Suffering from a slipped disk in his lower back, George Gund III entered the room in a wheelchair. Pushing the wheelchair was not the underling you might expect, but his brother and business partner, Gordon.

Gordon Gund is blind.

But Gordon wheeled George into that room, where George then sat off to the side, out of the spotlight, while Gordon stumbled to the podium to address the governors and take questions from the probing media.

"We must have made quite a first impression," Gund once said, laughing. "I think people felt sorry for us. I told them we were a hardship case."

Gordon Gund actually has refused to accept any semblance of that status, that way of thinking, in his life—despite his blindness. In fact, he remains ever the extrovert, the lead negotiator and deal-maker in most of the transactions the Gunds pursue. George prefers to stay in the background and has at times taken on the public persona of a cartoon character, although sister Agnes Gund once insisted to a reporter, "When he doesn't mumble, he's quite articulate."

George Gund, a former Marine, flies all over the world at a jet-setting pace estimated at nearly 500,000 miles per year. An avid fisherman, he has been known to pack his rod and reel and take off for a fishing hole halfway around the world on a moment's notice. If he wants to transplant a tree, as he has done many times, friends say he loads the tree on his private plane and is off to yet another destination. And if he wants to buy shoes or do a little sight-seeing in Italy or somewhere else in Europe, he does it. Travel can be that simple when you have several hundred million dollars and a private plane at your disposal 24 hours per day.

Yet George Gund is so shy and timid he will ask one of his employees with the Sharks or Cavaliers, in a barely discernible whisper, if he can take home a spare puck or an autographed basketball. Once he showed up late for a North Stars game, was denied entrance, and simply shrugged his shoulders and began to walk away before someone recognized him and insisted he be allowed in the very building he owned. Another time during a Cavs-Bulls' playoff game at the Coliseum, George the amateur photographer was spotted behind the Cleveland bench with a camera, angling to take some shots of Michael Jordan in action and clearly reveling in the moment. Can you imagine George Steinbrenner — or even Ted Stepien — doing any of these things?

Former North Stars president Lou Nanne once said of George Gund: "George is the kind of guy who will ask my permission to take a couple of hockey sticks. And I'll tell him, 'George, you don't have to ask me. They're yours. It's YOUR team!' "

Gordon Gund tends to fit the public's perception of what a professional sports owner should be more than George. Except the man has no sight. Forget this and you will not be reminded by Gordon, who greets folks with a smile, a firm handshake and his standard line, "Nice to see you again." He is so engaging, so intelligent and so friendly and so perceptive, it seems he really does see whatever life unfolds in front of him.

He doesn't, of course, except for astoundingly accurate mental images he can describe down to the tiniest detail. He hasn't had a clear view of the world in the accepted sense in nearly 30 years, since he started experiencing bright yellow and white spots flashing before his eyes at age 25. A former defenseman for the Harvard hockey team, avid skier, amateur photographer and private pilot, he could not comprehend what was happening to him shortly after he completed a tour of duty as a naval officer in the Pacific.

Eventually he was told he had retinitis pigmentosa, or RP, a degenerative eye disease, and at first the prognosis wasn't too grave.

"I was told I'd probably have my sight until I was in my 60s," Gund said. "When you're only 26 and you're young and strong, you don't worry too much about what your life will be like when you're in your 60s."

Gund, however, soon encountered great difficulty driving at night, fully aware by now that night blindness is one of the earliest symptoms of RP reaching an advanced stage. He returned to see his doctor, and this time the prognosis was not nearly as promising. He was told he was going blind. He was told his case of RP was advanced enough that he probably would have only limited and increasingly worsening vision for another five to 10 years. Furthermore, the stunned Gund learned there was no treatment for this terrible disease.

"So I know what it's like to be desperate, absolutely frantic," Gund has said.

Gund was so desperate and so frantic that he and his wife, Llura, began scouring the United States for help. Gund simply could not believe there was no cure for the darkness that was shrouding his otherwise seemingly perfect world. Finally, one doctor at Johns Hopkins Hospital in Maryland told him of a clinic in the Soviet Union that was doing experimental work. The doctor was blunt, though, and said he didn't think much of the experiment.

Grasping at what he figured was his last chance to recover his failing sight, Gund insisted on giving it a try anyway. His vision deteriorated rapidly while he waited for his visa application to be approved, and visas to the Soviet Union, at least in those times, were not easily obtained. Fortunately he was still able to see when his youngest son, Zachary, was born in October 1970. "Seeing my son's face is something I will always treasure," Gund said.

Two weeks later, his vision was gone. Completely. Shortly thereafter Gund received word that his visa had been approved, and his younger brother, Graham, traveled with him to the Russian city of Odessa on the Black Sea. The experience that followed was not pleasant, but left Gund with a fuller appreciation for life he did not have before going there.

In an interview with Terry Pluto of the *Akron Beacon-Journal* in 1989, Gund said of the Odessa experience: "The Soviet officials couldn't figure out why I came to Odessa when the U.S. was much farther along in terms of treatment and research of RP than the Russians. I think they thought I was up to spying or something because this was at the height of the Vietnam War. But I had exhausted everything (in terms of RP treatment) in the U.S.

"No one in the whole building spoke English. I couldn't even use sign language because I really couldn't see anyone. Getting to the bathroom was an ordeal. I learned how to trail the walls and I felt the paint peeling. The toilets didn't flush, and they had newspaper for toilet paper. We got one shower a week, so you can imagine the place didn't smell real terrific.

"I was eating something, but I couldn't see it, so I had no idea what it was. I was told that most of the lighting was bare bulbs hanging from the ceiling. The hospital had been built before the Russian revolution and apparently hadn't been touched since, and their methods of treatment were just about as backward."

Gund was receiving between eight and nine injections a day of bee pollen and animal placentas "with blunt needles, not the sharp disposable kind we have in the U.S." And not in the usual places, either. Many of the shots went right into his temple, just above the eyes. The bee pollen and animal placentas were supposed to revive the dead cells in his eyes.

"I had between 200 and 300 shots in the six weeks I was there, everywhere from my head to my shoulders to my buttocks," Gund later told Pluto. "It didn't take long for me to realize it wasn't working, that I had reached the end of my rope. I wasn't going to see again, and I had to dig down deep just to survive."

When Gordon's wife traveled to Odessa at the end of the six weeks to bring him home, she was shocked. He had lost so much weight, she almost didn't recognize him—later describing him as "a ghost."

In some ways, though, Gund was stronger than he had been before traveling to Odessa. Through time, he came to grips with his blindness and faced life with a renewed determination that seems to have gotten stronger with each passing year. Gordon Gund would need that strength to whip the Cavaliers into shape.

CHAPTER TWELVE

"The World According to World"

Only two legacies would survive and grow in strength from the Stepien era as the Gunds took over ownership of the team. One was that of Harry Weltman, who was one of the few to retain his job through a front-office purge and continued to "stop the laughing" via creative marketing devices and a slowly improving product on the court. The other was that of World B. Free, the enigmatic shooting guard acquired from Golden State for Ron Brewer in December of Stepien's last season as owner. Weltman engineered the deal.

"Ted gave his blessings and approval on it. With that, we got him," Weltman recalled. "I was very familiar with what World was, and what he wasn't. But I knew he could make a dramatic impact on our fortune, and we were lucky to get him. We didn't have to give up very much in return, because Ron Brewer was not playing very well at that point."

That was because Free, a prolific scorer who had a reputation for being one of the most selfish and egotistical players in the entire league, was considered a liability by most GMs at the time.

Shoots too much on the court. Shoots off his mouth too much away from it. Treats defense like a disease. That was the book on World B. Free when he arrived in Cleveland.

But, oh, Free could shoot. And he had a certain style, a real showman's flair. Plus when he arrived in Cleveland, the few fans the Cavs had left were starving for something, someone… anything at all they could applaud.

"Interest in the team had waned tremendously," Weltman said. "And he not only stopped that, but I think he started adding fans. People wanted to see him play, and we also knew the way Nissalke coached and the way the team played, we could keep the score close and we would have a shot at winning — because the guy could knock down five jumpers in a row that nobody in the world could stop. So all of a sudden, we started becoming a better team."

Free averaged 24.2 points over the last 54 games in 1982-83, and 22.3 in 1983-84, which was the Gunds' first season of ownership and would be Nissalke's last as coach. Even though the team had improved from 15 wins the year before he arrived to 23 and then 28 victories under Nissalke, Weltman wanted more.

Nissalke was reluctant to start younger players such as John Bagley and Roy Hinson. Weltman wanted them to start and play more minutes. Hinson, in particular, was an interesting prospect who was the direct result of the Gunds' first restored draft pick, purchased from the league thanks to their successful bargaining session with the other owners before they took over the team.

Weltman flew to Nissalke's offseason home in Salt Lake City, Utah, to ask him to resign in the spring of 1984. Nissalke reluctantly agreed. Then Nissalke got on the phone and told friends in the media he had been fired.

Regardless of the semantics, Nissalke was out. It was not a popular decision in Cleveland, where Nissalke had endeared himself to the local media and his methods obviously had brought about significant improvement on the court. The *Plain Dealer* would soon start referring to Weltman as "Hatchet Harry," noting that this was his second dismissal of a coach in barely two years on the job.

World B. Free was born Lloyd Free December 9, 1953, in the Brownsville section of Brooklyn, one of New York's roughest areas. Free always was quick to remind someone who suggested he was from Brooklyn that he actually hailed from Brownsville. He was intensely proud of where he grew up, and often returned to the ghetto during the summers when he wasn't playing in the NBA.

Free got out, but he wasn't like so many others who never went back. This despite the fact he says he was knifed and shot in the leg with a .22 while growing up in the projects.

"I remember when the gangs — the Roman Lords, the Jolly Knights — would come out and roam the streets at night. Families would gather up their kids and go inside, because they would cut your kids," Free said. "They would cut you, too, it didn't make no difference."

Yet Free once told a magazine reporter of his youth: "Growing up in Brownsville was a great experience. If I die and come back, I'd do it all over again. In Brownsville I learned how to be slick, how to lie, how to tell if someone's lying. If I get bad feelings about a person, I'll talk to him right now and then I'll never see him again. A knucklehead from the suburbs would keep on talking to the guy, and that's when he'd get ripped off."

Indeed, Free had learned to be slick by the time he joined the Cavaliers. He also had learned to shoot with amazing accuracy from 20 feet and beyond, and would not hesitate to display this talent anywhere, anytime, against anyone.

After one game-winning shot he hit, Free was asked by a reporter if he thought at the time the shot was going in.

"It left my wrist, didn't it?" was World's reply.

Free rapidly became a favorite with fans and media alike in Cleveland, although at the beginning of the 1984-85 season he had his problems with the new coach, George Karl.

"When I was younger," Free would tell reporters, "I jumped so high I needed an oxygen mask. Now I'm older, so I need to rely on that jumper more."

Noticing a crowd of reporters waiting to get into the locker room after another game, Free smiled and told them: "You don't even have to come in, boys. Just throw the notebooks into us, we'll fill 'em up and throw 'em back out."

He could fill up the basket and fill up a reporter's notebook, to be sure. He loved the spotlight. When the Cavs signed the then-free agent to a two-year contract extension prior to the 1984-85 season, it seemed fitting that he be flown in to the

Coliseum parking lot in a helicopter. The team even arranged to have a red carpet rolled out in front of him as he returned to earth, surprising a stunned group of media who had wondered why they were instructed to hang out in the parking lot for a news conference.

But that helicopter ride was not World's idea. Nor was it his idea of fun after it was suggested to him.

"He was scared out of his mind," said Weltman, "and he said that was the last time he was ever going to do that . . . But it really got tremendous press coverage, not only here but across the country. It was picked up by just about every major news organization across the country."

And for once, most of the news organizations weren't making fun of the Cleveland Cavaliers. It was perceived as a slick marketing move to promote the team's slickest player. All the team had to do now to begin earning nationwide respect in earnest was win.

Management approached the 1984 draft carefully, knowing the right move could put the team over the top and into the playoffs for the first time since 1978. With Nissalke removed and his replacement not yet named, there was no head coach. That left Weltman and Karl, then the team's director of player personnel and a man who at that point only aspired to be head coach, to determine the course of action the team should take. The Gunds' latest purchased pick was No. 12 in the first round.

They compiled a list of five players they really liked, and a sixth in case the other five were gone by the time they picked. The decision was made to move up in the draft, and they arranged to obtain the sixth pick from Washington in exchange for their own pick and productive forward Cliff Robinson, plus cash. The trade, however, would not be announced until after the draft — with both Washington and the Cavs aware of which players they were supposed to select and then exchange in the prearranged deal, depending on how the draft unfolded.

"We made that trade with the hope that Charles Barkley would drop to six," Karl said. "But we didn't get lucky. And then we had to take the player who we thought was the next-best player available in that draft."

It was Melvin Turpin, a 6-foot-11 mass of flesh from the University of Kentucky who possessed a sweet jump shot, a huge appetite for the finer things in life and a questionable work ethic.

"Mel really wasn't my guy," Weltman said. "George was the guy beating down the door to get him (if they couldn't get Barkley, who went to Philadelphia one pick earlier). George had done research where it told him the average team has a chance to draft a great center once every 11 years. And there was no question Melvin had talent.

"But let me tell you something: We probably were the first team to ever use psychological tests on potential draft choices. Now all the teams do it. And when we tested Turpin, he graded out very low in terms of self-confidence and self-motivation. This was a guy who was not going to respond well to someone yelling at him. The tests told us that would send him into a shell."

Keep in mind Karl had not yet been named coach. The perception was perhaps Weltman had hired him a year earlier for the player personnel job essentially as a coach-in-waiting. By accounts of both men and others, this was a false perception.

For starters, Karl wasn't even Weltman's first choice for the player personnel job. The GM initially offered it to NBA scout Al Menendez, who turned it down.

"When Nissalke went down," said Karl, "I had no vote whatsoever in that situation. Everyone seems to think I undermined Nissalke, but I thought Nissalke did a good job.

"The only thing that transpired at that time was that I had told Harry that I didn't think I liked the front office and that I was thinking about getting back into coaching. And if a situation came available, I said I would like to pursue it. I actually was pursuing assistant coaching positions at that time."

Turpin and Karl were on a collision course, and didn't even know it. After learning of the trade to the Cavs on draft day, Turpin gushed to reporters on a conference telephone hookup, "One of the reasons I'm so excited to come to Cleveland is the coach. I love the coach. The coach and me really hit it off."

There was one problem. The Cavs didn't have a coach at the time. Karl would not be named until more than a month later, and he insists to this day he never told Turpin beforehand that he was anything more than a candidate for the job.

"Ask him who the coach is," snickering reporters demanded of public relations director Harvey Greene, who quickly cut off the conference call to avoid Turpin further embarrassment. It was an omen of embarrassing times that lie ahead.

Turpin, whose listed weight was 260 pounds, showed up for training camp weighing closer to 300. Karl, who knew of the psychological evaluations on this sensitive big man, yelled at him anyway. Long and hard and often.

"You've got to go easy on the big fella," Weltman told Karl before camp opened.

"Don't worry about that," Karl said. "I'll handle him with kid gloves. He's my man."

Still the intense in-your-face competitor at age 33 that he was as a player at the University of North Carolina and briefly with the San Antonio Spurs in the ABA and NBA, the youngest coach in franchise history found he could not restrain himself when it came to berating Turpin. And that wasn't the only area in which Karl obviously lacked in self-restraint. In many ways, Karl was not ready for the head-coaching position handed him at such a young age.

Turpin wasn't the only player Karl clashed with right from the start. Free was another. The two had played against each other before a knee injury forced Karl to retire. Free was everything Karl was not, and vice versa.

As a player of marginal skills, Karl was like a kamikaze pilot. He would dive for loose balls, sling elbows to get rebounds and play a physical brand of defense, using his strength. Those were the things that kept him employed.

Free disdained playing defense, and Karl, from his playing days, knew it. A player of immense skill, the game came easily to World B. Free offensively. He laughed at the feeble attempts of players like Karl to stop him from scoring, which they rarely were able to do.

Now, though, it was not player vs. player. It was player vs. coach. And they were supposed to be on the same team.

"George was real high-strung when he first got the job," Phil Hubbard said. "He tried to play World in one-on-one (after practice) a few times. You know, he thought he was better than

World. He thought he could be physical with him and beat him. There was a little pushing and shoving, but then World was just blowing on by him."

Later, Karl admitted to a reporter: "I never beat World. I scored on World, but maybe you could have scored on World."

Karl wanted to change the team's offense from one that relied almost solely on Free to one in which everyone shared the spoils. The emphasis would be on defense anyway. Work on defense and share the ball on offense were Karl's themes, which sounded great in theory.

They didn't work so great in reality. The team lost its first nine games, won one, and lost three more. A second victory was followed by seven more losses, leaving the Cavs with a 2-19 record on December 12.

At one point during the slide, Free told reporters: "Sure, we're 2-13 and that's terrible. But I don't understand why everyone is so upset. We've only played 12 games or so." Someone mentioned that the Cavs looked like they might threaten the NBA's all-time worst record, set by the 1972-73 Philadelphia 76ers who went 9-73. Free laughed. "No way," he said. "I'll win nine games by myself."

Not everyone shared World's new-math optimism that there was plenty of time to turn around the season. Weltman was getting pounded daily by the news media, particularly the *Plain Dealer*, for making the change from Nissalke to Karl. And Karl was beginning to wonder if he really could coach, after all.

"George was getting upset. We all were," Weltman said. "We had been losing games, and I remember how downcast everyone was. There was some discussion like, 'Will this team win nine games? Or will they be the worst of all time?' "

Weltman called a meeting with Karl to discuss what was happening.

"We have nobody who can play in the post. We miss one easy shot after another. We have no post-up guy," Karl complained.

"You know, George, you're right," Weltman said. "We have nobody. Roy (Hinson) isn't ready at this stage of his career. Phil (Hubbard) isn't really that kind of a player. So why are we playing that kind of a game? If a guy can't hit a 6-footer, why have him take it?"

Karl came to realize he had been trying to force-feed his idea of how the game should be played on a team that simply did not have the talent to play that style. He also was running the team like a collegiate disciplinarian, and these were pros . . . seasoned veterans set in their ways. To change the direction in which the team was headed, he first had to make amends with Free.

"George, we can't be having these personality problems," Free agreed when they met. "We've got to work this out."

"OK, World, here's the deal," Karl replied. "Here's the compromise. I'll revamp the offense and get you more shots, and you treat me with a little more respect."

"How many more shots?" Free wanted to know.

"I'll get you 20 shots a game," Karl promised.

Now he was talking Free's language. The two agreed to give it a try.

In addition to providing the entire organization with a newfound sense of professionalism upon taking over, the Gunds also were inspired with a stroke of genius in deciding to rehire Joe Tait as the team's radio broadcaster. Tait spent the last two years of Stepien's ownership in exile, first doing New Jersey Nets' games, where he lived in the home of Yankees relief pitcher Rich "Goose" Gossage, and then doing Chicago Bulls' games, where he learned to despise then-Bulls coach Paul Westhead.

"Gossage had a great house in Jersey. But he only lived there during the baseball season, and he wanted someone responsible to live there and look after things. That part of it was great," Tait said.

The rest of his Stepien-imposed exile was not so great. Tait's heart belonged with the Cavaliers.

Gordon Gund wanted him back because he believed the fans identified with him, and also because he firmly believed Tait was one of the NBA's finest play-by-play men. Remember, the radio broadcast was one of Gund's primary sources of information gathering about the team. He has a direct radio feed of each game piped into his home in Princeton, N.J., and he also can dial a phone number from anywhere in the world and automatically get hooked up with a broadcast in progress. When he attends games in person, as he often does, Gund is outfitted with a headset and mentally meshes Tait's broadcast with the sounds of the arena.

"Being there adds another dimension," Gund said. "You hear the crowd, the sounds of the men on the court. You feel more of the total atmosphere. You get a real sense for how the game is played."

It helps having played the sport and having been a lifelong fan.

"Growing up, we had a hoop in our backyard," Gund said. "And with six kids in our family, we had plenty of spirited two-on-two and three-on-three games on that court. But in high school and college, I played ice hockey. So I had strong familiarity with both games before I lost my sight."

By the time Gund became co-owner of the Cavs in 1983, Gordon said he "had come to grips with the fact that I wasn't going to see games anymore, just as I can't see my children, or sunrises, or sunsets. That's simply fact."

So he turned to radio broadcasts of the games and sharpened his other senses to the point where he can accurately describe the assets and liabilities of virtually every single one of his employees. And action on the basketball court.

"Gordon is very perceptive. Amazingly perceptive," Tait said. "Sometimes I'll talk to him and he'll say, 'Boy, you sure were upset the other night on the air.' And then he'll add, 'I was mad, too. It seemed like we were playing lousy.' He usually is right on the mark."

Ask Gund to describe how he envisions someone like Michael Jordan playing basketball, and he might surprise the questioner. As in he can describe the indescribable better than most who have 20/20 vision.

"The man is an extraterrestrial flying machine," Gordon Gund once told the *Akron-Beacon Journal*'s Terry Pluto of Jordan. "He's 6-foot-6 or whatever, but he's long and lean and he doesn't seem as big as you'd expect for a player with his greatness. I see him having big hands and very long fingers. He can rule all the space around him as no basketball player ever has before.

"But there is the incongruity — the tongue that comes out. Usually, that indicates a person is not in control of something, but with Michael it means he's about to do something supernatural. That part is especially intriguing."

This from a man who has never actually seen Jordan play. Yet there have been nights when Gund swears he could see Jordan soaring or Brad Daugherty posting up and scoring on a soft jump hook over Robert Parish or Patrick Ewing. They are mental images, to be sure, but they are beautiful nonetheless. And beauty, in this case, is in the ear of the beholder. For that, Gund has Tait to thank.

"Radio paints as good a picture as I can get," Gund said.

The picture everyone was getting early in the 1984-85 season was fuzzy and not at all acceptable. Armed with their new agreement, however, Karl and Free began breaking new ground. Karl backed off of the other players, too, and began loosening the reins at least on offense. Let the players have some creative fun on offense, and maybe they'll give me a little more effort on defense, Karl thought.

It worked. John Bagley was somewhat erratic at point guard, but had, at least in Weltman's opinion, developed into "one of the top three or four penetrating guards in the game of basketball." Hubbard wasn't necessarily a post-up player, but he was a great garbage man who cleaned up around the offensive glass and supplied gritty defense. Roy Hinson was young and raw, but was showing All-Star potential as a shotblocker and high-flying dunker who also possessed a nice shooting touch from up to 18 feet. Mel Turpin and Mark West, the polar opposites of each other, teamed to at least provide an adequate two-headed center.

Turpin was the center with the soft head and the soft touch. West's nickname was "Hammer," and he didn't get it by singing rap songs or breakdancing. He was the most physical player on the team.

"I remember we used to play three-on-three after practice all the time, and then Turp and Mark West would play one-on-one," Karl said. "West would just beat on him. I bet you Mark West beat him 85 percent of the time. And I would say on 90 percent of the wins, West would dunk the last shot in Mel's face."

Free once brought a Cleveland Browns football helmet to practice and handed it to Turpin.

"Mel," said World, "you better start wearing this, because Hammer's going to hurt you so bad one day we're gonna have to take you to the hospital."

The final missing piece to the puzzle and a player who might have been just as physical as West was 6-foot-8, 275-pound Lonnie Shelton, obtained the previous season from Seattle in exchange for a second-round draft pick and cash.

"Lonnie could set a pick on the sun," Milwaukee Bucks forward Paul Pressey once said.

Setting immovable picks was a Shelton specialty. So was playing defense and roughing it up under the boards. He could rough it up off the court, too. One night Shelton chased New Jersey's Buck Williams into the stands to fight him. Another time, he and Pressey carried an on-court confrontation into the tunnel that led to the locker rooms at Richfield Coliseum.

But nothing topped one night when he went to a downtown restaurant for dinner with his girlfriend following a game. As Shelton and his girl left the restaurant, a man approached from behind with a gun and demanded Shelton hand over his wallet.

Shelton wheeled on the man and took the gun from him. Then he hit him in the head with a rock and sat on top of him until police arrived.

"Lonnie took the gun away from him, knocked him down, beat the crap out of him, and ended up sitting on him," Tait said. "Then he handed the gun to his girlfriend, because a big crowd had gathered around, and he told her: 'If anybody moves, shoot 'em.'

"When the cops show up, Lonnie lets the guy up — and as the guy is being led away by the police, he's saying, 'I'm going to change my life, Mr. Shelton, I promise you.' Because Lonnie had been talking to him the whole time he was sitting on top of him, telling him how this was wrong, you can't be doing this, you've got to change your life."

Boston Celtics center Kevin McHale later said of the incident: "If the guy had shot Lonnie, they never would have been able to find the bullet."

McHale was joking, but wasn't far off the mark. Shelton was out of shape and nursing a knee injury at the beginning of the '84-85 season, so he didn't play during the 2-19 start. Once he did begin playing and started shedding some pounds, the Cavs began winning.

They won 34 and lost 27 over the final 61 regular-season games, qualifying for the playoffs for the first time in seven years on April 9 when they beat New Jersey at the Coliseum. The team, led by Free, carried Karl off the court and then returned moments later to acknowledge a crowd of 10,185 that wouldn't leave that night.

"I think one of my fondest memories in all my coaching is the night an NBA team picked me up on their shoulders and carried me off the court," said Karl, who is now head coach of the Seattle SuperSonics. "I can't believe that happened. And I don't think it will ever happen to me again."

The team that turned it around so dramatically caught the fancy of the town's fans, who finally began returning to the fold after years of being turned off. After dropping two nip-and-tuck games by the combined total of five points in Boston to open their first-round playoff series vs. the vaunted Celtics, the Cavs were greeted by a sellout crowd of 20,900 when they returned to the Coliseum for Game 3 in the best-of-five affair.

The Cavs won, 105-98, snapping a 17-game losing streak to Boston as Free scored 32 points. The Celtics played that night without injured Larry Bird, and at the end of the game the crowd worked itself into a frenzy chanting, "We want Larry!" And "Bring on Bird!"

The next day at Boston's practice, the great Larry Bird was fuming.

"These fans here don't know basketball. They're a bunch of fuckin' farmers. If they want me, they'll get me. I'll come out with both barrels blazing tomorrow night," Bird told reporters.

He did. Still, the Cavs hung tough. With 4:08 left in Game 4 before another boisterous sellout crowd that booed every time Bird touched the ball, even in warmups, the Cavs led 109-104.

Then Bird scored six of Boston's last eight points, and a flurry by the Cavs at the end fell short. The Celts won the game, 117-115, and the series three games to one, despite another 30-point performance by Free. Each of the contests had been so close that the two teams scored exactly the same number of points in the series.

Weltman felt vindicated. The organization's future looked brighter than it had for nearly a decade. Karl even received some votes for the NBA's Coach of the Year award.

"Everything started coming together for us, and we ended up becoming the Cinderella team in the NBA that season," Weltman said. "Anyone who watched us play in the playoffs can tell you that we got screwed royally in Boston (by the officials).

"But the important thing was we were then poised to become a pretty good basketball team. We had won 36 games, and had we gotten past Boston I think we probably would have gone all the way to the NBA Finals. I really believe that. It was some turnaround. I was really proud of those guys."

CHAPTER THIRTEEN

"When the Ax Met Harry"

Draft day in June, 1985 was approached in much the same manner as the previous year's draft. Weltman, who received several votes for *Sporting News* Executive of the Year after the previous season's turnaround, was looking to make another deal. He also was conducting extensive research on a player named John "Hot Rod" Williams, a 6-foot-11 forward from Tulane who was embroiled in a point-shaving controversy that threatened his NBA career. Noting the mileage on Lonnie Shelton's aging knees, as well as that of key reserves such as Edgar Jones and Ben Poquette, Weltman knew the Cavs needed to inject some youth and size into their frontcourt.

"It came down to Keith Lee and Karl Malone for us," Weltman said. "It may sound funny to say now, but I think we deserve a little credit for wanting to go after Karl Malone. We didn't, but we saw something in him that a lot of other teams didn't . . . . He wouldn't have lasted until 13th in the draft if everyone had known what kind of player he would become. We were going to draft him at one point. We worked him out. I had dinner with him. We were very impressed with him as a prospect and a person."

Years later, Malone recalled coming to Cleveland to work out under the eyes of Weltman, the Cavs' coaches and scouts. "I remember coming to Cleveland very well. They brought me in before the draft, interviewed me and worked me out. They were very interested," Malone said.

"They put me up at the Holiday Inn near the Coliseum. I liked the area a lot. It was open, and there were a lot of trees. It reminded me of home (Summerfield, Louisiana). We talked for a long time and then they worked me out. They had me go one-on-one with Melvin Turpin. They were paying him over the summer to get into shape."

And just what did Malone think after going one-on-one against Turpin? "If I had any doubts about playing in the NBA, they ended then," he said. "I figured that if he could play in the NBA, I certainly could. And after my visit to Cleveland, I thought that is where I would be playing. I thought for sure they would draft me."

They didn't. Weltman said he was worried about Malone's lack of shooting range severely limiting his time on a team that needed more perimeter shooting. He feared Malone would be stuck behind Roy Hinson in Coach Karl's pecking order, and he felt the team needed someone who would contribute immediately. Lee possessed a nice touch on his outside shot, which was almost a set shot. He wasn't a runner and jumper like the athletic, muscular Malone, but Weltman liked his other basketball skills.

"Keith was a good low-post player with a nice outside shot," Weltman said. "Keith was a terrific shooter who also was a good rebounder and a good passer.

"We knew he couldn't run a whole lot, but we thought he would be able to play out on the floor a little bit more than a guy like Karl (Malone). And we needed that type of player more at that time. We looked at Keith Lee and said, 'Gee, we should be able to find a place on the floor for him for 30 minutes a game.' We didn't feel that would be the case with Karl Malone."

Another intriguing forward prospect available in that draft was Cleveland native Charles Oakley, a strong rebounder out of tiny Virginia Union. But the Cavs went into draft day set on Lee. They knew, however, that Chicago wanted Oakley — so they used their ninth pick in the draft to orchestrate a deal. Weltman told the Bulls he would take Oakley and trade him to them, along with a second-round pick that became guard Calvin Duncan, in exchange for Lee and guard Ennis Whatley, a promising veteran who would be entering his third NBA season.

"Everyone knew Charles Oakley was going to be a wonderful rebounder in the NBA. We knew it. Everyone knew it,"

Weltman said. "But we weren't so sure about the rest of his game, and we wanted a more complete player."

They wanted Keith Lee, and they got him.

The Cavs owned another second-round pick that year, the 45th overall. Weltman decided to use it to select Williams, even though Williams was about to stand trial in Louisiana on point-shaving charges and the NBA had issued a directive to all teams warning against drafting him. Prior to the point-shaving scandal breaking at Tulane, Williams had been projected as a first-round pick. The question was not his talent; it was more a legal matter casting the young man's character into question.

"The league had said there were no assurances that he would ever play, if someone drafted him. Even if he got cleared of the charges in court, the league had indicated that he still might not be allowed to play—at least not right away," Weltman said. "But we really did our research. I came to not only know John as a player, but also as a person. I came away feeling very confident that he would be found innocent of all charges against him.

"We kept it very quiet, what we intended to do. We were very careful about how we went about doing our research, and I told very few people even within the organization about my intentions to draft him. We did not want that leaking out."

The NBA and Stern, by then the commissioner, were not pleased when the Cavs called out Williams' name on draft day.

"I think they were a little pissed. They had sent out a memo warning against it. No, I don't think they were terribly pleased with my selection of John Williams in that draft. But I was convinced we were doing the right thing. Not only in terms of getting a good player — because everyone knew he was a first-round talent—but also in terms of doing the right thing for a guy who deserved it," Weltman said.

Williams would not play that season with the Cavs. His court case dragged on, and the NBA insisted on October 21, 1985 that the team withdraw its player contract to him at least temporarily. Lee signed his contract on October 4, then showed up for a news conference to announce the signing overweight and nursing a painful pulled muscle in his right thigh. He would miss all of training camp and the first 23 games of the season.

These were omens of how the 1985-86 season would unfold. The carryover euphoria from the previous season did not last very long, although there were some shining moments. On November 5, the Cavs whipped the Lakers 129-111 in Los Angeles on the very night the defending world champions received their NBA championship rings.

Afterward, as he was running up a $500 tab in the hotel bar, Karl ran from table to table shouting, "How did I do it?" To which one cynical observer added, "Gee, I must have missed something. Did George have a uniform on tonight?"

Actually, the enigmatic Edgar Jones had more to do with that victory than Karl or anyone else. He totaled 24 points, 12 rebounds, three steals and three blocks vs. the Lakers, once again making everyone wonder why he couldn't put up those kinds of numbers more often. He told Joe Tait on the post-game radio show of his shotblocking prowess: "Yeah, you should have seen me in college. I used to block 'em with my face."

No one doubted it. Jones had no front teeth. A 6-foot-10 forward acquired at midseason the year before from San Antonio, Jones also could give World B. Free a run for the title as the team's top talker. Appropriately enough, their locker stalls were located next to one another at the Coliseum.

"When I came out of college," said Jones, "I dunked on anything that moved. Nothing was safe. Nobody could sleep soundly. But I've dunked enough. Now I'm a jump shooter."

Jones played his college ball at Nevada-Reno, where an opponent's errant elbow knocked out his two front teeth and thusly earned him the nicknames "Count" and "Vampire Jones." But the EJ legend began developing even earlier.

There was the time before his collegiate career even started, when Jones burst into Coach Jerry Tarkanian's office at Nevada-Las Vegas.

"Here I am, Coach," Jones said.

"Who in the hell are you?" was Tarkanian's reply.

It was only then that Jones, a native of Newark, N.J., realized he had signed a national letter of intent to play basketball at the University of Nevada located in Reno, not Las Vegas.

"What the hell," said Jones later, "they're both gambling towns."

Jones loved telling stories about his years at Nevada-Reno, and usually they didn't relate to basketball. Listeners usually didn't know whether or not to believe him, either.

"I used to work splatter patrol," Jones once told a reporter.

"What was that?" the reporter inquired.

"You know, splatter patrol," Jones replied. "That's where you have to scrape the guys off the sidewalks after they jump from the tops of buildings. Happens all the time in Reno. A guy goes into a casino, loses his shirt, his house, everything he owns. Next thing you know there he is on top of the nearest building, threatening to jump. A lot of them did, too."

Another time, Jones said of life in Reno: "I used to gamble a little myself. In fact, I could take a few dollars and turn it into a few thousand in a matter of minutes at a blackjack table. It got so bad that when I would swing the doors open to certain casinos, the blackjack dealers would run for cover. Seriously, they would actually duck underneath their tables to avoid me."

As the 1985-86 season unfolded, it became increasingly obvious that a number of negative factors were at work ripping the team apart. Karl and Weltman weren't communicating. Injuries had left Karl relying too heavily on players like Jones, who didn't show up every night. The team floundered.

Part of the problem, at least in Joe Tait's opinion, was that the previous season's dramatic turnaround had convinced Karl "he was the greatest coach to ever come down the pike."

Others agreed. Karl verbally agreed to and then backed out of a contract extension commitment, believing he could do better. In the middle of the season, Karl began talking with the University of Pittsburgh about becoming their next head coach.

The Gunds were not pleased about this development. Neither was Weltman. They called Karl in for a chat.

"It reached the point where he basically was told to lay off the Pittsburgh thing, that he had plenty of time to figure out what he wanted to do — but not right now because we were in a fight to get back to the playoffs," Weltman said. "Not that we were playing anywhere near as well as we were the year before. We probably would have made the eighth (and final Eastern Conference) spot and been eliminated very quickly by Boston, because we were not going to surprise them this time."

Karl agreed to back off, but told the Gunds and Weltman he wanted to visit Pittsburgh one more time to talk with the dean of the school because Dean Smith, Karl's old coach at North Carolina, already had set up the meeting. George Gund offered to fly Karl and his wife, Kathy, to Pittsburgh in his private plane. Then Karl could fly on to Philadelphia to meet the team for that next evening's game.

Karl insisted on driving himself. But he left the Cavs' contingent with the feeling that his pursuit of the Pitt job was over.

The next night, Weltman arrived at the Spectrum in Philadelphia for the team's game with the 76ers. It was 90 minutes or so before tipoff, and Karl was being interviewed by the local cable station that did 76ers' games. The coach didn't know it, but the interview was being broadcast on closed circuit throughout the arena.

During the interview, Karl related that he was still very interested in the Pitt job, and that he believed he was still very much in the running. Weltman, listening elsewhere in the arena, could not believe what he was hearing.

"That son of a bitch!" Weltman muttered to himself.

It was at precisely that point in time that the decision was made to fire Karl, who later regretted his tenure with the club ended in such turmoil.

"I didn't want any of what happened to happen, even though I was perceived as the guy who initiated it all," Karl said years later. "All I wanted was a good contract. I mean, it was the first time in my life I was being offered a lot of money. And I'm not saying I didn't mishandle it. Maybe I did. But it's not what I wanted, for the relationship between Harry and I to fall apart like it did."

Gene Littles, left as Karl's top assistant after Weltman also fired Mo McHone earlier in the year, coached the team the last 15 games of the season, going 4-11. To illustrate the carefree hand with which Littles guided the team, World B. Free once demanded that the driver of the team bus pull over at a convenient store on the return trip to the team hotel after a game. The driver obliged. Free, now strength and conditioning coach for the Philadelphia '76ers, bounded out and into the store, from which he emerged moments later with a six-pack of Budweiser.

Weltman didn't know it yet, but he had signed his own pink slip. Since the firing of Karl — Weltman's third of a coach in four seasons on the job — the GM had been getting hammered unmercifully in the *Plain Dealer* and on radio talk shows. The Hatchet Harry moniker was revived in full force, and the Gunds did not like the mounting negative publicity.

Only 10 weeks earlier, Weltman had received the prestigious Pride of Cleveland award from the Sports Media Association of Cleveland and Ohio (SMACO). Weltman began his acceptance speech with a tribute to the Gunds, although Gordon Gund later claimed it was around then that the owners began considering not to renew Weltman's contract.

This Weltman disputes. He claims he reached a verbal agreement with the Gunds on a three-year contract extension.

Whatever, he was out of a job on April 16, 1986, less than a month after dismissing Karl. The Gunds had decided to move "in a new direction."

Said Gordon Gund at the time: "Harry Weltman made some very strong contributions that helped result in significant progress by this franchise . . . .We just feel that if we are to continue progression toward our goal of becoming a contender, now is the time to bring in someone with a fresh approach who hopefully will help us reach our objective that much more quickly and effectively."

Weltman left a mixed legacy. Attendance under him improved from an average of 6,200 when he took over to 8,767 when he left. The team had improved from one that won 15 games the year before he arrived to one that won 36 and 29 his last two seasons, including the thrilling playoff season of '84-85. But Weltman failed in his working relationships with three coaches, two of which he handpicked for the job himself.

He also made some dubious choices in the draft, opting for players such as Mel Turpin and Keith Lee who turned out to be stiffs with deplorable work ethics. Then again, he had the guts to draft John Williams when no one else in the NBA did — and Williams, once cleared of the point-shaving charges as Weltman steadfastly had believed, would go on to become a productive player in Cleveland for years to come. Weltman also drafted Roy Hinson, who soon would be used by the new incoming regime to acquire one of the greatest players in franchise history. And he traded for World B. Free, one of the most popular players in franchise history.

The firings of Weltman and Karl left the Cavaliers with no general manager and no coach entering what would prove to be the most important draft in franchise history. When interim head coach Gene Littles bolted for Chicago to become a Bulls' assistant coach just weeks before the 1986 draft, that left only director of player personnel Barry Hecker and assistant coach Ed Gregory behind to attempt plotting the club's future.

Gordon Gund, of course, had a new GM in mind. He was Wayne Embry, who previously had served in that capacity for six years with the Milwaukee Bucks and now was employed as a consultant with the Indiana Pacers. But Embry had helped scout the draft for the Pacers, and felt obligated to stay with them until its conclusion. He would not come aboard in Cleveland until afterward.

At the draft lottery, even before Gund had decided on Embry as his new GM, the Cleveland owner sat at a table with legendary NBA mover-and-shaker Red Auerbach of the Boston Celtics. He asked Auerbach who he would take if he had the No. 1 pick in the draft.

"I guess he's usually pretty canny in conversations like that, like you usually don't know what agenda he's got. But at the time, it did not look like we would end up with the No. 1 pick. I'm sure he might not have been so candid if he had known that was going to be the case, but I didn't even know it at the time," Gund said.

So Auerbach was honest.

"If you can pick a center, get one. And the best one in this draft is North Carolina's Brad Daugherty. If I was picking No. 1, that's who I would take. That's what you build from," Auerbach told Gund.

Shortly thereafter, the Philadelphia 76ers let it be known throughout the league that they were willing to part with the No. 1 pick in the draft. This in part came about because Richard Watson, Gordon Gund's legal counsel and a minority owner with the Cavs, informed the Sixers that they would never be able to sign the No. 1 pick and stay under their salary cap. Watson was an expert on the complicated cap, and had even worked with the NBA to help revise it. Talks subsequently escalated between Philadelphia and Cleveland, with the Sixers wanting Roy Hinson and a sizable amount of cash in return for the top pick. Hecker did not want to part with Hinson. Gregory wasn't so sure.

Gund was certain of one thing. If he was going to permit such a trade, he wanted the man who would be running the team to be aware of its possibility. He phoned Embry in Indianapolis.

"If we have a chance to get the No. 1 pick in the draft, should we do it?" Gund asked.

"Absolutely," Embry answered. "Especially if that's all you have to give up to get it."

"Who should we take with the pick?" Gund asked.

"No question. Take Brad Daugherty, the center out of North Carolina," Embry replied.

So the Cavs traded for the No. 1 pick, surrendering the popular and still-improving Hinson and $800,000 in cash to Philadelphia on the morning of the draft. Despite a crowd of 2,000 or so chanting Len Bias' name at a draft-day party at Stouffer's in downtown Cleveland, the Cavs subsequently selected Daugherty. Bias, the talented forward out of Maryland, went to Boston one pick later. Several hours later, Bias was dead of cocaine ingestion.

"The fact that we ended up with Brad and Boston took Bias is a tremendous irony in hindsight," Gund said years later. "I think everyone felt that Len Bias was the best athlete in the draft."

But based partly on Auerbach's advice, Gund entered draft day convinced the Cavs had to come away with a center. Cleveland still owned the eighth pick in the first round as well. Hecker had been a big fan of Ron Harper for months, and most scouts had Harper, from Miami of Ohio, rated very highly. It was a no-brainer. The Cavs took Harper.

As the second round began to unfold, the Hecker-Gregory team pulled off one of the great trades in NBA history. On the first pick of the second round, 25th overall, the Dallas Mavericks selected point guard Mark Price from Georgia Tech. The Cavs called and acquired Price for the mere price of a 1989 second-round draft pick and $50,000 in cash.

"Mark Price dropped like a rock in that draft," Gregory later said. "I couldn't believe he fell out of the first round like he did."

Gregory said he got on the phone to Dallas GM Norm Sonju.

"The Mavericks had two second-round picks that season," Gregory said. "They wanted to get rid of one of them. Up until the week of the draft, they wanted $250,000 for that 25th pick. As the week approached, they kept dropping their asking price.

"About 10 minutes before the first of Dallas' second-round picks came up, I telephoned them. I said we'd give them the $50,000 and a second-rounder for the pick if they would take Mark Price with it and trade him to us. They agreed to do it."

This is where the whole thing gets a little weird. At virtually the same time Gregory was making his deal with Sonju, Embry, working for the Pacers, was on the phone with Mavs player personnel director Rick Sund — negotiating a similar deal for Indiana.

Minutes after Embry thought he had struck a deal with Sund, though, he received a return telephone call from Dallas. Sund told him the deal was off, that the Mavericks already had made a deal with Cleveland for Price.

"I told them I couldn't understand how this could have happened," Embry said. "They said it did and that was that."

The Pacers did not understand how it could have happened, either. To this day, they suspect foul play. Embry said Pacers owner Herb Simon was not pleased when he told him what had happened.

"He was upset. He was very upset. In fact, he went ballistic," Embry said. "I told him that I had no idea what was going on with Cleveland, that he had to trust my integrity. I couldn't believe the irony of the whole thing."

Neither could the Pacers, who remain steamed about losing Price. "Looking back," said Embry, "I'm happy with the way it turned out. I stayed with the Pacers until after the draft because I tried to use a degree of integrity and do what I felt was right. I did let the Cavs know which players I preferred, but I don't think there was any conflict of interest on my part.

"I know (the Pacers) were upset about Mark Price because they wanted him, too. But I had nothing to do with that trade from the Cleveland end. I knew nothing about it until after it happened."

Later in the second round, the Cavs also selected swingman Johnny Newman from Richmond, completing a most productive day. Two days later, Embry was officially named vice president and general manager at a news conference. "I think you have to establish a goal of winning an NBA championship," Embry said then. "If you establish a goal of just making the playoffs and you fall short of that, you're nowhere."

One more factor contributed to making the week of June 16, 1986 what Gordon Gund would later call "probably the most pivotal week in franchise history." On the eve of the draft, the Cavs received word that John "Hot Rod" Williams had been found innocent of the point-shaving charges against him at Tulane. He would be available to play, beginning in the 1986-87 season. All the Cavs and their new GM had to do now was name a new coach.

CHAPTER FOURTEEN

"Trader Wayne and Cool Hand Lenny"

Even before he had been named general manager of the Cavaliers, Wayne Embry ran into Lenny Wilkens at the Big East Basketball Tournament at Madison Square Garden in New York, where both were scouting collegiate players. Wilkens, then 48, was serving as GM of the Seattle SuperSonics at the time. But after a combined 13 seasons coaching the Sonics and Portland, the former Cavalier player was struggling with the transition to the front office.

"If you ever get back into it (being a GM) somewhere," Wilkens told Embry, "think of me when it comes time to bring a new coach in. I miss coaching."

Embry filed the suggestion away.

It wasn't long thereafter that he pulled the file and gave Wilkens a call. From the beginning of Embry's search for a coach, Wilkens was the frontrunner. Others interviewed included Willis Reed and three relatively unknown but respected assistant coaches — Dick Harter, Ed Badger and John Wetzel. It didn't take Embry long to settle on Wilkens.

Embry is black. So is Wilkens.

Much was made at first of this union of two black men in the highest echelon of professional sports. No other franchise in any major American sport at the time employed blacks at the two key positions of coach and general manager, and they would go on to become very successful in Cleveland.

Both men attempted to downplay it. Embry often laughed when, during interviews, the interviewer almost always assumed he and Wilkens were close friends from the old school. After all, they were former players, weren't they? And they were black.

But they weren't close friends. They knew each other enough to say hello and make small talk in passing, and that was about it. They admired each other professionally, but that was the extent of their relationship prior to July 9, 1986, the day Wilkens was hired.

"I wonder what people would think if Lenny and I were white," Embry said once. "Would anyone have said (then-Detroit GM) Jack McCloskey hired Chuck Daly because they're friends? Aren't they both white?

"I just wish the black-white thing wasn't even an issue in today's society. That may be somewhat unrealistic, but that's the way I feel. I don't base giving a man a job on his skin color or whether or not he is my friend. I don't judge people that way. I wish everyone could say the same."

Of their playing days, Wilkens once remarked: "He respected the way I played and I respected the way he played. We were always friendly, but never friends because our lives seemed to go in different directions. There was one common element — respect for each other."

Embry and Wilkens had similar, yet diverse backgrounds. Both experienced racial prejudice in the 1940s and 1950s. Embry, though, grew up on a farm outside Springfield, Ohio. Wilkens was raised in the Bedford-Stuyvesant section of Brooklyn, N.Y.

The farm Embry grew up on was owned by his grandparents. "My father and his two brothers built homes on the farm, which was about 70 acres," said Embry. "My grandparents (Will and Alice) were the patriarch and matriarch of the compound. Between them and my parents (Floyd and Anna), there was a lot of discipline instilled there."

Floyd Embry worked at an auto body shop in Springfield. Anna Embry worked at Wright-Patterson Air Force base in nearby Dayton. Springfield's black population was small in the 1940s. "We could not eat at the restaurants in town," said Embry.

"We just accepted it." Not being allowed to eat at the restaurants in town was only a small portion of the problems the Embrys endured.

"Our farm was shot at by the Ku Klux Klan," said Embry. "Crosses were burned. As kids, we thought of it as being like the old Hatfields and McCoys. There were times I feared for my life."

Embry was the only black student when he enrolled at Olive Branch High School. "I didn't have any friends and was the victim of racial slurs," said Embry. After the second day of school, he came home and made an announcement to his grandfather, Will.

"He was doing some chores, I think cutting alfalfa," said Embry. "I told him I was quitting school so I would be able to help him work the farm. I figured this would be no problem. Only about two or three in our family went past the ninth grade."

Will Embry listened to his grandson. "Then he told me I was not quitting," said Embry. "He told me I was going back to school. He told me that I was going to go back there and prove that I was as good as anyone else. He had a way of being very persuasive. The way was the use of a switch. I had a deep fear of the switch."

Embry went back to school. "When I went back," he said, "I went back with a completely different attitude. I dedicated myself to being the very best person, the very best student and the very best basketball player I could be.

"I was driven to excel because if that's what I had to do to gain respect, that's what I did. It's a legacy I continue to live by. Look, I could carry scars until the day I die, but what I think I've done is establish an attitude that, yes, those were tough times and there was bitterness, but I'd rather dwell on how to turn a negative into a positive."

The Bedford-Stuyvesant area in Brooklyn where Wilkens grew up had no farms. It was a ghetto. Wilkens, whose mother Henrietta is white, grew up a devout Catholic. He was less than three years old when his father, James, a chauffeur, died suddenly of a bleeding ulcer.

Wilkens' surrogate father became the priest at the parish he attended, Father Thomas Mannion. "At the time," Wilkens said, "he appeared larger than life to me."

Wilkens encountered his share of prejudice. He usually dealt with it in a cerebral manner, indicative of his reflective, quiet nature. Jack Bagshaw, a former college roommate who is a doctor in San Francisco, told a magazine reporter of incidents at Providence where Wilkens starred in basketball.

"There were times when he was rejected by white girls just because he was black," said Bagshaw. "He'd disappear. I'd find him back in our room. We had some profoundly candid discussions about those moments."

Another time, after Wilkens had played a couple NBA seasons with the St. Louis Hawks, he and his wife, Marilyn, went looking for a larger home in the St. Louis suburb of DePere, an area they thought they would like. They spotted one home they were interested in, but when they went for a second look, the real estate agent told them their prospective neighbors had gotten together and approached him.

"They asked that no black families be allowed to move into that home," the real estate agent bluntly told the Wilkens'.

Wilkens later discussed the incident in his book, *The Lenny Wilkens Story*. In it, he said he decided not to make a big deal out of the snub because he and Marilyn ended up not liking the house very much anyway. But he added, "Later, as fate would have it, I was invited to speak at a luncheon in DePere. Well, I considered opening my talk by saying, 'I can't live here, but I can speak here, so at least I can get into your neighborhood one way.' Instead, I simply rejected the speaking request."

Embry and Wilkens played against each other for years in the NBA. Embry was a burly center who spent most of his 11-year career with the Cincinnati Royals. Wilkens' 15-year Hall of Fame career included stops at St. Louis, Seattle, Cleveland and Portland.

Embry gained a reputation as being a tough guy whose principal duties were to rebound and set wall-like picks for Royals teammate Oscar Robertson. Embry loved to mix it up in the paint.

Wilkens joined the NBA in 1960. He had to be talked into it. After earning a degree in economics at Providence, Wilkens planned to teach as a graduate assistant while earning his masters. He did not seriously consider the NBA until attending a Hawks-Celtics game at Boston Garden during their 1959-60 championship series.

"After that," said Wilkens, "I was hooked. It was so exciting. I thought I was better than most of the guards on the floor that day, so I thought I would enjoy pretty good success."

He did, being named to the All-Star Game nine times. Embry played in five All-Star Games. He admired Wilkens as a player.

"I respected Lenny as a player and as a coach in Seattle," said Embry. "In the back of my mind, I always thought he would be good to work with."

An incident in Milwaukee had soured Embry on hiring a close friend to coach. "I would never have hired Lenny to be my coach if we were real tight friends," Embry told Terry Pluto of the *Akron (Ohio) Beacon-Journal*. "I did that once. The guy was my old roommate with the Boston Celtics, and he turned out not to be my friend at all."

That was in 1970, when Embry talked Don Nelson into taking his first coaching job. Several years later, Embry was shoved aside in a subsequent power struggle that left Nelson serving as coach and general manager of the Bucks.

In Wilkens, Embry foresaw no such conflicts. Wilkens, meanwhile, was simply glad to be back in coaching — though he reminded the media early in his first season that "a coach is only as good as his players."

As Wilkens and Embry pored over the roster left behind by the Weltman-Karl regime, they did not like much of what they saw. The three leading scorers from that team were World B. Free, Roy Hinson and Mel Turpin. Free was a free agent, Hinson was gone to Philadelphia, and Turpin, well, was Turpin. Immediately, decisions were made on basically the bottom third of the remaining roster. Those guys — including the flamboyant but highly erratic Edgar Jones — were not asked to return.

Jones, though, did hang around for awhile at the start of training camp, claiming he was injured. Even after the Cavs released him, he showed up at a preseason game in Akron dressed to the nines and signing autographs as if he still were a part of the team. He later threatened to sue the club, claiming they released him while he was injured.

He was, of course, injured throughout much of his brief stint in Cleveland. One time Jones missed a series of practices and games with "a pulled chest muscle." Another time, he sat out several days with a sore knee when no one could find anything wrong. When trainer Gary Briggs told Jones he might have to undergo arthroscopic surgery to determine the problem, Jones suited up for the very next practice.

"You notice how fast EJ got out there once they told him he might have to have microscopic surgery," Free told reporters.

"Uh, World, that's arthroscopic surgery," one replied.

"Whatever," Free said.

Free, meanwhile, had his own problems as the new regime took over. Despite averaging 23.4 points the previous season, he had little leverage in contract negotiations with Embry, who did not particularly want him on the team. Age was one factor. Free was 32 years old, and Embry believed guards' legs began to go at around that age. In addition, the new GM was not enamored with Free's reputation as a selfish player; nor was he convinced Free was needed to continue putting people in the seats at the Coliseum. The drafting of Ron Harper also made World expendable, regardless of whatever Free had done for the sagging franchise in the past.

Wilkens wanted Free on the roster, but with the understanding that World would accept a reduced role and help aid the development of Harper. Along with the reduced role, the Cavs planned to offer Free a reduced salary. Free made $675,000 the previous season, and wanted a two-year guaranteed contract worth around $1.5 million.

Embry countered with a one-year offer worth $400,000, only half of which was guaranteed. The implication was clear: If World did his job of teaching Harper well enough, he would be gone by midseason at no extra cost to the Cavaliers.

The two parties met in Windsor, Canada, where a rookie camp was being held over the summer. Free told friends the Cavs had called with an invitation to meet with him "overseas." But nothing was resolved that night across the Detroit River. And when training camp passed and the season began, Embry said all offers to Free were off the table.

Thus, World B. Free's existence as a Cavalier came to a quiet end. He eventually signed a one-year deal with Philadelphia, and played out his career with the 76ers and Houston, never again averaging more than 6.4 points.

"I've always been one of those guys who says World B. Free's number should be retired," Joe Tait said. "I don't care. I see those other numbers up there (the retired numbers of Austin Carr, Nate Thurmond and Bingo Smith), and a couple of them I have questions about. But I have no question about the fact that World should be up there, because he carried this franchise on his back. I mean, the people who came out to see this team during the time World was on the team, they were coming out to see World score 40.

"I don't care what kind of guy people say World was. I heard he was a bad guy in Philly. I heard he was a bad guy in L.A. (sic). I don't know about all that. But in the years he was here, he was a fan favorite. He played to the fans. He would do anything for them. He would stop during warmups to go over and get his picture taken with kids. I mean, he was all they had."

Even his teammates, who sometimes took World with a few thousand grains of salt, said they were going to miss him.

"Any person who would change their name to World, well, you know they have a big ego," Phil Hubbard said. "But as a person, World was all right. The only thing was that World sometimes thought he was the only guy on the team because he was scoring all the points. Well hell, somebody has to get the rebounds, play defense, do all of those things, too.

"But none of us really ever got upset at World over that. He was a fun-loving guy . . . . He put up numbers and he sold tickets. We needed everybody, but he was the main cog."

By the beginning of the 1986-87 season, he also was history.

Five promising rookies, comprising more than 40 percent of Wilkens' first roster, made that season an interesting one to watch. The team would go on to win only 31 games and lose 51, missing the playoffs again, but somehow this time it was different. There were nights when Harper, Brad Daugherty, John Williams, Mark Price and even Johnny Newman made the future look incredibly bright. Embry and Director of Player Personnel Gary Fitzsimmons also came up with a couple of brilliant midseason pickups who had been rejected by other teams — swingman Craig Ehlo and small forward Tyrone Corbin.

Harper, who led the Cavs in scoring his rookie season with a 22.9 average, was the most exciting of the bunch. Opposing coaches called him "a poor man's Michael Jordan." Signing him, though, was not easy.

Harper and his agent, Cleveland-based Mark Termini, wanted more than $2 million over four years. The Cavs countered with $1.2 million over four.

"When Wayne came in with that offer, I got up and left. I said, 'Nobody insults me like that. I may not be too bright, but I'm brighter than that.' I knew it wasn't a fair offer," Harper said. "Wayne was saying all this stuff like, 'Well you can't shoot and you can't dribble.' And I said, 'Damn, then, what the hell did you draft me for?' "

Harper wasn't always brimming with such self-confidence. When he arrived at the same Miami University in Oxford, Ohio, attended years earlier by shy Wayne Embry, Harper suffered so badly from a speech impediment that he almost quit school and gave up on a basketball career that by 1986 was set to earn him millions.

"I was never a great basketball player until I got over my speech problem. Getting my speech problem under control gave me confidence in myself, and then I had more confidence in my basketball game, too," Harper said.

Nice story, but Embry still wanted to play hardball at the negotiating table with Harper the rookie in '86. When Harper got up and walked out of their first session like that, Embry called after him. "You'll never recoup the money you're walking away from," Embry said.

Replied Harper: "Wayne, you don't understand. Where I come from we have a saying: 'What you never have is never yours. So I won't miss it.' "

Eventually, Harper signed for $2.15 million over four years. But he reported to training camp late, and at first that was a concern. Soon, though, it became readily apparent that in the open court, there were few in the league who were better. He was out of control at times and committed too many turnovers as a result, but Wilkens loved him and set about beginning to teach him the finer points of the game.

"Ron always listened. He was very coachable. You have to be careful with a player like that, though, because you don't want to pull in the reins too tight on him. You don't want him to lose his creativity altogether, although you do want him to start playing more under control," Wilkens said.

Harper finished second that season in Rookie of the Year balloting behind Indiana's Chuck Person, and he, Daugherty and Williams were named to the NBA's All-Rookie team.

Williams was the unlikeliest of the talented rookie trio to attain such lofty recognition. Not because of his skills as a player or because he was a bad person, but because of what he had endured to get to that station in life.

When Williams was just eight months old in Sorrento, Louisiana, his mother Annie died. His father, claiming he had a funeral to attend, left the infant with his maternal grandfather, Felton Williams — who was 78 years old at the time and blind.

The father, John Washington, never returned to pick up his son. It wasn't until a neighbor, Barbara Colar, grew weary of hearing the infant sobbing on Felton Williams' porch that John Williams at last found himself a home. She took him in and eventually gave him the nickname "Hot Rod" because of the way he speedily scooted around on the floor of his trailer home, making enginelike noises. The nickname stuck.

When Williams was about 12 years old, Colar took him aside and told him he was adopted. Hot Rod immediately burst into tears and began screaming, "No, you be my real mama!" To this day, he still refers to Colar as his mother.

Around the same time Colar told him he was adopted, Williams also saw his father for the first time since infancy. "He tried to give me $5, but I gave it back. That isn't what I wanted from him," Williams said.

By the time he was in high school, Williams had grown to 6-foot-9 and college recruiters were hot after him. He played in and was named Most Valuable Player in a high-school All-Star game that also featured future NBA stars Karl Malone and Joe Dumars. One day shortly thereafter, a man showed up at Barbara Colar's trailer and handed over a shoebox with $10,000 enclosed. "We would really appreciate it if John went to Tulane," the man told Colar.

The college did not seem to mind that Williams had struggled to maintain a "C" average in high school; nor that he had fared poorly on his SAT exam, scoring a 470 when the average for an entering freshman at Tulane was closer to 1,100.

This kid could play basketball, and soon he began regularly receiving envelopes containing $1,000.

"They would slide them under my mama's door while I was out playin' ball," Williams said. "Where they came from, I don't know. Was I wrong for taking the money? I don't think so.

"My mama and I had nothing. I mean nothing. I needed clothes. I needed shoes. I never sat down and read the NCAA rules. If my mama and I needed help like that today and someone was willing to give it to us, I think I would do the same thing."

Later, though, Tulane teammates Jon Johnson and Clyde Eads approached Williams about altering the outcome of games for additional money. Williams insists to this day that he said no — but that moment marked the beginning of a nightmare that nearly cost him an NBA career and millions.

In early 1985, amid rumors that the Tulane basketball team was being investigated for point-shaving and drug charges, police raided the home Williams shared with Barbara Colar. Suddenly he faced not only the end of his promising basketball career, but also a possible 17 years in prison and $35,000 in fines.

"There were sirens, dogs, everything. First they accused me of robbing a bank — just to try and scare me, I think," Williams said. "There must have been 50 or more police there the day they came to get me. They thought I was hiding. They treated me like I was some kind of animal."

Williams, the star of that Tulane team, eventually was cleared of charges that he helped fix games against Southern Mississippi and Memphis State. Opposing coaches and films of the games in question ultimately proved his best defense witnesses.

Embry, meanwhile, took a look at the Cleveland roster after Williams' rookie season and still did not like much of what remained. Turpin, for instance, was still around. So was Keith Lee. It wasn't that these two lacked skills. Each possessed some.

Mentally, though, they were basket cases. Especially Turpin. The idea behind keeping former Kentucky point guard Dirk Minnifield two years earlier, for instance, was so Minnifield could keep Turpin in line. Instead, they kept each other out late most nights on the road — and then could be spotted the next morning, once as early as 6:30 a.m., dining on chili dogs and french fries at an airport eatery.

When a newspaper story broke in Lexington, Kentucky, about how several former UK players had been paid for their services, neither Minnifield nor Turpin denied it. Turpin, in fact, was upset because the story identified other players who received considerably more than he did.

"I was underpaid," he said, obviously angry.

This is the same character who signed a contract with the Cavs that paid him a total of more than $1 million his first three seasons, much of which he had to give back because he failed to fulfill a weight clause. It was a reasonable clause, calling for him to maintain 13 percent body fat. Yet after a time, Turpin wouldn't even weigh in on the designated dates because he knew he had no chance to reach it. He simply would hand over the prescribed portion of his paycheck.

"He paid $90,000 that first year alone," remembered Harry Weltman.

"His first year in the league," said George Karl, "we all bought color TVs on Turp. The truck backed up to the Coliseum, and emptied a bunch of 25-inch Sonys."

One time during Wilkens' first season as coach, team captain Phil Hubbard approached Turpin during a team flight.

"Mark Price is getting married. We're kicking in $20 apiece to get him a nice wedding present," Hubbard said.

"Damn, Hubs. I can't be givin' up no greenbacks to a rookie. I don't hardly know the guy," responded Turpin, whose salary was $650,000 that season.

"You've got to be kidding me. All the money you make, and you can't kick in 20 bucks?" said Hubbard, who was growing angrier by the minute.

"Sorry, but I don't hardly know the guy," Turpin said again.

"Fine. Forget it, you asshole. I'll kick in the $20 for you," Hubbard said as he stormed off.

"He was making way more than I was at the time," said Hubbard later, "but he wouldn't give it up. So I put in for him.

"That was Turp, though. That was the kind of guy you were dealing with. We were trying to form a little bit of unity. You're not a team without unity."

Turpin's highly questionable attitude and life habits carried over to the court.

"Turp had all this talent," Hubbard said. "We all expected more, but we didn't get it. Somewhere down the line, he just didn't have the desire. I tried to talk to him. We all did. We were always trying to push him. Always."

Sometime during Turpin's third season in the league, and the first for Embry and Wilkens in Cleveland, Hubbard pulled the big fella aside one last time.

"Turp," said Hubbard, "you can make a lot of money when the next contract comes up. But you have to start working harder and getting your act together. If not, you're gonna be out of the league."

There was no fourth season for Turpin in Cleveland. In a trade that proved outstanding more for what was shipped out than what was received, Embry orchestrated a three-way deal with New Jersey and Utah prior to the 1987-88 season. Turpin was sent to Utah, Lee and John Bagley to New Jersey to be reunited with new Nets GM Harry Weltman. In exchange, the Cavs received promising young sharpshooter Dell Curry and a pair of aging veterans who were nearing the ends of their careers, James Bailey and Kent Benson.

One final footnote on Turpin: After telling reporters in Cleveland he weighed 287 the day of the trade, he officially weighed in at 301 just a couple days later in Utah.

"How could you gain 14 pounds during the flight from Cleveland to Utah?" a reporter inquired.

"What can I say? I love airline food," Turpin replied.

Two years later, Turpin was out of the league.

With Williams and Daugherty manning the frontcourt, and Harper and Price roaming the backcourt, the Cavs began to show marked improvement. Price, in particular, was the showstopper in 1987-88.

For one thing, Harper suffered a severe ankle sprain in the season's second game and was out until late December. Daugherty was a plodding-type center with a soft touch around the goal who rarely inspired crowds to offer a standing ovation — even though he did scorch legendary Boston center Robert Parish for a career-high 44 points late in his second season. Williams, like Daugherty, was steady and efficient but largely unspectacular.

Then there was Price. Ignored in the first round by every team in the league coming out of Georgia Tech, he hardly proved them wrong with a mediocre rookie season during which he suffered appendicitis and shot only 40 percent from the field. The Cavs themselves were so impressed they used their 1987 first-round draft pick, seventh overall, to select another point guard — Kevin Johnson from California.

Training camp in 1987 was the first time Cleveland witnessed Price's true and rare level of competitiveness. With Bagley traded and out of the picture, the starting point-guard position was up for grabs. Price seized it.

"It wasn't until he came back that next year, healthy and after they had drafted Kevin Johnson, that he really started to show what he could do," Hubbard said. "And he really did kick it in that next year. He saw an opportunity, took advantage of it, and never looked back. You have to give him credit for that."

Price basically kicked the highly-touted rookie's butt every day in practice. Wilkens had no choice but to start the second-year man, drafted in the second round a year earlier, over Johnson, the lottery selection.

As the season progressed, it became clearer that Price, the supposedly physically disadvantaged white kid who stands a shade under 6 feet, was something special. He had a picture-perfect jump shot honed through years of work with his father, Denny, a former NBA assistant coach under John MacLeod in Phoenix. He had quickness. He had heart. Price had so much of the total package,

Johnson was deemed expendable midway through his first NBA season.

Just before the trading deadline in February of 1988, Embry went to work again. In a deal that would prove controversial for years to come, he dealt Johnson, Tyrone Corbin and the hard-working Mark West to Phoenix for former All-Star Larry Nance and Mike Sanders. The teams also flip-flopped first-round draft picks, meaning the Cavs would pick eight spots higher than they would have in the upcoming 1988 draft. And finally, the Cavs threw in two future second-round draft choices.

It was a stunning trade. The entire city of Cleveland buzzed about it for days, weeks . . . more than a year and beyond. Callers to radio talk shows still debate its merit today.

Larry Nance would prove to be a player the likes of which Cleveland fans had never seen. But Kevin Johnson also would go on to enjoy great success — and the flip-flopping of first-round-ers enabled Phoenix to land Dan Majerle, while the Cavs were forced to settle for the forgettable Randolph Keys.

The bottom line, though, is that the trade would never have been possible if not for Price's rapid and remarkable improvement. The team finished its second season under Wilkens 42-40 and lost in five games to Chicago in the first round of the playoffs, despite leading by 17 points early in Game 5 at Chicago Stadium. Michael Jordan took over in the second half of that game, however, scoring 21 of his 39 points and foreshadowing an event the following season that would impact the Cleveland franchise's future in a way no one could have imagined.

CHAPTER FIFTEEN

"Curse of Michael"

As long as basketball is played in Cleveland, the 1988-89 season will remain special. It was a season in which everything fell into place — until a Monday in May when Michael Jordan hit a shot for the ages, a shot that many still say altered the course of the franchise.

It is Brad Daugherty who probably best summed up the 1988-89 season. Years later, in a discussion during a break in All-Star weekend festivities, Daugherty said, "There are a lot of things I will remember about that season. The thing I'll remember the most, though, is coming onto the floor before so many of those games. Especially the home games.

"There was this feeling we had. You could sense it. It was a feeling that we knew that everyone we played knew we were going to kick their asses. It was an amazing feeling, one that I never had before and one that I've never had since."

The Cavaliers compiled some stunning numbers in 1988-89. Their average margin of victory at the Coliseum was 15.1 points. They were 37-4 at home, where they ran off a franchise-record 22 straight victories from mid-December to early March. They were 38-4 when holding their opponents under 100 points; 52-4 when leading at the start of the fourth quarter. They went for the jugular. Thirty-nine of the 57 victories were won by 10 or more points. They never lost more than two consecutive games.

The season began like many NBA seasons begin for many NBA teams — with high hopes. Daugherty was 22. Mark Price and Ron Harper were 24. Larry Nance was 29 and about to play his first full season with the team. Mike Sanders, a role player who fit in with the cast of scoring characters around him, was 28. Coming off the bench were John (Hot Rod) Williams, who was 26 and Craig Ehlo, 27. Key additions included backup center Wayne (Tree) Rollins, 33, and backup point guard Darnell Valentine, 29. Also in reserve was veteran forward Phil Hubbard, 32.

There were a few questions when the Cavaliers, who were coming off a 42-40 season — a season in which they were eliminated by the Jordan-led Bulls in the playoffs — reported to Wilkens. Questions such as: Would the five-year, $5-million offer sheet made to Price by the Washington Bullets and matched by the Cavaliers cause any friction among the players? Would the foot and ankle injuries that Harper suffered the previous season that limited him to 57 games have any lingering effects?

Harper was asked if the 1987-88 season, one in which he averaged a modest 15.4 points, humbled him. "Humble me? Me? The only thing that humbled me," he said, "is that I had to go to Phil Hubbard's game."

He cackled, then added, "Right now, I feel great. There is some soreness in the foot after I play, but I never think about it when I'm on the court. No more shot-blocking for me, though. I'm now leaving that up to Tree, Hot Rod and Larry."

Price's outrageous — at the time — contract was the talk of training camp. "I think it's great," said Harper. "Now, when it's my turn, I can start at $1 million, look at the $3 million Michael Jordan is getting and say, 'Go ahead, pick a number in between.'"

The Cavaliers also had their critics. They said this was a team that was better suited for the less-physical, more up-tempo Western Conference. "To say the West is finesse and the East is power is something I don't pay any attention to," said Wilkens. "Many times labels are pinned on teams without much research."

It also was said that a team could not win big with a small forward like Mike Sanders starting. The small forward was the NBA's glamour spot. It's where Larry Bird started, Charles Barkley started, James Worthy started. Not guys like Mike Sanders.

Sanders was not a prototype small forward. He was a former center under Larry Brown at UCLA in the early 1980s. He was 6-foot-6, did not jump particularly well, did not scare anyone with his long-range shooting and did not have the quickness to create his own moves to the basket.

No flash on the court, no flash off the court. Sanders was a quiet, friendly man, the youngest from a family of eight children. At the time of his birth, Sanders' parents — Steve and Olivea — worked as cotton pickers on a plantation in Vidalia, Louisiana.

"My mother told me that she picked cotton up to the day I was born," said Sanders. "She said that even after I was born, she would wrap me up in a blanket, take me out to the fields and make a tent from sheets to shield me from the sun."

The Cavaliers were 8-3 in the 11 games Sanders started for them in 1987-88. "I feel I fit into this system very well," he said.

Training camp went smoothly. Early in camp, the Cavaliers were asked by the publicity department to fill out a questionnaire. Among the questions for the media guide: Name the person you'd most like to meet. Chris Dudley's answer: Mrs. Chris Dudley.

Nance was participating in his first training camp with the Cavaliers after a February 1987 trade that brought him and Sanders from Phoenix. Cleveland in February is not like Phoenix in February. Asked how he liked the change in climates, Nance said, "The weather in Phoenix is beautiful, but to win games and play for the type of team I'm playing with now, I'd travel to the North Pole."

The first exhibition game was in Providence, Rhode Island, against the Boston Celtics. The score: Cavaliers 121, Boston 80. After three quarters, the Cavaliers led, 99-59. They led by 42 points three times. On one of those occasions, during a timeout, trainer Gary Briggs looked over to the three Cleveland-area writers, pointed up and asked, "Is that scoreboard right?"

It was. Nance made all nine shots he attempted, scoring 24 points. "I am going to miss this year," he said. He smiled, then added, "I feel very comfortable with this team. I feel like I belong. The way the system is here, if you do exactly what Coach Wilkens says, you will win. He is a great coach."

Exhibition game or not, Celtics coach Jimmy Rodgers appeared stunned after absorbing the worst exhibition loss in the Larry Bird era. "If ever I had a fear of waking up from a nightmare and seeing it become reality," said Rodgers, "this is it." Bird was impressed. "The Cavaliers have a chance at becoming a very good team," he said. "They hit the open man and they play good defense."

The next night, the Cavaliers played the New York Knicks in Madison Square Garden. Twice in the second half, they led by 37 points. They won, 122-106. "We are not going to go 82-0," said GM Wayne Embry, who was in attendance. Knicks coach Rick Pitino looked as shell-shocked as Rodgers did one night earlier in Providence.

"The Cavaliers," said Pitino, "are playing like they've been in training camp for six weeks, not one week."

The Cavaliers continued winning, beating Miami, 106-89, and Milwaukee, 106-99. One area where Wilkens wanted to see improvement was in Dudley's free-throw shooting. Dudley was a monster under the boards who was also a monster from the free-throw line. He shot 56 percent from the line as a rookie in 1987-88.

"We see improvement," said Wilkens. "When Chris came here, he had three hitches in his stroke. We've got him down to one."

The preseason maulings continued. The Cavaliers crushed the Pistons, 120-102, in Dayton, Ohio. Wilkens said the victory was important. "We didn't want to go up against a premier team and play poorly," he said. "Then, people would be saying our other victories were a fluke."

Pistons coach Chuck Daly was not talking fluke. "The Cavaliers are for real," he said. "Just like I predicted they would be." Moments later, Daly talked about a dream he had during the summer. "This is no joke," said Daly in discussing the midsummer's night dream. "I had a dream and in it I watched the NBA Finals."

The participants? "The Cavaliers and Utah Jazz," said Daly. Daly's dream was replayed for Embry. "That's nice," said Embry, "but Chuck is just trying to take the monkey off his back and put it on ours."

The Pistons were not happy about being shelled by the Cavaliers — even if it was during the preseason in Dayton.

"They are going to have to play like this all the time," said Pistons reserve John Salley. "Not only that, we're the type of team that gets mad when we're embarrassed." Asked to comment on the Cavaliers, Pistons center Bill Laimbeer reacted with expected sarcasm. "They are the best team in the East," he said. "Give them the trophy now."

The Cavaliers had the perfect preseason. There were no holdouts, no serious injuries, no one reporting to training camp at 400 pounds. They went 8-0, playing in places like Fayetteville, North Carolina; Jonesboro, Arkansas; Winston Salem, North Carolina; and Daytona Beach. "By now," said Ehlo, "I think we just figure we are part of a barnstorming tour."

The Cavaliers opened the regular-season in Charlotte, where the expansion Hornets were playing their first game. On hand were the governors from two states — North Carolina and South Carolina. The Charlotte symphony orchestra played. The national anthem was sung by David Clayton Thomas, formerly of Blood Sweat and Tears. Many in the crowd of more than 23,000 wore tuxedos.

About 90 friends of Daugherty made the drive across the state from his hometown of Black Mountain, North Carolina, near Asheville. Asked if they wore tuxes, Daugherty said, "Tuxes? They came in overalls."

The Cavaliers took some of the starch out of the tuxes. They won, 133-93.

A small group of family and friends met the Cavaliers at the airport in Cleveland after victories in Charlotte and Indianapolis. The four-year-old triplet sons of television commentator Jim Chones — Kameron, Kyle and Kendall — were there to greet their dad. One of them tugged at Chones' arm. He had a question. "Where's Michael Jordan?," he asked.

The Cavaliers opened the season with four straight victories. They held the lead for 185 minutes and 37 seconds out of 192 total minutes. They won by an average of 22 points. All, though, was not perfect. Dudley was 1 of 14 from the free throw line, having missed 11 straight. Dudley, a Yale graduate, was baffled.

"The funny thing is that I've reached a point where my form is not that bad," Dudley said. "I've seen a lot uglier strokes at the line, but they go in."

It was suggested that maybe the Cavaliers should try a tactic the Hawks tried several years earlier with center Jon Koncak. Koncak made three straight free throws when the lights were turned out after a Hawks practice. When the lights were turned back on, he resumed missing.

The Cavaliers made it four victories in a row with a 108-91 rout of the Los Angeles Clippers. Midway in the third quarter of the game, Price threw a perfect alley-oop pass to Nance, who slammed the ball home. Nance's leaping ability amazed Price. "Sometimes," said Price, "I think I will throw one extremely high, just to see if Larry can't get it. Very few guys have the body control he does. I am just very glad he's in Cleveland."

In his younger days, when Nance won the NBA's Slam Dunk Contest, he was called the Highatollah of Slamola. "After I throw the ball," said Price, "to be honest, I just stand there and take pictures. I just watch Larry go up and become a fan as much as anyone else."

Playing the Clippers brought back cruel memories for Price's backup, former Clippers guard Darnell Valentine. "Playing for the Clippers," said Valentine, who played for them 2 1/2 seasons, "was like playing in the twilight zone. We were the Murphy's Law of the NBA. With the Clippers, it was a matter of individual survival. You like to have enjoyment playing this game. With them, there was nothing but gloom."

In the 13th game of the season, Dudley ended his string of missed free throws at 11. It ended when he banked a shot off the board and through the basket in the Cavaliers 112-84 victory over the Celtics. The crowd of 19,148 roared.

"Really," said Dudley, "it was no big deal. It would have been a big deal had I made six in a row."

The Cavaliers prepared for a home game against the Doug Moe-coached Denver Nuggets. The Nuggets led the league in scoring, averaging 133 points a game. Moe-coached teams are virtually impossible to scout. Years earlier, when Moe coached the San Antonio Spurs, then-Cavaliers coach Bill Fitch dispatched assistant Jimmy Rodgers to scout them. Fitch asked to see some of the Spurs plays after Rodgers returned.

"I don't have any," said Rodgers.

"Why not?," asked Fitch.

"Because," said Rodgers, "they don't run any plays."

It was much the same with the Nuggets in 1988.

While they averaged a league-high 133 points a game, they also gave up more than anyone else — 123. "We're only the second worst defensive team in the league," said Moe. "The worst is whoever is playing us." The Cavaliers defeated the Nuggets, 122-103. "Our defense was like jelly," said Moe. "We have some games where we can't guard me."

After 16 games, the Cavaliers were 12-4. Only the defending champion Los Angeles Lakers (13-4) and runner-up Detroit Pistons (15-4) topped them. Wilkens was asked if his team should be mentioned in the same breath as the Lakers and Pistons. "Not yet," he said. "It's too soon to label us up there. We are good, though."

The Cavaliers beat the Mavericks, 102-98 in Dallas, behind Price's 22 points. Mavericks coach John MacLeod first saw Price play more than a decade earlier when Price was a mere nine years old.

"Mark was at a basketball camp I conducted when I was at the University of Oklahoma," said MacLeod. "He was dribbling behind his back and running the break just like he does now. You can never project someone being an NBA player at that age. I knew, though, that he would be terrific."

The Cavaliers defeated Atlanta, 120-94, to give them the best record in the NBA at 15-5.

"I've got a lot of confidence in this team," said Harper. "As long as we maintain our health, we've got a good chance for everything. We might be a team that is playing until June."

The Chicago Bulls played the Cavaliers for the first time since eliminating them in the first round of the playoffs the previous spring. The Cavs won, 107-96, and Michael Jordan came away impressed by them.

"The Cavaliers, I'm sorry to say," said Jordan, "are now the team to beat in the East. They are much better than they were last year."

Erica Lyn Ehlo, four months old, attended her first NBA game, a 122-98 Cavaliers victory over Charlotte. Her father, Craig Ehlo, had 13 points and nine rebounds. How did Erica Lyn Ehlo like her first game?

"Fine," said her father. "She did cry, though, when coach took me out in the first half."

Ehlo, then in his second full season with the club, originally was signed to a 10-day contract in January 1987. He had been playing for the CBA's Mississippi Gulf Coast Jets, who were owned by Ted Stepien. The Jets played in Biloxi, Mississippi, where Ehlo once counted precisely 25 fans in attendance at a game. Shortly after his arrival in Cleveland, he mentioned to a reporter that Stepien still owed him one week's pay — $396.

A few days later, Ehlo was shooting around at the Coliseum about an hour before tipoff of a home game. A young woman called out his name and approached him on the baseline.

"Craig Ehlo, you better watch what you say in the newspaper! You shouldn't be so ungrateful to those who help you out! You shouldn't be so quick to burn your bridges, because you could be back in the CBA looking for a job tomorrow!" the woman yelled, loud enough for bystanders to hear.

Ehlo was dumbfounded.

Then the woman said she was one of Ted Stepien's daughters.

"He gave you a chance! He helped you get to where you are today! And besides, my father says he doesn't owe you any money," Ms. Stepien told Ehlo in no uncertain terms.

Ehlo laughed. He was used to getting little or no respect.

"When I signed my first contract with Houston in 1983," said Ehlo, "I got a $5,000 signing bonus. I thought I was rich. They asked me how I wanted it, and at first I didn't know what they meant. Then I told them to give it to me in 10s and 20s, so it would look like I had a real wad.

"Heck to me, that was a real wad. I was going to buy a new truck, but decided against it. I got scared because I didn't know how long this would last and I wasn't sure I could afford something like that. So I put the money away."

"Where? In a bank account?" asked a reporter.

"No, in a coffee can, which I then hid somewhere," deadpanned Ehlo. "And I won't tell you where."

Ehlo's coach in Houston was Bill Fitch, the former Cavaliers coach. "Fitch had guys sit on his bench according to pecking order," Ehlo said. "Since I was 12th man, I got the 12th chair. I was so far away from the coach, it was like I was in another country."

It was in Houston where Ehlo earned his nickname, "Eggs." He used to play shooting games after practice against then-teammate John Lucas, who now coaches the Philadelphia 76ers.

"We used to play for breakfast," Lucas said. "I beat him so often and won so many breakfasts, I started calling him Eggs."

The nickname stuck. Eggs Ehlo's finest moment in a Rockets uniform came during Game 6 of the 1986 NBA Finals between Boston and Houston.

"It was in the Boston Garden and the final seconds were ticking down. They had already won it, and there was a horde of Celtic fans dressed in green ready to rush the court," Ehlo said years later. "So I was faced with a dilemma: Do I keep the ball as a souvenir and run off the court? Or do I try to score one last bucket before the final buzzer? Obviously, being the scrub I was at the time, the decision was easy.

"So I got the ball at halfcourt with four or five seconds left and weaved my way through this green maze to the basket. Some guy was bold enough to jump against me, and I dunked on him. I scored the last two points of the 1986 Finals over some Celtic fan. It felt great."

Fitch, meanwhile, kept saying Ehlo would be a fine NBA player. But he never played him, and eventually cut him so he could keep someone named Conner Henry on the Rockets roster prior to the 1986-87 season. Getting cut from the Rockets was devastating for the native of Lubbock, Texas, but then Ehlo was used to being scorched in his home state.

He loved to tell the story about how Abe Lemons recruited him out of high school to play for the University of Texas, which was a Texas schoolboy's dream.

"Lemons came to recruit me, smacked me on the back and said, 'Son, I want you to be a Longhorn.' Then he slapped a Texas U. sticker right on my chest," Ehlo said.

"But the very next day, Texas fired Abe Lemons."

So Texas suddenly was out. From there, it was on to Odessa Junior College and Washington State for Ehlo before the pros. Years later, he reflected on making it in the NBA.

"I just can't believe I own a home now," Ehlo said. "I lived in an apartment for so long, I can't believe I have a lawn to mow now."

By 1988, though, Ehlo was an established player with the Cavaliers, a scrambling type who backed up Ron Harper at shooting guard and could change the complexion of a game with his all-out hustle, determination and improved outside shot. But he still wasn't getting much respect in Lubbock, where he fulfilled a request from a friend for a charity auction and sent along a signed jersey one summer.

"No one bid on it except my friend," Ehlo said. "He had to buy it back. I told him, 'Shoot, I could have gotten you one for free.'

"They follow me and root for me down there in Lubbock, I guess, but they're just not what you would call basketball fanatics. Football is the biggest sport in Texas."

The '88-89 Cavaliers continued to mow down the opposition, moving out to a record of 21-5 with a 127-110 victory over Washington on December 30. But they denied they were among the NBA's elite at that point.

"We have no championship rings," Harper said. "The only teams I see with championship rings are the Los Angeles Lakers and Boston Celtics."

The only Cavaliers player who had ever appeared in an NBA Finals was Ehlo, who claimed these Cavs were a better team than the '86 Rockets. "It's a little better because of attitude," said Ehlo. "There were some real egotistical individuals on that Rockets team. There is egotism here, but it is a team thing. There was a lot of arguing, almost dissension on that team. Here, there are pranks and there is teasing. So far, it has not gone beyond that."

By early January, Cleveland was buried in snow. "Some people in Phoenix are going to find this tough to believe," said Nance, who spent 6 1/2 years playing for the Suns before being traded to the Cavaliers, "but the other night after we beat Indiana and it was so bad driving home, I actually went for a walk in the snow in the woods behind my place. And I really enjoyed it."

Nance blocked a career-high and franchise-record 11 shots in a 104-96 victory over the Knicks. "They (the Knicks) kept coming at me," said Nance, "and I just kept blocking them." The team followed his lead. They blocked 21 New York shots in all, tying an NBA record as they won their 11th straight game, pushing them to 24-5.

Asked to comment on the difference between his leaping ability and Nance's, Daugherty said, "There is one big difference when Larry and I go up in the air. When I go up, I come down. When Larry goes up, he stays there."

Even in losing, the Cavaliers gained praise. After handing them their worst loss of the season, 116-95, Lakers coach Pat Riley likened the Cavs to the Lakers of the early 1980s.

"It's an innocent climb they are making," said Riley. "It's got to be fun for them, because they are learning about themselves. We were that way back in 1980. I guess we should check back in nine years to see if the Cavaliers are still together. They know they are talented, but they don't have to play yet with a lot of expectations. It's easy to play from that position. It's going to be interesting to see if they can sustain it in the second half of the season. I think they will."

Everyone was jumping on the Cavaliers bandwagon. "There is no doubt they can win the whole thing," said Eddie Johnson of Phoenix, after the Suns were blasted, 126-110. "They have had trouble with the Lakers, but if they played them for seven games, I would put my money on Cleveland. They're an awesome team. They have a good mix of players and they handle the ball well."

Pacers coach Dick Versace called the Cavs "the finest basketball team on the planet. I don't see any weaknesses on that team."

Golden State brought an eight-game winning streak to Richfield and was rocked, 142-109, as the Cavs set a franchise record for most points scored in a regulation game. "The Cavaliers were awesome," said Golden State coach Don Nelson. "I knew they were awesome from the films, but you never really know until you play them.

"They're the best team and the best-coached team I've seen this season. They're definitely contenders for the championship if they keep their heads straight. I wouldn't want to play them in the playoffs. They're just so sound. And, they are going to get better."

Cavaliers reserve forward Hubbard was an 11-year veteran in the twilight of his career in 1988. He wasn't playing much, but scored the basket that established the franchise scoring record in the win vs. Golden State. "We're winning," said Hubbard, "so I won't complain. What can I complain about? I've had 10 great years in the league. If it ended today, I would go out a happy man."

Boston's Larry Bird once described Hubbard as one of the best defenders to ever play against him. Hubbard said that reputation wasn't earned easily.

"He was the best," Hubbard said of Bird years later. "But you have to remember that with a guy like that, he's going to take 20-25 shots a game. What the fuck are you gonna do? If he's any good at all, he's going to make at least 10 out of 25. That gives him 20 points right there.

"You're not going to completely keep a guy like that from getting his points. You can't stop a guy like that. You can try to beat him up, push him around. But you can't stop him . . . . The thing I thought that made him so tough to guard was that he was so offensively focused. When you run into a guy who is that offensively focused and they're setting picks for him like crazy so he can get open and get the ball, it doesn't matter what you do. You just hope he doesn't get 50 — because if he's gonna get 50 off me, I figure I won't be around much longer. I'm going to be up there in the stands watching him like everyone else."

By 1988, Hubbard knew he wasn't going to be around much longer. Still, teammates like Daugherty appreciated the wily veteran.

"People think the whole game is what they see out on the court," said Daugherty, "but where it really starts is in the locker room and upstairs in the practice gym, and that is where Phil is so valuable. I feel lucky to have him here with us. So much of what he does is unseen. People see myself or Ron Harper or Mark Price, but they don't see and probably don't appreciate how much Phil Hubbard has meant to our success."

A game against the Pistons in late January, 1989, became Friday night at the fights. Laimbeer put a bear-hug on Daugherty, who broke loose and was grabbed by Isiah Thomas in a Cavaliers 80-79 victory over the Pistons. Laimbeer connected with a right cross to Daugherty's face. Both players were ejected.

Minutes later, Rick Mahorn initiated some fisticuffs with Nance. "I'm not sure if they tried to start something or not," said Daugherty. "Maybe they did, maybe they didn't." Daugherty and Laimbeer were fined $5,000 each and suspended for one game apiece.

"No class," said Embry, who was fined $1,000 for going onto the court during the melee. "Neither one (Laimbeer, Mahorn) of them has any class. There is no place in the game for what those two did."

"If this was a preview," said Daly, "the playoffs are going to be incredible."

The mild-mannered Daugherty was livid at the fine and suspension. "For some reason," said Daugherty, "people around the league think we are going to take the sort of crap the Pistons deal out. Well, we won't, and now they know we won't. Look, I like to be as physical as anyone. The most physical guy in the league is Moses Malone and I love playing against him."

Asked if Laimbeer's right cross to his face hurt Daugherty, he said, "Not at all. Laimbeer punches like a girl."

Daugherty was not finished. "He (Laimbeer) does this kind of thing now because his basketball game isn't what it used to be," Daugherty said. "The fact that the Pistons are trying to project this image of being street-tough is bull. If they want to really fight, I'll be glad to go out, get some of my teammates, and fight them all night. The thing that really bothers me is the league is putting me on the same level as him."

Laimbeer was seething, too. His consecutive game streak ended at 685, fourth-longest in NBA history.

Daugherty served his one-game suspension two nights later when the Cavaliers lost, 122-117, in overtime to the Bullets in Baltimore. More significantly, Nance suffered what was diagnosed as a sprain above his left ankle.

"It's really strange," said Nance. "It is hurting just above the ankle. I've never had anything like this before."

Three Cavaliers — Price, Daugherty and Nance — were named to the All-Star Game. Harper was not. Angered, he took it out on the Sixers with a triple-double — 25 points, 10 rebounds, 10 assists.

"I took my frustrations out," said Harper. "In my case, once I get mad, I play good basketball. What I did, though, is no consolation for not being named to the team."

Kings coach Jerry Reynolds lauded the Cavaliers after losing to them, 110-94. "Cleveland and the Lakers are the two best teams in the league," he said. "I don't know if the Cavaliers are quite as gifted, but they're the most solid. They could be wearing rings the next three, four years."

Daugherty had 23 points, nine rebounds and six assists against a Hornets trio of Earl Cureton, Tim Kempton and Dave Hoppen in the pivot during another Cleveland victory. Kempton is best known for being able to eat a Burger King Whopper in one bite.

"We have no answer to their center," said Hornets coach Dick Harter. "I don't know what James Naismith had in mind when he invented the game and put the basket at 10 feet. For us, he should have put it at seven feet."

Before the game, an imposter slipped into the Hornets locker room at Charlotte Coliseum and started to put on Rickey Green's uniform. He was escorted out by Coliseum security. Passing Price on his way out, the would-be imposter said, "I was going to hold you scoreless today."

Another fan, standing up when North Carolinian Daugherty was announced in the pre-game introductions, un-furled a sign that read, obviously in reference to the recent fight with Laimbeer, "Please don't hit me, Mr. Daugherty."

Price, Daugherty and Nance appeared in the All-Star game at Houston, and Wilkens coached the East team. East teammate Isiah Thomas said Price is the toughest point guard he faces.

"That little shit can flat-out play," said Thomas. "He is faster than me and he is quicker than me. The thing I can't believe about him is how he has gotten to the point where he is now in such a short time."

The West All-Stars won, 143-134, in the game played at the Astrodome. Price had nine points and one assist in 20 minutes, Daugherty no points in 15 minutes, Nance 10 points and six rebounds in 17 minutes.

Injuries kept superstars Bird and Magic Johnson out of the game. Did that take something away from it? No, said Wilkens. "Someday," he said, "both of them will retire. What happens then? Do we just drop the game?"

Cavaliers assistant coach Dick Helm made it to the game, but his clothes didn't. Team owner Gordon Gund gave him a suit. "You can have everything but my shorts," Gund told Helm.

Helm said he thought about asking Embry for a suit. "I didn't think anyone would be able to see me, though, if I put on one of his suits," said the rather average-sized Helm. Embry, of course, is a 6-foot-8, 300-plus pounder.

The Cavaliers improved to 38-12 after a 118-100 victory over Philadelphia, but Sixers guard Gerald Henderson issued a rare note of skepticism.

"At this point," he said, "the Cavaliers are the best team in the league, but it remains to be seen how they will play when it gets real tight. In a seven-game series, you've got older veterans doing tricky things to you."

Two days later, the Cavaliers played their first nationally televised game in 11 years. "We're not playing for CBS," said Price, who scored 27 points by making 10 of 12 shots in a 110-90 victory over Houston. "What we really wanted to do was show people how good we are, rather than have them hear it through the grapevine."

The Cavaliers bandwagon continued to swell. "They are scary," said Houston coach Don Chaney. "They impress me more than the Lakers."

Tom Heinsohn was on the CBS telecast team. "I'm picking them to win the whole ball of wax," said Heinsohn. "They have all the ingredients. They all operate on the same page. Lenny Wilkens knows how to win four games in a best-of-seven series. He's not like some college coach coming into the league who doesn't have the experience."

Heinsohn talked about the Chicago Bulls, who were 29-20 and trailing the Cavaliers by 8 1/2 games in he Central Division.

"They've made Michael Jordan a gate attraction — a monster," he said. "I saw (coach) Doug Collins try to get everyone involved, but then give up on it too soon."

The streak at home hit 20 with a 128-91 victory over Portland. "I think the most amazing thing about this streak at home," said Ehlo, "is that no one talks about it."

In the final seconds of the third quarter, Daugherty hit a long shot that appeared to be the first 3-pointer of his career.

Official Jack Nies, though, ruled that Daugherty's right foot was on the 3-point line. "It's a conspiracy," said Daugherty, smiling. "No one wants to believe big guys can shoot 3-pointers."

The Detroit Pistons sent Adrian Dantley to Dallas for Mark Aguirre. Indiana coach Dick Versace, a former Pistons assistant, said the trade assured Detroit of a return trip to the NBA Finals.

"I don't know about that remark," said Embry. "The game is still played on the floor."

Next up was the rematch with the Pistons. "Hey," said Daugherty, when asked to discuss going up against Laimbeer for the first time since their fight, "I'm not going to go out there and spit in the guy's face at the center circle. I'm here to play basketball."

Laimbeer begrudgingly had been taking notice of the Cavaliers. "They are like the Mike Tyson of the NBA," he said. "We have to play hard against them for 48 minutes or it will be all over."

After practice for the Pistons game, rookie Randolph Keys spotted teammate Wayne (Tree) Rollins.

"You taking me out to dinner tonight?" asked Keys.

"No," said Rollins. "I've already got two kids I'm taking to dinner."

At tipoff of the Cavaliers' 115-99 victory over the Pistons, Laimbeer looked at Daugherty and pointed to a sign in the upper-reaches of the Coliseum.

It read: Daugherty — Nice Punch Alice.

Alice Daugherty had 20 points and 13 rebounds. Laimbeer countered with eight and nine. The Cavaliers raised their season record against the Pistons to 3-0. "There is no big secret why they are 3-0," said Isiah Thomas. "The Cavaliers are a better team than we are."

But in the waning minutes of the game, Price was guarding Thomas. As Price passed Pistons forward Rick Mahorn, 6-foot-10 and 250 pounds, Mahorn threw an elbow in the direction of the 6-foot, 175-pound Price's head. It connected. Price left the game with 6:10 to go, and later was diagnosed with a concussion.

Price said he was guarding Thomas at the time of the incident. "He was bringing the ball up and I was looking at him," said Price. "Mahorn was nowhere near me, but he went by me and hit me with his elbow. I went down." No foul was called by the officiating crew of Jake O'Donnell, Jimmy Clark and Derrick Stafford.

The Cavaliers sent a videotape of the incident to NBA headquarters. "You can't tell me it was an accident," said Wilkens. "Mahorn could seriously have hurt Mark. This has to be addressed very strongly. Either we're going to have the best basketball played or we're going to have fights. You see this crap happen all the time. I just don't believe those two guys (Laimbeer and Mahorn) don't perpetuate this stuff."

The Cavaliers were 43-12, leading the Pistons by five games in the Central Division. But Price sat out when the Pistons defeated the Cavaliers for the first time, 96-90, on March 3. The NBA fined Mahorn $5,000, but did not suspend him.

"As far as I'm concerned," said Price, "this is a slap on the wrist. Somehow this sort of thing has to be stopped and I don't think a fine such as this is going to do it."

Nonetheless, the $5,000 fine levied was the largest ever by the NBA for elbowing.

"This is a joke," said Mahorn. "I was just running down the court with no intention of hurting anyone . . . . If I really wanted to hurt someone, I could really do it."

Some Pistons fans started to take the Cavaliers seriously. The Northfield Hilton Hotel, where the Cavaliers stayed in the Detroit area, received a telephone call at 4:15 p.m. The caller said a bomb was set to go off at 4:45. The hotel was emptied at 4:30 and the Cavaliers boarded a bus to drive around the area for about 45 minutes.

"At first I thought this was all a joke," said Wilkens, who received a telephoned death threat about one hour before the hotel received the bomb threat. "When I realized it wasn't, I hung up. It's a sad commentary when something like this happens."

Price returned to play 43 minutes and score 23 points in a 105-95 victory at Sacramento. "The headaches are gone," he said. Kings coach Jerry Reynolds said he couldn't believe how Price was not selected until the 25th pick of the 1986 draft.

"Everyone in the league should feel like fools for letting him go until the second round of that draft," said Reynolds. "The Cavaliers have a great team. I really like them a lot. The key, though, is Price. He is an MVP candidate. He won't get it, though. There is a rule that the little-bitty guys can't get it. But he is as deserving as anyone."

Two nights later, Price tied a club-record with six 3-pointers, but it was not enough to avert a 120-114 defeat at Golden State. When Price was taken out for a rest in the third quarter, the 15,025 at the Oakland Coliseum Arena gave him a standing ovation. "We beat the best team in basketball," said Warriors coach Don Nelson.

Others weren't so sure. Pacers coach Dick Versace, a former Pistons assistant, said he thought Detroit was now the favorite to win the Central Division race. "The Cavaliers are a great team. Lenny Wilkens has done a masterful job," Versace said. "I don't know, though, if they could do the same thing the Pistons have done if they, for instance, lost someone like Larry Nance. I like the Pistons because they have more depth."

Interestingly, the strained tendon above Nance's left ankle continued to be bothersome. His scoring average dipped to 17.6 points a game. "It's taking away some of my mobility," said Nance.

Before a 109-100 loss to the Cavaliers at the end of March, Bulls assistant coach John Bach watched a videotape of the Cavs-Bulls game two weeks earlier. Price hit a 20-foot jumper.

"Amazing," said Bach. "Get a look at his wrists. The ball just explodes out of his hands."

By early April, the Pistons were gaining ground in the Central Division standings almost daily on the slumping Cavaliers. Even after the Cavs defeated Philadelphia, 92-90, Sixers star Charles Barkley was not impressed.

"Cleveland can't beat Detroit," he said. "You know that. I know that. Look at how they keep winning with Isiah Thomas out (broken bone in left hand). Cleveland has a good team, but Detroit is awesome. Their bench is too deep."

Commenting on Detroit's Bad Boy image, Barkley added, "It intimidates a lot of teams. It takes a strong man to win against that."

Indeed, the Cavs, who had owned the best record in all of the NBA for nearly two-thirds of the season, soon found themselves trailing the Pistons in the Central Division. Before a 107-95 loss to the Pistons at the Palace in Auburn Hills, a loss that virtually ended Cleveland's divisional title aspirations, a television reporter approached Bill Laimbeer and requested an interview.

"Where you from?," Laimbeer asked.

"Cleveland," the reporter said.

"Well," said Laimbeer, "fuck you, you fucking asshole."

After the game, the Pistons were more smug. "The Cavaliers might as well rest their guys," said Isiah Thomas, "because this race is over."

Price remained upbeat. "People forget that we are new at this type of thing," he said. "You've got to realize that Detroit has been through these types of wars the last five years. How many times did they go up against Boston late in the playoffs and come up short?

"I'm sure we're going to have to go through a lot of games like these, just like the Pistons did all those years, before we can take the next step."

Pistons coach Chuck Daly was weary of the constant carping from around the league concerning the team he coached. He was particularly upset with Embry. "Apparently," said Daly, "Wayne Embry wants to be the commissioner."

Embry refused to back down. "Chuck certainly has a right to defend himself," said Embry, "and the Pistons do play a good, aggressive-type of basketball. My point is that Bill Laimbeer and Rick Mahorn don't have to try to hurt a guy every time he goes in for a shot. And, the fact that the Pistons are allowed to promote and encourage their Bad Boy image is entirely wrong.

"I do a lot of business in Detroit. I talk to people there all the time who say they are embarrassed they have to be associated with that sort of image. I don't think it's necessary for Rick Mahorn to take out Mark Price, and I'm disappointed Chuck Daly thinks that's the price we have to pay."

The Cavaliers ended the season with a 90-84 victory over Chicago, making them 6-0 against the Bulls. They were heavily favored to beat the Bulls in the first round of the playoffs. Yet Michael Jordan claimed the Bulls had the Cavaliers right where they wanted them.

"I know everyone is expecting us to be swept in three," said Jordan. "We want to prove them wrong. This is a whole new season. We've got everyone back and ready to play. The pressure is on the Cavaliers, not us. Everyone is expecting us to lose."

Jordan was asked for a prediction. "Bulls in four," he said.

Before Game 1, Price viewed the Cavaliers' 90-minute practice from a stationary bicycle, where he was trying to nurse a pulled groin muscle back to health. He hit 9 of 10 shots in a 3-point shooting drill, but was ruled out.

"This could not have come at a worse time for me," Price said. Or the Cavaliers. They were upset, 95-88, in Game 1 at Richfield.

"With Mark Price," said Bulls forward Scottie Pippen, "they are a great team. Without him, they are a totally different team."

The Cavaliers evened the best-of-five series in Game 2, winning 96-88 on Harper's 31 points. Price returned to score 15 points. But Ehlo sprained his right ankle with 30 minutes remaining in the Cavaliers practice for Game 3. "I was playing Michael Jordan against our first team," he said, "and just came down on it funny."

The series returned to Chicago for Game 3. Ehlo was out and the Bulls romped, 101-94, to take a 2-1 lead. "Now," said Jordan, who scored 44 points, "we control our own destiny."

The Cavaliers forced a fifth game, defeating the Bulls in overtime, 108-105, in Game 4. "We do not want to go on vacation," said Nance, who had 27 points, nine rebounds and three blocked shots. Price scored 24 points and Harper 17 to offset Jordan's 50.

"Michael Jordan is beyond description," said Embry.

Added Ehlo: "When that tongue comes out, you know you're in trouble."

Game 5 was played at the Coliseum on May 7, 1989, and the Cavaliers led by a point with three seconds left on the clock. The Cavs led, 100-99, after Ehlo and Nance executed a perfect give-and-go from out of bounds at midcourt. Ehlo, inbounding the ball to Nance, blew past Bulls defender B.J. Armstrong, took a return pass and made a driving layup.

"I fell asleep on the play," said Armstrong. "I was jumping up and down in front of Ehlo and when he passed it in and made the cut he blew by me, whiff, like I wasn't there. I slipped."

Time out, Bulls. As they walked to the bench, Jordan looked at Armstrong and said, "Don't worry, I'm going to get the basket."

Three seconds remained.

Bulls forward Brad Sellers was ready to inbound the ball. Time out, Cavaliers. As Jordan walked back to the Bulls bench, he looked at Wilkens and smiled.

Three seconds still remained to be played. Sellers inbounded the ball to Jordan, guarded by Ehlo.

"We drew up a play," said Jordan, "where I would back-pick for Bill Cartwright and then pop out to the ball."

That play was thwarted when Nance came up to help Ehlo double-team Jordan. "I had to fake and cut real hard," said Jordan, "and both of them went for the fake."

Jordan had the ball 30 feet from the basket. The game clock was winding down.

"Ehlo was on me and it seemed like he was trying to foul me," said Jordan. "But then I was able to get past him and, to be honest, I was kind of surprised I had that easy a shot, although there was a guy flying at me."

The guy was Ehlo. Jordan rose up near the free-throw line, hung as Ehlo flew by, and put up the shot that will forever be frozen in the minds of the 20,273 fans at the Coliseum on that day in May.

The ball sailed through the rim and net.

Bulls 101, Cavaliers 100.

End of game.

End of season for the Cavs.

"I have seen Michael Jordan do a lot of things," said Daugherty. "I cannot believe he hit that shot, though. I cannot believe it. He had three seconds to do it.

"I saw people run at him. I don't see how he stayed in the air that long and double-pumped like he did. I have seen him do some amazing things, but . . . they had to expect a miracle. They got it. His name is Michael Jordan. I just can't fathom how in the world our season has ended. Just one man took it to us, all by himself.

"Amazing. Michael is just amazing."

All the Cavs were stunned.

Nance: "That is why they call him Michael Jordan, super-star."

Ehlo: "I am going to try to forget this as soon as I can, because he did hit that shot on me. We did what we wanted to do . . . It's like a nightmare."

Not for Jordan.

"I wanted my teammates to believe they could beat Cleveland, even after losing to them six times in the regular season. That's why I made the prediction of Bulls in four. You've got to believe it first before you can actually do it," Jordan said.

For the Cavaliers, seeing was not believing.

"It is not over," Harper said. "I refuse to believe it is over."

But he was wrong.

Just like that, it was over.

CHAPTER SIXTEEN

"Team of the '90s"

The Shot by Jordan seemed to push the Cavaliers down a long, winding path of irreversible poor luck, beginning the moment he ended their 1988-89 season and continuing in training camp the very next fall. Brad Daugherty reported to camp fresh off what was supposed to be minor foot surgery and tried to play, but couldn't. He was dispatched to the Cleveland Clinic for what he thought was routine treatment for an infection — and stayed there for several weeks. He missed the first 41 games of the 1990-91 season.

"I thought I was going to get an examination, get some stitches, and go home," Daugherty said. "Staying there so long was driving me crazy. I was bored stiff. You can watch only so many Andy Griffith reruns (on television)."

Larry Nance also was out at the beginning of the season, having not fully recovered from surgery to repair a shredded tendon in his left ankle. He missed the first 17 games. And Mark Price, the team's third All-Star from the previous season, sat out eight of the first 15 games with a sprained right foot.

The injuries were devastating to the group Magic Johnson had ordained "the team of the '90s." But even more so was a chain of events that led to perhaps the most controversial trade in franchise history on November 16, 1989.

For months, rumors had swirled throughout town and the NBA about enigmatic guard Ron Harper. Not just trade rumors, though there were plenty of those; but damaging rumors reflecting poorly on his lifestyle off the court. He also was entering the final year of the four-year, $2.15 million deal he signed after difficult negotiations as a rookie, and already had begun making noise in the newspapers about wanting "a Chris Mullin-type contract." Mullin had just signed a long-term pact with the Golden State Warriors worth between $2.5 million and $2.6 million annually.

"That was the going rate for starting 'two guards' in the league. I felt I deserved it," Harper said.

Embry wasn't so sure.

Other teams were actively pursuing Harper in trade talks with the Cleveland GM prior to the 1989 draft in June. Embry listened, but did not bite. He knew Harper was talented, even if he also felt he knew some things about the young man that made him more than a little nervous.

The previous season, Harper was crushed when his three teammates made the All-Star team and he didn't. He felt he deserved the honor, too. While Daugherty, Nance and Price were quiet guys who disdained all the hoopla that had become part of NBA All-Star Weekend, Harper so enjoyed the extravaganza that he made a habit of going even when he wasn't invited.

As a rookie, Harper competed in the Slam Dunk contest in Seattle. The next year, in Chicago, he was just coming off an ankle injury and again was invited to compete, but declined at the very last minute. He still showed up, though, and as usual arrived at the All-Star affair with a sizable entourage in tow.

The NBA's security people took notice of the people Harper was running with. After one particular All-Star Weekend, they called Embry and warned him that some of the folks Harper was associating with were suspected drug dealers and gamblers, the worst mix imaginable for a professional athlete. They urged Embry to talk with his young star.

He did, but Harper didn't want to hear it.

"I didn't give a shit. I didn't pay them no mind," Harper said. "I told them I was old enough to judge my friends and choose who my friends were. I told them they should choose their own friends, mind their own damn business, and stay out of my personal business."

Embry fumed. Harper began to believe the club had hired private detectives to follow him around town and even on the road. A short while later, he was called into Embry's office again.

"We heard you went to a club in Cleveland, and went into this room where there was a tray of drugs being passed around," Embry told him.

"It was a club I had never, ever heard of in my life in Cleveland," Harper said. "Then one day I was riding through downtown and I saw the place — the club they were talking about. It was run down, like a shack. And I said to myself, 'Wow, I'm really glad these are the kinds of places they think I'm hanging out in.' "

Harper never denied that he enjoyed a little of the nightlife. He often could be spotted at various clubs in the Flats or elsewhere, sipping on beers or mixed drinks and mingling with the public.

"I was a 21-year-old kid when I got into the NBA. What is a 21-year-old kid going to do? Sit at home and watch TV? I didn't see nothing wrong with going out and hanging out. But the places I was going were not the places they thought I was going."

Embry worried about Harper's influence on younger players. He worried about the people with whom Harper was associating. Perhaps most of all, he worried that someday he would wake up to learn Harper had been arrested for some drug-related charge. And then the Cavs would lose a valuable asset with no chance to receive anything in return.

By the beginning of the 1989-90 season, the situation was about to boil to a head.

Gordon Gund called a meeting at the Sheraton hotel at Cleveland Hopkins International Airport. Embry arrived to find Gund sitting with team legal counsel Richard Watson and Horace Balmer, head of NBA security.

"The DEA (Drug Enforcement Administration) has just informed us that Ronnie is associating with known drug dealers," Balmer told the assembled group. "They believe his car has been used in at least one deal that they know of. They believe he has given money to these guys."

Shortly thereafter, Lenny Wilkens arrived at the meeting.

"Tell Lenny what you just told us," Embry implored Balmer.

Balmer repeated the bombshell allegations. The room fell into a dead silence, after which Balmer soon left, leaving the Cleveland contingent to collect their thoughts in private.

Gordon Gund spoke next.

"I want him the fuck off my team — NOW!" Gund said emphatically.

Wilkens later told others that what surprised him the most at that instant was that he never before had heard Gund curse.

"What did you just say?" Wilkens asked.

"I want him the fuck off my team — NOW!" Gund repeated.

Then Gund turned to Embry and added, "Make the best deal you can as quickly as possible. I want him out of here certainly within a week."

Wilkens attempted to talk Gund out of the decision at first, but saw it was futile. The coach's belief was that Harper was innocent until proven guilty, and that no formal charges had been brought against the player. He wanted to see more facts backing up the allegations.

Embry drove Wilkens home from the airport. During their drive, the GM convinced the coach of the perceived need to move Harper and of Gund's unwavering intention to do so. Reluctantly, Wilkens agreed it was for the best.

Word soon got out around the league about the allegations concerning Harper, and of the Cavs' intentions to move him. For obvious reasons, teams weren't lining up with dazzling offers for Embry. The best he could do — which, indeed, is all Gund requested — was a deal with the woebegone Clippers for the rights to Danny Ferry, who was playing in Italy and had no intentions of ever signing with the Clips.

Even then, the Clips demanded Embry throw in two future first-round draft picks "as an insurance policy in case Harper went to the can," as one source put it. Embry had the Clips throw in troubled shooting guard Reggie Williams for a second-rounder just so the Cavs would have someone to play the position in Harper's sudden absence.

Harper heard he was going to be traded to the Clippers two days before the deal actually went down. He heard it from teammate Randolph Keys, who read it in Peter Vescey's column in the *New York Post* while Harper, Keys and Tree Rollins were dining in a restaurant near the team hotel on the morning of a game at New Jersey.

At the team's shootaround later, Harper arrived wearing all his Cavs' gear inside-out "in a protest." He joked about the trade rumors, but by this time actually believed them to be true.

Harper's teammates laughed, but his coach did not. Wilkens took one look at Harper with his practice uniform turned inside-out and pulled the player aside for a long talk.

"No matter what happens, you'll still be playing in the NBA," Wilkens told him. "No matter what happens, promise me you'll keep playing hard. Don't worry about some of the things that are being said about you. Just go out and play."

Replied Harper: "Yeah, well, I'm still going to keep wearing this shit the wrong way until I see what happens."

Two nights later, during a heavy Cleveland snowstorm, the Cavaliers called a downtown news conference to announce they had traded Harper, two first-round draft choices and a second-rounder to the Clips for the rights to Ferry, plus Williams. Since Ferry was playing in Italy, the only immediate arrival in Cleveland would be Williams.

Embry called Harper to inform him of the trade. Harper hung up on him.

It was their last conversation.

No drug charges were ever filed against Harper, although he did testify before a grand jury in Dayton concerning $18,000 he loaned to childhood friend Mark Jones in 1988. Both Jones and Harper said the money was used to help Jones open a popular nightclub called "Dymond's" in Harper's hometown. Though the federal grand jury later indicted Jones on "one count of knowingly, intentionally and unlawfully attempting to possess with attempt to distribute in excess of 500 grams of cocaine," he was never convicted.

Of all the allegations about drug use and involvement with drug dealers, Harper's agent, Mark Termini, later said: "No one made those allegations directly. If anybody had made them formally, there would have been a libel or a slander action sent forth.

"In regards to any rumors there were about anything amiss with Ron, I think time has proven how unfounded any of those things were. I don't recall anyone ever putting a name behind any of the accusations. And I think that tells you what substance the rumors had. I think Ron got a bad rap. Any speculation to that effect about why Ron got traded has been very unfair to Ron. I think time has proven that out."

Harper later said that he believed his ongoing battles with Embry over a number of things, but especially who he was hanging out with, played a key role in the decision to trade him.

"Thinking back, I'm sure that our very first (contract) negotiation played a role in why Wayne never liked me and eventually got rid of me. I was young and arrogant. If I didn't like something, I came right out and said so. I wasn't afraid to tell them to fuck off. Wayne and I just did not get off on the right foot, and nothing ever changed."

The morning after the Harper trade was made, and even before it had been announced to the media, the Cavs gathered for their usual morning workout on the Loge Level II practice court at the Coliseum. Among the first to arrive were Craig Ehlo and Steve Kerr, who were surprised to see Coach Wilkens already in the gym.

As they entered, Wilkens, sitting on a bench just inside the door, did not even look up. He sat with his head cradled in his hands and appeared not to even notice the two players.

"I thought he was sick," Kerr would later say.

Added Ehlo: "I thought maybe a family member had died. That's how bad he looked. We said, 'Coach, are you all right? Is everything OK?' And when he looked up at us, it was like his face had lost a lot of its color."

It wasn't until later that they understood. Wilkens had argued against the trading of Harper, a player he respected and looked forward to working with in the coming years. Even if Embry eventually got Wilkens to go along with the decision to move him, in his heart Wilkens believed it was a mistake.

"Ron can be out of control at times and do some things that will make you as a coach pull your hair out," Wilkens once said. "But he works hard, he's always on time for practices and planes, and he's a tremendous talent. Other than Michael Jordan, there isn't another player in the league who can do what he does when he gets the ball in the open court."

Later, in front of the media, Wilkens held up his end to make it look like a united front. He had been out-voted on the trade issue behind closed doors, but he would not let that be known publicly. At least not yet. Years later, Wilkens would hint at it just enough that most everyone began to suspect he never wanted it, which in turn infuriated Embry, who felt in the end all parties had agreed on the trade.

Shortly after the deal went down, the Cavs encountered a serious slump. Players were angry with management that Harper (and also the two first-round draft picks) had been dealt away for Ferry, who was playing once a week 7,000 miles away in Italy and as yet had admitted to no definite intentions of ever coming to Cleveland.

Williams became somewhat of a scapegoat, and it didn't help matters that he played poorly and didn't seem to want to be in Cleveland. During what would become an incredibly brief stay with the Cavs, Williams was always the last to arrive at practices and the first to leave. At one point, following a loss at home, an angry Wilkens chastised his players for what he perceived as a poor attitude.

"Look," fumed Wilkens, "I don't like this trade any more than you guys do. But we have to stick together and fight through this thing."

As Wilkens said that, Williams sat in his locker stall just a few feet away. "He didn't have much confidence when he got here," said one teammate, "but that little speech seemed to sap whatever little he had left right out of him. You could almost see Reggie shrink deeper into his chair. He probably felt about two inches tall right about then."

Meanwhile, thousands of miles away in Rome, Ferry was living the life of royalty. Il Messaggero Roma of the Italian League lured him away from the NBA for a salary of $2 million a year and such perks as a 13th-century, five-story piazza in the prestigious Trastevevre section of Rome. The luxurious rent-free home included a pair of maids who fawned over him, baking cookies, preparing grand five-course meals, and doing his laundry. He drove a $75,000 BMW, courtesy of the team.

With all this already his, Ferry was sitting in a unique position of fantastic leverage when the Cavaliers acquired his rights. Agents marveled that no player, except perhaps David Robinson, had ever entered contract negotiations with a team armed with so much leverage. Robinson was drafted by the Spurs in 1987, and they had one year to sign him or he would go back into the 1988 draft. The catch: Robinson wouldn't play until completing a two-year stint in the Navy, so he was in no hurry to sign unless the money was right.

Ferry was in a similar situation. The Cavs owned his rights indefinitely as long as he played for pay elsewhere. But he could sit out a year and re-enter the draft as Robinson had threatened. Or he could simply continue pulling down millions for playing one game a week in Italy. Though Ferry was careful not to say so, even his Italian coach, Valerio Bianchini, suspected Ferry wanted all along to pursue the NBA.

Bianchini, known in European coaching circles as "The Great Philosopher" for obvious reasons, put it this way in an interview shortly after the Cavs acquired Ferry's rights: "There is a famous opera house in Milan called La Scala. Now if you are a great singer, you can be gratified to sing in Philadelphia, Boston or New York. I'm certain that all three have opera houses that are quite nice.

"But most great opera singers have a burning desire to sing at La Scala in Milano — because there is no place else like it in this world, no place better. Only after performing there can a great singer know his true level of talent."

The NBA is basketball's La Scala. Ferry knew it. So did Bianchini, the owners of Il Messaggero Roma and the Cavaliers.

On June 1, 1990, Ferry signed with the Cavs. The deal was stunning: 10 years, $34 million. Though it was rumored and written that only seven years were guaranteed, a buyout clause insured that Ferry would indeed receive virtually all of the $34 million no matter what happened.

Of course, he expected to be a star. So did Cleveland management. Embry said on the day the club acquired his rights: "Boston waited a year for Larry Bird. San Antonio waited two years for David Robinson. You will see — Danny Ferry will be well worth the wait, too." Embry also predicted Ferry would be able to play small forward in the NBA and average close to 20 points a game. He added that "the owners, coaches, staff and players here have one goal — an NBA championship for Cleveland. Danny Ferry and Reggie Williams will help get us there."

Williams lasted only 32 games. The Cavs waived him before the 1989-90 season even concluded. Ferry arrived a year later, and it quickly became apparent he wasn't quite the player they had expected.

Assessing the damage done by the trade, Larry Nance was asked what he thought of it late in the 42-40 season that was 1989-90. He answered the question with a thoughtful question of his own. "Excuse me," replied Nance, "but didn't we win 57 games last year with the team just the way it was?"

He needed to say no more.

If the Cavaliers thought 1989-90 was a lost season, they were in for a real shock. The next season would prove much, much worse. After starting the season 6-3 and leading the Central Division early on, John Williams went down with a badly sprained left foot November 16 in a game vs. Milwaukee. He missed the next 37 games. And as if that were not bad enough, Mark Price suffered a torn anterior cruciate ligament in his left knee on November 30 at Atlanta.

Williams' injury, though serious, was not nearly as much of a concern as Price's. Only a few years earlier, a torn ACL usually meant the end of a player's career. At the very least, it meant Price would be sidelined an entire year. Replacing him at the point were guys like Darnell Valentine, who only a couple months earlier was playing professionally in Mexico; forgettable first-round draft pick John Morton; and Kerr, who rarely got the call from Coach Lenny Wilkens. With Price out, the season was an unavoidable disaster, and the team went on to finish 33-49 and out of the playoffs for the first time in four seasons.

Williams eventually returned that season, but appeared in only 43 games and averaged just 11.7 points — well below the numbers he posted the previous season. The irony of it all was that Williams made $5 million for those 43 games in '90-91, or roughly $116,279 per game.

How this came about is an intriguing and complex tale, and some of it had to do with the huge contract granted Ferry by the club a year earlier. Knowing Williams was to become a restricted free agent in the summer of 1990, the Cavs offered him a three-year extension worth $4.2 million in October of 1989.

Noting that Atlanta's Jon Koncak, a player clearly of lesser abilities, had just signed a six-year deal worth $13.2 million, Williams declined on the advice of his agent, Chicago-based Mark Bartelstein. They also were well aware that the Cavs had opened the vault door much wider for Ferry.

Actually, Bartelstein was more than an agent to Hot Rod. He had stood by Williams since the point-shaving scandal at Tulane. The two young men had become close friends, and Williams trusted Bartelstein to plot his financial future in the NBA.

In January of 1990, the Cavs upped their offer to $10 million over five years. But on the advice of Bartelstein, Williams by then had taken out a $5 million insurance policy on himself and felt he could do better. "I knew I would get the $5 million if I got hurt, so I felt more secure," Williams said.

This is where Gordon Gund and Wayne Embry dropped the ball in the Williams contract negotiations. Bartelstein came up with a counterproposal of $11.8 million over five years. Williams was ready to sign if the club agreed to it, but he and Bartelstein issued specific instructions giving the Cavs only until the end of the All-Star break on February 11 to decide.

The Cavs did not respond until near the end of March, saying then that they accepted the terms spelled out in the counterproposal. But by then the deal was off the table, according to Bartelstein, who had taken note of a six-year, $18-million offer Dallas made to unrestricted free agent-to-be Sam Perkins. Williams also was appealing to the NBA to make himself an unrestricted free agent, as opposed to restricted, the difference being that a player's current team can match any offer made to a restricted free agent within 15 days. An unrestricted free agent is free to sign with whomever he chooses, and his current team has no right to match the offer.

Eventually, the NBA ruled that Williams was a restricted free agent. While this was good news for the team, Williams again rejected the Cavs' latest proposal of $13.5 million over five years. He was peeved because the team gave him and Bartelstein only three days to make a decision on it, and then yanked it from the table. About this time, July of 1990, another factor came into play when Il Messaggero Roma, Ferry's old Italian League team, came out of nowhere with a two-year offer worth $9 million for Williams, who strongly considered it before eventually deciding he did not want to leave the United States.

Now the Cavs were in a bad negotiating position. All they could do is wait to see what other offers would be made to Williams from other teams in the NBA. They figured they then would simply match whichever one Williams decided was the best.

On August 29, though, they and the rest of the NBA were stunned to learn the details of Williams' signed offer sheet with the Miami Heat: seven years, $26.5 million. And much of the money was to be delivered up front.

"Matching the Miami offer wasn't a difficult decision. It was something we felt we had to do," Embry said. "We couldn't afford to lose a player of Hot Rod's caliber and get absolutely nothing in return."

Of course, they could sign him and trade him — which they fully intended to do. But only with Williams' approval. Hot Rod had Bartelstein write that into the contract, too. So when the Cavs attempted to deal him to Seattle for Xavier McDaniel and Nate McMillan, Williams flew to Seattle, had a look around, and decided he would rather stay in Cleveland. He turned the trade down.

The Williams deal sent the Cavs soaring over the NBA's salary cap, set at $11.871 million for the 1990-91 season. This would hamper them for years to come, virtually tying their hands anytime they attempted to work a trade.

Meanwhile, Williams — the player the Cavs could have had at a fraction of the cost had they responded more quickly to Bartelstein's counterproposal the previous February — made up in a big way for the lost time and lost wages his court battle had cost him years earlier.

He missed what would have been his rookie year because of the point-shaving charges brought against him at Tulane. Had it not been for former Cleveland GM Harry Weltman, in fact, Williams may not have been drafted at all in 1985.

"My agent figures that missing my rookie year cost me about $1 million. It cost me $450,000 in attorney fees alone, and it also cost me the money I would have made if I had been drafted in the first round instead of the second round," Williams said.

Williams made $600,000 in 1989-90. On September 15, 1990, the Cavs delivered him a lump-sum payment of $5 million. He would make more in that one day than any other player in professional basketball would make in the subsequent year, including Michael Jordan. On September 15 of each of the next four years, he would receive additional lump-sum payments of $4 million.

"I never had the dream of being the highest-paid player in the NBA," Williams said. "But when I look back on what I made — $125,000 my first year, $200,000 my second year and $250,000 my third year — I don't feel bad about it.

"Guys like Mel Turpin were making $1 million, and they weren't even playing. I was making $800,000 less and playing 38 and 40 minutes a night, but I didn't gripe. When they re-did the contracts of Mark Price, Larry Nance and Brad Daugherty, I didn't gripe. I just kept my mouth shut, did what they asked, and played as hard as I could."

The difference, of course, was that Price, Nance and Daugherty were former and future All-Stars. Williams, while a valuable and talented player, was the team's sixth man.

And just what did Hot Rod do with all that sudden wealth? He built an unbelievable home in his native state of Louisiana, and he bought lots of toys.

Yes, toys. For his children, John Jr., Johnfrancis, Johnna and Johnpaul — so named because Williams wants them to always remember they have a caring father, something he never had as an abandoned child.

"He really loves those kids," teammate Craig Ehlo said. "You should see the basement in his house. It looks like a Toys-R-Us."

CHAPTER SEVENTEEN

"Pick-and-Roll Perfection"

As the Cavaliers convened for the 1991-92 season, the general feeling was that their luck had to change. The talent, if it ever could get healthy at the same time and the right time, was in place to make a run for the Eastern Conference championship, Michael Jordan and the Chicago Bulls notwithstanding. But Mark Price was not due to return until mid-December, and no one was certain he would be the same player he was before he suffered his knee injury in November of 1990.

Price, of course, had some doubts himself. He wondered if he would be as quick as before, but also took solace in two basic facts.

"It's not like I was a high-flyer who went around dunking on people before the injury," he said. "I'm a shooter. I don't see why I shouldn't be able to shoot the ball just as well as I did before, and that has been my greatest strength."

That has been Mark Price's greatest strength on the court since he was a little boy, born in Bartlesville, Oklahoma, and raised mostly in a nearby town named Enid. By the time he was 10 years old, Price had spent a lifetime around basketball. His father, Denny, a lifelong player and coach who was an NBA assistant in Phoenix under John MacLeod for two seasons, said he realized his oldest son had unique potential by the time Mark reached the age of nine.

The revelation came during the first basketball camp attended by Mark at Oklahoma University, where Denny also had worked as an assistant coach with MacLeod.

"He was only 9 years old, but the way he could handle the ball and shoot was really something," Denny Price said. "It was probably at that time that I realized he would become pretty good and have a chance to play collegiately somewhere. I didn't really think beyond that."

But Mark did. His mother remembers watching him attend Suns practices and games in Phoenix. While the rest of the players' and coaches' kids ran amok as youngsters are wont to do, Mark never did. He would sit intently, as if memorizing the action on the court.

Then Mark Price would go home and practice the moves he saw the pros make. Hour after hour after hour.

"Mark would never miss many days of shooting," Denny Price said. "We always had a goal up in our driveway while he was growing up. Many times I can remember seeing him shoot until it was so dark he couldn't see anymore."

Then, reluctantly, Mark Price would go into the house and find something else to do. As he got older and his high school buddies started going out, Mark found gyms where he could shoot through the darkness of night. It was a sacrifice, but it didn't seem so to young Mark Price, who loved it.

"I think my Dad put a basketball in my hands at about 7 years old. It was like I fell in love with it right from the beginning," he said. "I was always fascinated with it. I'd go home in the backyard and pretend I was Dick Van Arsdale, a player with the Suns back then."

By 1990, it was becoming clear that Price, the point guard they said was too slow and too small coming out of Georgia Tech, was as good an NBA player or better than Van Arsdale, who scored 15,079 points during a distinguished 12-year career that included three All-Star appearances. Then came the collision with the rolling sign at the Omni in Atlanta, when Price's foot got wedged between the floor and the sign that buffeted the scorer's table. When something had to give, it was the anterior cruciate ligament in Price's left knee.

"I've spent my whole career getting knocked around by 7-foot, 260-pound guys, but it's a scorer's table and a rolling sign that takes me out. That's too weird," Price said.

Eleven months later, Price thought he was ready to test the knee in real NBA wars again. Coach Lenny Wilkens wasn't so sure. But when the team began the season by losing four of five games, and Price kept insisting he was ready, team doctors agreed to let him give it a try.

Price took off and so did the team. Following one particularly hot shooting night shortly after his return, a reporter told Price it looked like he still had the ol' shooting touch.

"Well," Price said in his slow Oklahoma drawl, "I didn't have surgery on my hands."

On December 17 at the Coliseum, the Cavs set an NBA record for largest margin of victory with an amazing 68-point rout of the Miami Heat, 148-80. It was the most points ever scored by the Cavs in a regulation game, and the 27 points they held the Heat to in the second half set another club record. It was a night when everything clicked just right for the Cavs, and everything went wrong for the Heat.

Even Steve Kerr, who by then was playing little, logged 11 minutes in the rout after being the last Cav put in by Wilkens.

"Eleven minutes of pure garbage time. Man, that's unheard of," Kerr said. "Still, I was beginning to wonder when I was going to get in there. We built a double-digit lead early, and I started thinking, 'OK, if we can just keep it to 15 points or so, I might get in for a few minutes at the end.'

"Then we got it up to 20, then 30, then 40, and I started thinking, 'Come on coach, put me in there. What are you waiting for?' Even I couldn't blow a 40- or 50-point lead in less than a quarter."

From December 20 through January 11, the Cavs did not lose a game, tying a franchise record with 11 consecutive victories. They also tied a team record with seven straight wins on the road. They were rolling, and Price was rolling right along with them. In the month of January, Price averaged 20.4 points in just 30.4 minutes a night, as Wilkens continued to limit his minutes to lessen the strain on Price's left knee.

On January 2, the Cavs beat the Knicks in New York, 110-103. Knicks coach Pat Riley took note of the way Price played.

"I look at Mark Price and see him all the way back (from knee surgery)," Riley said. "There are basically about five players in this league who make a difference, really make a difference, and he is one of them. He is the most productive point guard in the league, according to the way we rate players.

"I know when Mark probably looks at his numbers, he would say he's not even there yet. And he's probably right. But he's just waiting to become greater. That's bad news for a lot of teams, including us. I'm not being the courier of good news for the rest of the league here."

Off the top of his head, Riley listed Michael Jordan, David Robinson, Larry Bird and Patrick Ewing as the types of players who compare to Price. He also said Magic Johnson was that type of player before his sudden retirement prior to the 1991-92 season after testing positive for the virus that causes AIDS.

"You lose a presence more than anything else when you lose a player like that," Riley said. "You lose something that touches everyone else. It's their leadership, their ability to hit the big shots, make the right passes . . . all those things."

In February, Riley and the rest of the Eastern Conference coaches voted Price onto his second All-Star team. Fans name the starters, but coaches name the reserves — and Price, like most players, considered it a greater honor to be recognized one of the best by the coaches instead of the fans.

Only one other player in the history of the NBA had made it back to an All-Star Game after suffering a torn ACL, and that player, Bernard King, took six years to do it. Price accomplished it in a little over one year, a remarkable feat. Yet when Price arrived in Orlando for All-Star Weekend in 1992, he was not nearly as big a story as King had been the previous year.

Price, in fact, was catching serious flak for some things he had said about Magic Johnson's plans to appear in the All-Star Game. Price, being perfectly honest, said bluntly that he wasn't all that crazy about playing against someone who had tested HIV-positive.

A devout Christian who sings gospel music in the offseason and has even cut one gospel album, it was no secret that Price did not approve of the lifestyle Magic Johnson led. Price admired him as a player, but not as a person.

On at least three separate occasions leading up to All-Star Weekend, Price told reporters he wasn't thrilled that Johnson, who was retired anyway, would be playing in the All-Star Game.

"The NBA ought to take a long, hard look at the situation," Price said. "It is a relatively new disease. I don't feel enough is known about how it might be transmitted."

When Price arrived in Orlando and attended a news conference mandatory for all players, though, he was in for a shock. Johnson was at the same news conference. Hordes of reporters from all around the country and even the world descended on Price and demanded to know why the Cleveland point guard was anti-Magic, anti-AIDS and anti-establishment during a weekend that was supposed to represent a lovefest between Magic, the NBA and the AIDS research community.

Stunned, Price backpedaled. At one point, he even denied saying the very things he was on record as saying on at least three previous occasions.

Later, he admitted the media crush flustered him.

"My main thing all along was that if someone had concerns, they had a right to voice them," Price said. "But I was never anti-Magic, and I never said I didn't want to play against him or wouldn't play against him. I care about Magic Johnson. I want him to get healthy.

"All I said is that I had some concerns and the NBA should take a look at it. My concern was that it would get swept under the table without being talked about."

Ironically, it ended up getting talked about so much that Price's remarkable comeback was almost overlooked during what became a tumultuous All-Star Weekend.

Price wasn't the only repeat All-Star the Cavs had in Cleveland that year. Center Brad Daugherty, playing some of the best basketball of his career, became the first player in franchise history to be named to his fourth All-Star team at a mere 26 years of age. Ironically, though, whenever All-Star Weekend rolled around, Daugherty professed that there were other places he would rather be.

When he made his first All-Star team in 1988 at age 22, for instance, Daugherty wasn't exactly bristling with excitement. "Man, if I were home right now, I'd have been out in the woods hunting for about a week. It's that time of year," he said then.

Home is Black Mountain, North Carolina. For years, Daugherty kept an 80-acre ranch nearby and spent his offseasons there. Even though by 1992 he was more into tending to his wife, Heidi, and their budding family in a new home on the oceanfront in Ormand Beach, Florida, Daugherty never has forgotten the memories of growing up in Black Mountain.

His parents, Roy and Dorothy, decided to move Brad and his two older brothers to western North Carolina from New Rochelle, New York, shortly before Brad's birth in 1965. "They decided it would be a better life for us to grow up as country kids," Brad said.

Roy Daugherty, a master drill sergeant in the Army for 25 years, instilled discipline and respect for other people in his three boys. But they still were boys ... and boys will be boys at times. Roy Daugherty knew how to deal with that, too.

"You had to obey and respect him, but it wasn't too bad," Brad said. "If you wanted a whipping, he would give you one — but it usually came about because you deserved it. His lectures were worse than any whippings, because you knew you had done something really bad. I feared them more."

The worst, though, was the combination lecture-whipping. Young, adventuresome Brad Daugherty found himself on the wrong end of those a few times as well.

"For awhile I was really into scaring my mom with snakes and frogs and stuff I would catch out in the woods. (My father) thought it was funny at first, but it got to the point where I was scarin' the hell out of my mom. I would sneak up on her while she was in the kitchen cooking, and drop a snake or something on the floor behind her," Brad said.

"My father finally told me that was no way to act toward my mother, but I kept on with it anyway because I thought it was funny. Then one day I brought a little baby copperhead into the house and it got loose — a damn poisonous snake in the house, and we couldn't find it for a couple of days. I ended up gettin' a whippin' for that."

As he grew older, he found other diversions. Like basketball. His hoops career got off to an inauspicious start when his father nailed an 8 1/2-foot high basket to an oak tree in their backyard.

Brad would battle with brothers Greg, who was 10 years older, and Steve, who was five years older, on that dirt court. Greg would one day grow to 7-foot and play collegiately at West

Carolina, while Steve, who grew to 6-7, went on to play collegiately at East Carolina and professionally for a brief while in Europe.

"I would get into backyard games with my older brothers," said Brad, "and they would pop me upside the head, smack me around, and try to make me cry. Then, as I got a little older, they would go to play in pickup games and I would beg them to let me come along. The only way they would let me play is if I promised to do nothing but pass them the ball all day long."

So as he grew into a larger and more experienced player, Daugherty rather naturally evolved into the rare big fella who thought "pass" first. Bill Burrows, the coach at nearby Charles D. Owen High School, took notice — especially when Daugherty sprouted from 6-foot-3 as a sophomore to 6-11 1/2 as a senior.

College recruiters took notice, too. Daugherty received about 300 letters from interested schools. One day, as Daugherty sat in Burrows' office with his coach, Indiana University coach Bob Knight called and asked to speak with Brad.

"Coach," Daugherty candidly told Knight, "I am not interested in Indiana. I don't want to play for another coach who hollers and screams."

Said Burrows later: "I got a kick out of that. I still kid him about it."

Daugherty already was younger than many of his classmates because he began first grade a year earlier, and then he tested out of a year in high school. So he graduated at age 16, barely giving himself enough time to get his driver's license.

Not that would he let such a technicality keep him off the roads earlier.

"I had this old Volkswagon that I let guys on the basketball team drive," Burrows said. "One day I'm driving down the road with one of my assistants and here comes my old VW the other way. All I can see on the driver's side of the car are knees and elbows.

"We turned around — and when we caught up with them, it must have taken Brad five minutes to get out of that car."

Burrows remembers another time at the McDonald's All-American game in Chicago after Daugherty's senior year in high school. "Brad ate nine Big Macs in one sitting. That's the truth," he said.

By the time Daugherty came to the Cavaliers in 1986, though, he was mature beyond his 20 years. Four seasons at the

University of North Carolina under Coach Dean Smith, a man Daugherty greatly respects, taught him much about the fundamentals of life as well as about basketball. The lessons began even before Daugherty signed the bottom line on the national letter of intent to attend North Carolina, which, led by a junior-to-be named Michael Jordan, was coming off its only national championship season the year he was recruited.

While other coaches applied the full-court press in an attempt to lure Daugherty to their schools ("Lefty Driesell about lived in my town, he wanted me to go to Maryland so bad," Brad said), Coach Smith took a different approach. He went to watch Daugherty practice once, and then made precisely one visit to the Daugherty home in Black Mountain.

"The amazing thing was that my parents and I sat there and Coach Smith never said a word about basketball. Not a single word," Daugherty said.

Instead, Smith showed Daugherty the Carolina media guide, turning to a page that revealed a list of Carolina graduates who had gone on to become doctors, lawyers and coaches. It was a list, Daugherty later said, "of real people with degrees and good jobs."

This method of recruiting, in Daugherty's own words, "blew me away. I was so used to coaches saying they were going to build their programs around me — that sort of crap. Coach Smith just said I could have a scholarship if I wanted one and that I'd get a good education. He never promised anything else."

Smith's values impressed Roy Daugherty and his 16-year-old manchild of a son. Any preconceived notion that Brad would be pampered at North Carolina disappeared the day he arrived in Chapel Hill. Shortly after someone carried Daugherty's bags to his room for him, Smith delivered his first lecture.

"This is the last time anyone will carry your bags here. From now on, you're like everyone else. We all carry our own bags. We do things for ourselves," Smith told Daugherty.

Smith also stressed the importance of attending class and being on time. He rewarded good students with more freedom. He helped prepare Daugherty to succeed in life, whether or not he succeeded in the NBA, and at age 20 Daugherty graduated with a degree in geography and social studies, ready to take on the world.

By the middle of the 1991-92 season, Daugherty and Price had developed into a very special pair on the basketball court. Former NBA coach Jack Ramsay called them "the two best offensive players at their position in the game."

Golden State coach Don Nelson told the *San Francisco Chronicle* of Daugherty: "To me, Daugherty is the most well-rounded center of them all, and that includes David Robinson and Patrick Ewing and Hakeem Olajuwon. Of any of them, he's got the best passing skills, he's the best defensively, he can score, and he can rebound. He's got it all."

Indeed, he had it all, including Price to throw him the ball. Daugherty remembered playing against Price in college, and he remembers what crossed his mind when the skeptics were saying Mark Price was not quick enough to play in the pros after the Cavs first drafted him.

"I cannot fathom why anyone would say or think Mark Price is not quick," Daugherty said. "Not quick enough? Mark is one of the three quickest players I've ever played with. Kenny Smith was the quickest, and Michael Jordan is probably second. But Mark is right there with those guys in terms of quickness."

By 1991, Daugherty and Price had made an art of the pick-and-roll, one of basketball's simplest yet deadliest plays if properly executed. No one in the league executed it better, and opponents constantly fretted over how to defend against it.

"In a sense," said Cavs GM Wayne Embry, "Brad and Mark remind me of Oscar Robertson and myself when I played. It all starts with the pick. If you don't set a solid one, you can forget the rest of it. The play is dead.

"But Brad has made it a science in setting a solid screen, and he knows how to make himself a good target as he rolls to the basket. Mark knows how to use the pick, too. It's a hell of a problem for the opposing defense. If they don't jump out to help on Mark, he'll hit the shot. If they do, he'll hit Brad rolling to the basket for a layup or dunk.

"The pick-and-roll is designed to create situations. It forces the defense to rotate, and even if it rotates fast enough to cover Brad as he rolls to the basket, that only means someone else is open. And if either Mark or Brad has the ball, they will find that open man."

Embry is so fond of the play that he named the boat he owns the "Pick-and-Roll." To his delight, the Cavs of '91-92 were widely recognized as the most unselfish and best passing team in basketball. They ranked first in the NBA in the all-important assists-to-turnovers ratio, and backed up that offensive efficiency with a defense that led the league in blocked shots. Their average of 7.57 blocks per game was highest in club history.

For once the playoffs approached with the team reasonably healthy. Daugherty and Price showed everyone they were ready by scoring 40 and 35 points, respectively, in Game 1 of their first-round playoff series against New Jersey. The 40 points by Daugherty represented another club record, and the Cavs quickly dispatched the Bill Fitch-coached Nets three games to one.

This was important because it represented the first time in Lenny Wilkens' six years as coach that the team had won a playoff series, setting up a showdown with aging, but still dangerous Boston in the Eastern Conference semifinals. The Cavs had tied their club record, set in 1988-89, with 57 victories during the regular season; the Celtics, in Larry Bird's final season, had won 51, edging New York in a tiebreaker on the final day of the season to capture yet another Atlantic Division title.

Daugherty again set an aggressive tone for the Cavs in Game 1 of the best-of-seven series, totaling 26 points and 17 rebounds in a 101-76 romp at the Coliseum. The Celtics, however, took the next two games to surge into a 2-1 lead — with Game 4 to be played in Boston Garden.

On a Sunday afternoon in front of the usual packed house and a national television audience, the Cavs and Celtics put on a real show. Larry Nance was the star, scoring 32 points as the Cavs eventually pulled out a thrilling 114-112 victory in overtime to even the series. It would prove to be a pivotal game, and the Cavs won the series by capturing two of the next three games in blow-out fashion at home.

In Game 7 at the Coliseum, Wilkens instructed small forward Mike Sanders to stick to Bird like they were wearing the same uniform. Though Bird still wasn't in the best of health because of a bad back, Wilkens was well aware of how great players could rise to the occasion at precisely the most pressurized moments.

Sanders simply did not permit it this time, limiting Bird to 12 points and four assists while disrupting everything the

Celtics tried to do offensively. The Cavs won, 122-104, in front of a boisterous sellout crowd of 20,273.

"Even when he went out to the 3-point line, I went with him," Sanders said. "We were trying to take away his passing opportunities, because his passes are what make everyone else better. He gets their whole team involved with his passing. You try to stop his passing first, his shooting second."

Stop Bird in either phase and you stop the Celtics. The Cavs, at least at the most crucial of moments, accomplished exactly that to advance to the Eastern Conference Finals for the first time since the Miracle of Richfield season 16 years earlier.

Their opponent: The Chicago Bulls, led by Michael Jordan. Despite their 57 wins — six more than the Atlantic Division champion Celtics — the Cavs of course had finished second again to the Bulls and Jordan in the Central Division. Everywhere they turned, Jordan seemed to be blocking the path they wanted to pursue.

"There is a great sense of accomplishment in what we've done," said Daugherty after finishing off the Celtics. "But we're not satisfied yet. I always thought we had a good basketball team — but people got traded, people got injured, and we had to go through a lot to get where we are today. That makes it all the more worthwhile.

"At the same time, we know we're going on now to play another great basketball team. We've got a lot more work left ahead of us."

With Jordan again having his way against Craig Ehlo and company, scoring 33 points, the Bulls embarrassed the Cavs in Game 1 at Chicago Stadium, 103-89. The national media — and the Chicago media in particular — railed on the Clevelanders, calling them "Stay-Puft marshmallow men" and "cream puffs" for their listless effort in what obviously was one of the biggest games of their lives. A headline in the *Chicago Sun-Times* declared bluntly that the Cavs were "too polite to stand a chance against the Bulls."

"I even got it from a cabbie on the way to (Game 2 at Chicago Stadium)," Cleveland scout Ron Meikle later said. "I told him I worked for the Cavs, and he asked me what we were even doing in the Eastern Conference finals against his Bulls. He told me that at least the Knicks gave them a good series (in the East semifinals)."

At issue was the old widely-held belief that the Cavs were soft, not physically or mentally tough enough to compete with the big boys come playoff time when no blood means no foul call. As usual, this kind of talk riled Embry and infuriated Wilkens.

"We have one bad game and labels are thrown on us right away," Wilkens said. "We heard what the critics had to say, but the thing is that we're upset with ourselves after playing a bad game. No one has to tell us."

Added Embry: "That (criticism) was ridiculous, just so ridiculous. This team has won too many games to be treated like that."

To make matters worse for Larry Nance, his wife, Jaynee, returned to her downtown Chicago hotel room after Game 1 to discover all her jewelry stolen. The jewelry, including a Rolex watch worth $12,000, was worth an estimated $40,000, but at least was insured.

Nance and the Cavs rebounded to win Game 2 in a rout at Chicago Stadium, temporarily silencing all the critics. But only temporarily. When they dropped three of the next four games to rather meekly succumb four games to two in the series, the Bulls advanced to the NBA Finals and the Cavs went home wondering how they could improve without any room to maneuver on the salary cap and no first-round draft pick — both adverse side effects of the Ron Harper/Danny Ferry trade and Ferry's subsequent signing, plus the subsequent signing of John "Hot Rod" Williams.

CHAPTER EIGHTEEN

"A Time to Leave"

Wilkens spent the following summer working as an assistant coach under Chuck Daly on the U.S. Olympic basketball team — the Dream Team, as it had come to be called. And with good reason. The Dream Team was led by Michael Jordan, Magic Johnson, Larry Bird and a host of other NBA superstars Wilkens ironically had spent the previous six seasons trying to beat.

"Watching these guys play has been just awesome," Wilkens said after the team gathered for a week of training in June of 1992 at La Jolla, California. "They are so good. Then you look down the bench at the guys not even out there, and you think, 'Those guys are still so good.'

"They've been a real joy to be around. I know a lot of people joked that we would need 25 basketballs to keep all of them happy, but it hasn't been like that at all. They're really receptive to what we as coaches have to say."

The experience soured somewhat on Wilkens during his last week in Barcelona, Spain for the Summer Games. During a pickup basketball game against some workers at the practice facility where the Dream Team held its workouts, Wilkens felt something pop in the back of his left foot. He had ruptured his left Achilles' tendon.

"I guess it was a stupid thing to be doing, playing pickup ball like that at my age (then 54). But I've always stayed active," said Wilkens, who was used to regularly playing tennis or even a little 2-on-2 or 3-on-3 basketball with writers after Cavs' practices.

Upon returning to Cleveland from Barcelona and undergoing surgery at the Cleveland Clinic on August 13, Wilkens thought his health problems were mostly behind him. They weren't. One night about a month later, Wilkens suddenly encountered difficulty breathing and had to be rushed to a hospital from his offseason home in Seattle.

He spent the next five days in the hospital recovering from a pulmonary embolism — meaning two blood clots had formed on his lungs. It is a condition that occurs on occasion after someone undergoes major surgery. It also is a complication that can be fatal, a fact Wilkens was well aware of.

"I'm not afraid to admit I was scared. Sure I was," Wilkens said. "At night, even though I hadn't had a good night's rest in I don't know how long, I was afraid to go to sleep. I was afraid I might go to sleep and never wake up again. So I watched the clock . . . just stared at it for what seemed like hours on end."

By the time training camp was set to begin for the Cavs each October, Wilkens usually felt rested and raring to go. But not this time. He tried to talk a good game and tell everyone he was feeling better, but his foot remained in a cast and he continued to use one crutch to get around. It was evident he often was in pain and weary.

Coaching, for perhaps the first time in Wilkens' life, became a monumental struggle. Getting through the day without collapsing from physical exhaustion was even a test of strength.

"Lenny is a man of great habit," Joe Tait said. "He puts his offseasons together like his in-seasons. Then you throw the Dream Team in there, Barcelona, the dumb thing where he played the pickup game and blew out his Achilles', got the blood clot. Suddenly camp was here and he found himself totally unprepared for it. It was just a real struggle for him."

It didn't help that the team struggled to start the regular season as well, losing Daugherty for nine games because of tendinitis and bursitis in his left knee. Free-agent pickup Gerald Wilkins, who had spent the previous seven seasons in New York, struggled at first as he tried to fit in. The team seemed disjointed, out of sync.

One day early in the season, Tait was sitting with the coach in Wilkens' office.

"I can't get a read on these guys," Wilkens told Tait. "It's really strange. I've always in the past known how this team was going to play on a given night, and therefore I could make changes based on that feel. I don't have that feel for this team at all. It scares me a little."

Upon Daugherty's return, however, the Cavs regrouped — and by February, a month during which they won 12 of 13 games, Wilkens felt the team was playing as well as it ever had under him. Gerald Wilkins began playing better, too, and the whole team finally seemed to be clicking.

Heading into a March 13 encounter vs. the lowly Bullets in Baltimore, the Cavs had won 11 of 13 games and owned a record of 40-21. The club arrived in Baltimore just ahead of a fierce blizzard, and the game was postponed from a Saturday to the following Monday night. That Sunday, Wilkens talked expansively about his team's chances of capturing an NBA championship.

"The league is tougher, but I think we're better, too," Wilkens said. "I think the team is reaching a point of maturity. Plus we added a key player, I think, in Gerald Wilkins. He gives us another big guard to help defend other teams who come at us with size at that position.

"I feel we're good, and we're playing very well right now. What we need to do is finish up strong heading into the playoffs. If we continue to play well, we're as capable as anyone."

The next night, though, the Cavs played miserably in losing to the Bullets, 105-101. When Wilkens met with the media afterward, he seemingly blamed everyone and everything but his own players for the loss. He blamed the blizzard. He complained about not having enough athletic tape to hold a decent practice, which forced his players "to sit around at the hotel and do nothing for three days." He ripped the NBA for not playing the game on Saturday in the first place, pointing out that the team and officials were all in town.

Privately, Cavs general manager Wayne Embry was incensed over the coach's reaction to the loss in Baltimore. He felt Wilkens was making excuses. When the team lost six of its next nine games, Embry's concerns grew greater. He began to wonder if Wilkens was losing touch with the players, if he was pampering them too much on occasions when a heavy hand might be the more productive method of motivation.

Though the Cavs promptly won their next five games, Embry remained unimpressed. Two of the victories were made possible on last-second shots by Danny Ferry, one of which clearly should not have been allowed by officials in a win at Atlanta. The GM addressed his concerns during a subsequent informal chat with the coaching staff.

"I'm concerned about how the team is playing," Embry told Wilkens and his assistant coaches, Dick Helm and Brian Winters.

"But Wayne, we've won five in a row," Helm responded.

"I think it's a soft winning streak and we've got problems. Better to address them now before the playoffs are upon us and it's too late," Embry said.

"We're fine," Wilkens insisted. "Just relax. We're winning games and we're in good shape. Whatever problems we've got, we'll get them cleared up."

Embry wasn't so sure. As the discussion broke up, he wondered to himself if the coaches were being honest with themselves, or simply seeing what they wanted to see.

Wilkens, meanwhile, felt as long as the team was winning, all was well. And the team did keep winning — capturing 10 in a row and 11 of its last 12 games to close the regular season.

The first-round playoff opponent was an old foe coached by yet another old friend, the New Jersey Nets and Chuck Daly, who had replaced Bill Fitch after the Cavs defeated the Nets in the first round a year earlier. The Nets were hurting. Star point guard Kenny Anderson was out with a broken wrist, for one thing, and he was considered the key to everything the team tried to do offensively.

Game 1 in the best-of-five series was all too easy for the Cavs, who won 114-98 as nine players scored in double figures. The usually closemouthed Cavs even started hinting about a possible sweep. But Daly met with the media following a New Jersey workout one day later and projected his team as one that felt it had nothing to lose. Why not let it all hang out in Game 2?

Daly also joked about his 93 days as coach of the Cavs under Ted Stepien in 1981. He reiterated that he "liked Ted socially and all that. There was some confusion about who was advising who, that's all." And then he told a story about returning to the Coliseum as coach of the defending NBA champion Pistons and running into Stepien, by then the silent season-ticket holder.

"(Former Cav) James Edwards came into the locker room and said, 'Ted's out there. Why don't you go say hello?' So I went out," Daly said.

Stepien looked at Daly and said: "Isn't this something? You coaching the Pistons, with Bill Laimbeer and James Edwards, two players we had right here in Cleveland when you were the coach ... and you guys are winning championships. We couldn't win a game when you guys were together here."

Daly laughed and replied: "Ted, remember the one time we were driving in your car on the way to a meeting or something downtown, and I told you that I sensed we had something there in Edwards and Laimbeer? I told you they could be a great inside-outside combination for us, that we could be set at the center position for years to come. Do you remember that?"

Naturally, Stepien didn't remember the conversation.

But this was 1993, and Daly had more than reminiscing about the past on his mind. He also talked of the Cavaliers' chances to capture a championship before their "window of opportunity" escaped them.

"A team this good can go the other way real quick. They've got a good roster, a good coach and a good GM. People talk about how they need to break up the team if they don't win it this year, but they'd better be real careful before doing something like that," Daly said.

"I've heard all the talk about them being soft. We should all be so soft as a franchise. There are only so many windows of opportunity that you get to win a championship. Age is the one big factor. Players get older, and it's not easy to replace great players. They've got some great players in guys like Price, Daugherty and Nance. This is a big window of opportunity for them this year. They don't want it to close on them without taking advantage, and I think they sense that."

Then Daly talked about his Nets.

"The perception is that we're going to go in three (straight losses) in this series," Daly said. "I told our players we can go kicking and screaming, or we can go with our heads tucked between our legs. I like to fight."

And with that, the Nets fought their way to a 101-99 victory in Game 2 at the Coliseum. Suddenly, the Cavs — whose critics said they would rather fish than fight — were thinking about not a sweep, but about survival. The next two games would be played at Brendan Byrne Arena in New Jersey.

Somewhere between Cleveland and New Jersey, the rumors started. They may have been swirling before, but now they were in full force. Lenny Wilkens was in trouble. If his Cavs couldn't escape their first-round encounter with the injury-ravaged Nets, then perhaps a coaching change was in order.

Cavs GM Wayne Embry heard the rumors.

And said nothing.

Cavs owner Gordon Gund heard the rumors.

And said nothing.

"If Lenny Wilkens truly is in trouble, God help us all," Daly said. "If Lenny becomes a free agent, just watch. He'll get snatched up so fast your head will spin."

Needing strong performances to dissuade the mounting wave of negative publicity in what should have been a shining moment, the Cavs came up with back-to-back listless performances in the Meadowlands. They won Game 3, 93-84, but fell behind by 14 points by halftime in Game 4 and ended up scoring a playoff franchise-low 79 points in an embarrassing 96-79 loss that sent the series back to Cleveland for Game 5. All indications were that a loss in Game 5 would send Wilkens, who had one year left on his contract, looking for employment elsewhere.

The Cavs won Game 5 and the series, but no one seemed too happy about it. They had not played very well, and they knew it.

Waiting in the next round was the team they didn't want to play, with the player they knew they couldn't stop: the two-time defending champion Bulls and Michael Jordan.

The best-of-seven series with the Bulls was short and not very sweet from the Cavs' perspective. Chicago won it in four straight.

Making matters worse was the way the Bulls won Game 4, 103-101, in front of 20,273 at the Coliseum. In an incredible repeat of The Shot that altered the Cavs' future in the 1989 playoffs, Jordan hit another fadeaway jumper from about 18 feet at the final buzzer over Gerald Wilkins and an onrushing Larry Nance.

"I had a hand in his face," Wilkins said. "But he just knew it was going in and he had ended our season. He just knew it. He ruled."

Again.

"Yeah, he did it to us again. Can you believe it?" John "Hot Rod" Williams said. "Every time that guy has to step up in a clutch situation and hit the big shot, he does it. I've never seen anything like it."

Except, of course, in 1989 — when Williams and the rest of the Cavs saw something exactly like it. Jordan recalled The Shot, which came in Game 5 of a best-of-five first-round series to give the Bulls a 101-100 victory, and compared it to the sequel.

"Both of them have been very gratifying," Jordan said. "But the other one actually was a little tougher because if I missed it, we lose and go home. If I missed this one, we go to overtime. Plus we had a 3-0 lead in games this time. So the pressure wasn't quite the same, but the result is the same."

Along the way to the same old results against Jordan and the Bulls, Wilkens twice benched Price in favor of second-year point guard Terrell Brandon for crucial stretches in the fourth quarter. Price wasn't pleased. Worse yet, after the first benching, Wilkens didn't get around to explaining his thinking behind the move to Price until both he and Price first tried to explain it to the media.

Bad move. For the biggest games of the year, Wilkens was in danger of losing his star point guard to a major pouting act.

Price, of course, also was nursing a sore right thumb. He constantly reminded the media of this, as he often does when fighting through a nagging injury. This sometimes annoyed his teammates, especially when they saw Hot Rod Williams playing with a far more damaged hand throughout much of the season and saying very little about it.

Truth be known, a couple other small things about Price annoyed his teammates at times, as much as they respected his overall abilities and knew they needed him at the top of his game to have their best shot at winning.

If he drove to the basket and didn't receive a foul call he thought he should get, for instance, he often would pout and fail to run back to the other end on defense. "If Craig Ehlo did that," said one teammate, "Lenny would have been all over him. But Craig would never do something like that. Mark did it all the time, and Lenny never said a word to him."

Finally, a teammate approached a reporter one day and advised him to watch Price at the end of quarters. "If he has the ball and doesn't think he has a chance to make the shot, he won't try a desperation heave from like halfcourt or beyond because he figures it will affect his shooting percentage," the player said. "I guess he doesn't care that the one time he might get lucky on a shot like that might win us a game."

For whatever reasons, Price was largely ineffective in the 1992 playoffs. He shot just 44 percent and averaged 13 points, well below his regular-season numbers.

Then there was Daugherty. Overall, his numbers were great in the 1992 postseason. But he did nothing to dispel the growing belief that he didn't want the ball with the game on the line. In the season's final loss to the Bulls, he was dominating during the first three quarters, totaling 25 points and 12 rebounds, but disappeared in the fourth, when he failed to score and grabbed only one rebound. Critics took note that this was not the first time something like this had happened in a big game.

The team's most consistent, hardest-working players in the playoffs turned out to be 34-year-old Larry Nance and Gerald Wilkins, the new arrival.

For the coach, the abrupt end to the season was met, strangely, with silence. Management did not spring to his defense. Neither did his players.

After a final team meeting at the Coliseum, Gerald Wilkins angrily stowed gear in the trunk of his Mercedes and talked about what he believed was going to come down.

"Something is going to happen," he said. "You should have seen it (in the locker room). No one could look anyone else in the eye.

"Changes are coming. You can feel it. Maybe we need someone to come in (as coach) who is a little bit of a madman. Someone who will make us do one-handed pushups and run through brick walls for him. Maybe that's exactly what we need."

"Someone like Pat Riley?" a grinning reporter asked, knowing full well Wilkins had his problems with Riley in New York.

"Hell no! That motherfucker is crazy!" replied Wilkins, laughing as he jumped into the car and drove off.

For Lenny Wilkens, the coach, it was time to get away and do some serious thinking with wife Marilyn, his kindred spirit. After tying up a few loose ends, they were off to New England to visit with friends and contemplate Lenny's future.

When Wilkens returned to Cleveland the following Monday, he made it easy on Embry and owner Gordon Gund. He resigned.

"It was a tough decision for me because I like it here," Wilkens said at the time. "And I felt we had made some in-roads toward becoming an outstanding team. But the playoffs determined that we are not where we want to be. That was the first time that I felt the players did not play hard.

"It was a tough playoffs because we lost the fire. How that was and whose fault it was, I honestly don't know. But I do know that if you don't play with fire in the playoffs, you're not going to get very far. It was very hard to watch that happen. I'm a very competitive person — so, for me, it was very hard."

Embry and Gund, who had planned to meet with Wilkens later in the week and reach some kind of mutual agreement, were caught a little off-guard by Wilkens' sudden resignation. But they obviously were not upset by it.

"All of us ought to applaud the job he did here," Embry said. "He deserves a lot of credit for our success — but it was a limited success. We didn't reach our goal of winning a world championship. We did achieve the level of true contender, I think, and for that Lenny deserves a great deal of credit."

Added Gund: "I was very disappointed in our performance in the playoffs. I certainly felt we had the chance to at least give a much better showing against the Bulls. In the past, we had demonstrated the ability to play with a lot more enthusiasm and determination.

"So we were disappointed in that, no question. We were going to address that with Lenny in meetings this week."

The meetings never came. Instead, Wilkens promptly met with representatives from the Los Angeles Clippers and Atlanta Hawks. His agent, Lonnie Cooper, also talked with the Indiana Pacers. All three teams were looking for a high-profile coach, ready and willing to open up their checkbooks for multi-year deals guaranteeing millions of dollars. Wilkens had realized this during his soul-searching post-mortem in New England.

That made his decision easy. Why beg Embry and Gund to return for the final year of his deal in Cleveland, which offered no security beyond that, when he could go elsewhere and be set for his coaching life?

"Lenny burned out here, that's all," Joe Tait said. "It happens in this league when a coach is with the same team for a long time. Chuck Daly said the same thing when he left Detroit and went to New Jersey. When you've been with the same team for seven years, they've heard all your little speeches and know all your little tricks.

"Plus Lenny didn't have the same feel for the club that he had in years past. He said so himself. So that was the main thing: He never developed that feeling for the club at all. And toward the end he just developed a bunker mentality, where he didn't want to talk to anyone. He didn't want to talk to me, he didn't want to talk to the media. And if he did talk to you, he had to be sarcastic, defensive.

"It got to the point where our pre-game interviews, which had been going 4 1/2 minutes, were down to a minute, 45 seconds by the time the playoffs came around. He just didn't want to talk to me or anyone else. . . . Plus he and Wayne didn't get on the right page (the last season) and he became way too permissive with the team."

This was evident in the way the Cavs had begun traveling since ceasing to fly commercial when the Gunds bought them their own plane in 1991. Wilkens often would solicit the opinions of players as to when they wanted to travel, and sometimes even let them take a vote on when to practice or even whether or not to practice.

"If the players had their way, we would have flown home after every West Coast game," Tait said. "Mark and Brad were the leaders. They were always saying, 'Let's go home.' And Lenny was way too permissive with that."

"It was a tough year for me because of coming off the surgery and then also having the pulmonary embolism," Wilkens said. "That kind of stuff takes a lot out of you, and I was on medication (blood thinners to clear up the clots in his lungs) throughout November, December and January. I didn't really start to feel good again until around the end of April.

"Still, we had a good year. We won 54 games. People talked about us making excuses and all that, but the reality is that we had players who were hurt. Hot Rod was not 100 percent physically because of his hand. He just couldn't grasp the ball the way he normally could. Mark had the thumb injury. Those two guys being hurt took away some of our depth and flexibility. Those aren't excuses; just facts."

Eight days after resigning in Cleveland, Wilkens signed a five-year deal worth an estimated $6.5 million to coach the Atlanta Hawks. Later asked about the Cavs' playoff collapse, he said simply, "I've moved beyond that. A team can be off in a short series like that. We lost an edge some way or another, and I never really was sure why. But I didn't waste a lot of time thinking about it, either. I moved beyond it and on to other things."

The Cavs, meanwhile, were left without a coach at the end of the 1992-93 season — and with a roster that was beginning to show its age, especially in the frontcourt. The future was getting cloudier by the minute.

CHAPTER NINETEEN

"Czar of the Cavs"

Wilkens' sudden resignation as coach of the Cavaliers set off widespread speculation about who would surface as his replacement. One of the first candidates mentioned both in the rumor mill and behind closed doors in the front office by Embry and Gordon Gund was Mike Fratello, former head coach of the Atlanta Hawks and from 1990 through 1993 a colorful analyst for NBA telecasts on NBC-TV.

In Fratello they had a candidate who was everything they were looking for: A high-profile "name" whose reputation was that of a fiery motivator, tireless worker and upbeat personality. While at NBC, venerable play-by-play man Marv Albert dubbed his broadcast partner "Czar of the Telestrator" because of the way Fratello artfully dissected plays and explained them to viewers.

"I've always liked his enthusiasm and knowledge of the game," Embry said. "During our discussions of a coach, we kept coming back to Mike."

Added Gund: "He was clearly our No. 1 choice. We got the feeling that his goal was the same as ours — and that is to win a championship. He has a real handle on what coaching in the NBA is all about."

Fratello was named coach June 17, 1993. Embry immediately sought to discourage members of the media from comparing the arriving Fratello to the departed Wilkens. In turn, members of the media argued that such comparisons were inevitable — especially since Fratello signed a five-year, $6.5 million contract almost identical to the one Wilkens had landed less than a month earlier from Fratello's former employer in Atlanta. Negotiating both deals separately for the two coaches was the same agent, Atlanta-based Lonnie Cooper.

Embry's futile plea was like a respected statesman discouraging comparisons between the Bush and Clinton administrations upon the latter's takeover, simply because they were two distinctly different personalities with varying views on how to best tackle the formidable task at hand.

Wilkens was the devout churchgoer who had been named Catholic Man of the Year by the Cleveland diocese the previous year. He often left tickets at will call for nuns from his Cleveland-area parish, and once had the class to phone a reporter and offer condolences after the reporter's wife suffered a miscarriage. On the court, he was a master strategist who was as good as anyone in the NBA at drawing up workable plays in the closing seconds of a tight game. He coached the game in Cleveland the way he had played it: In a cerebral and quietly efficient manner, and with his face acting as a mask that refused to betray his innermost emotions.

Off the court, Wilkens loved good books, conservative but classy suits, and quiet meals with his wife, Marilyn, and some of their closest friends. He was the consummate family man, or at least as much of one as coaching in the NBA permits. After an important and exhilarating playoff win against the Celtics in 1992 earned the Cavs a berth in the Eastern Conference Finals, a reporter asked Wilkens if he was experiencing "one of the most thrilling moments of his life." Without hesitation, Wilkens replied, "No, it doesn't compare. This is satisfying, yes, but the most thrilling moments of my life came when my children were born."

At the same time, Wilkens also could seem distant and aloof to those outside his close inner circle — not only to the media but to some of his players and, at times, to those in the Cavs' own front office. He expected the players to motivate themselves. As professional athletes, Wilkens figured it was their responsibility — and ultimately, at least in his final playoff series as the team's coach, the players failed him in this most basic duty.

Fratello arrived in Cleveland like a lightning bolt. He loved his cellular phone, flashy clothes and long talks into the night about life and basketball (mostly basketball) with assistant coaches Ron Rothstein and Richie Adubato. He would go weeks or even months at a time without seeing his wife, Susan, and their two children, Kristi and Marc.

As head coach in Atlanta, he earned the reputation of a screamer who did not discriminate: He would yell at Dominique Wilkins the same way he would John Battle or some other lesser player. It was his way of motivating, which he believed a must for all coaches, even those at the highest level. His choice of words when routinely dressing down players would have shocked priests and nuns. But the bottom line, at least in Embry's eyes, was that Fratello's teams always played hard and with great intensity.

"I always admired how Mike's teams played in Atlanta," Embry said. "Regardless of how they got there, they won a lot of games. There's nothing wrong with bringing his kind of intensity to the job, or having his kind of passion for winning. That's what competition is all about."

Off the court, Fratello could turn his charm on and off at will — like the most skilled politician. He established the fact that he was a quick wit who knew how to deliver clever lines to the press; and at the same time, he immediately let it be known he was a control freak. Nothing written or said about him or his team escaped his scrutiny. Whereas Wilkens often said he didn't read the newspapers, for instance, Fratello had articles faxed to him from the Cleveland-area newspapers every day during training camp and for the remainder of the season whenever the Cavs went on the road. Occasionally he would even critique the articles in front of the reporters who wrote them.

Training camp was not held at the Coliseum — where Wilkens had held it each of his seven years. Fratello took the team to Wright State University in Fairborn, Ohio, just outside of Dayton "to avoid all possible distractions and make it clear that we as a coaching staff intend to get down to business. We're going down there to work."

He also announced that not only would training camp practices be closed to the media, but so would the locker room afterward. This new policy would remain in force for the entire season "at the players' request," even though the players later denied they ever made such a request.

Asked shortly after appointment of the new coach what Fratello's arrival would mean, Battle, who played for him six years in Atlanta, replied: "Longer practices and lots more four-letter words."

Spud Webb, another ex-Hawk who happened to stop in Cleveland over the summer to work Ron Harper's basketball camp, said Fratello was a tough but fair coach who could be exactly what the rather laid-back Cavaliers needed. "Mike is a very tough guy," Webb said. "Mike doesn't like players who are soft. He likes players who can take a lick and hand one out."

Long before he was Czar of the Telestrator for NBC, Fratello was Czar of the Sideline in Atlanta. His Hawks' players once met at the home of Dominique Wilkins, Gerald's older brother, to discuss ways to get him fired. Battle himself took great pleasure in telling the story prior to being reunited with the coach in Cleveland.

"Mike was all right at first, but after awhile he got a little too crazy," Battle said years earlier, after first joining the Cavs. "So we met at 'Nique's house and talked about how we could get rid of him. I'll never forget it because (Hawks teammate) Scott Hastings arrived late, listened to what we were talking about for awhile, and then said, 'Look guys, I'm in the last year of my contract and I'm just not that good a player. So I don't care what you guys do, but I'm going to keep kissing Coach's butt every way I can.'

"Then Hastings left, and we all just broke out laughing. You had to sort of respect the way he at least came to the meeting and told us that."

It was ironic, then, that Battle and Fratello found themselves reunited four years or so later in Cleveland. Since Battle had played little in Wilkens' final season as coach, he welcomed the change.

"Mike will give you a real chance to compete for playing time. That's all I'm asking for," Battle said as training camp opened. "Mike is the kind of coach who wants you to get up in a guy's face, pressure him, play all-out defense. Then when you get the ball, he wants you to get out and run, force the issue. But most of all, Mike just wants to win. And then he wants to hug you and high-five you after it's all over."

That became evident more quickly than even Battle could have imagined. When Battle hit a last-second jump shot to send the Cavs' first exhibition game under Fratello into overtime vs. Boston at Wright State, the first person to greet Battle on the court was the coach himself, who delivered a bear hug and the requisite high five. Observers obsessed with comparisons could not help noticing this was something the unemotional Wilkens never would have done.

Fratello grew up in Hackensack, New Jersey, where his father, Vincent, was a former Golden Gloves boxing champion who fought professionally 66 times and became known as the Hackensack Hurricane. The son brings the same kind of single-minded fury to coaching that the father used in the ring.

"I was about 11 years old when I decided I wanted to be a coach," said Fratello, "and I never changed my mind about it again."

In high school — at Hackensack High, of course — Fratello starred in baseball, basketball and football. He was best in football, where he earned all-state honors as a linebacker and center despite standing just 5-6 and weighing 145 pounds. He usually found himself matched up against opposing players who stood six or seven inches taller and were 70 or more pounds heavier. He even played nose tackle one season at Montclair State in New Jersey, where he lettered four years in football and one in basketball. "Yeah, I played nose tackle one season," said Fratello, "but our defense stunk that year."

Nonetheless, it was during those formative years that Fratello established himself as a tough guy, despite his diminutive physical stature. It also was around that time when he met Hubie Brown, then a basketball coach at Fairlawn High in New Jersey. Brown was so impressed by the feisty player that one time, when Fratello hurt his knee playing against Brown's team, Brown took Fratello to his home afterward to treat the sore knee.

Others in Fratello's Hackensack neighborhood were busy going to drive-ins or out for hamburgers and Cokes. Fratello was talking hoops with Hubie Brown, the legendary Jersey prep coach who soon would head for the NBA. It was an association that eventually led Fratello to the NBA as well.

Another high school coach in the area at the time was Adubato, who received a telephone call from Fratello shortly after Fratello's playing days ended at Montclair State.

"I would like to work your summer camp," Fratello told Adubato.

"I don't know," Adubato replied. "The coaching staff for the camp is set. And there's limited space at the place where we're holding it this year."

"I don't care. I'll sleep on a floor. I'll work it for free," Fratello said.

So Fratello joined the staff at Adubato's camp. The year was 1968, and accommodations at the rural site fell far short of luxurious.

"He worked the whole week for nothing, 18 and 19 hours a day," Adubato said. "If you saw the brochures we sent out for this camp, it made it look like a country club. But when we got up there, the basketball courts were actually converted tennis courts, with grass growing up in between the cracks. And the pool, which looked like it was Olympic-sized in the brochure, was about 8 by 10 (feet)."

The cabins where the coaches and campers slept, Fratello joked years later, "looked like they were made out of matchsticks."

"Yeah," agreed Adubato, "they were kind of timbery, I guess you could say. They looked like they could go up at any moment."

Fratello didn't care. It was a place to eat, drink, sleep and talk basketball 24 hours a day. Fratello, Adubato and the Cavs' other current assistant coach, Ron Rothstein, later worked Five-Star Basketball Camps all over New Jersey, New York and Pennsylvania in the summertime. One summer a camp was held in the Pocono Mountains in Pennsylvania over Labor Day weekend.

"It would get cold up there, and the cabins had no heat," Adubato said. "Well, you would work the camp all day until like 11:30 or 12 at night. Then we would go back to our cabins and stay up until 3 or 4 in the morning, just talking basketball.

"One night we were so cold we were breaking up furniture and taking things off the walls for firewood. (Howard) Garfinkel (who ran the camp) was going to fire us for that, the very next day. It seemed like every year he would always fire me, Ronnie and Mike about five times each, but never really go through with it."

Another time, three police cars descended on a gathering of coaches outside a local tavern at 3 a.m. in Elmwood, New Jersey, where the group, including Fratello and Adubato, had earlier in the day conducted a basketball camp before meeting at the tavern for dinner and eventually closing it down. People in the normally quiet neighborhood had called to report loud noises that sounded like garbage cans rattling.

What the arriving police discovered were seven grown men — Hubie Brown, Dick Vitale, Brendan Malone, Brendan Suhr, Brian Hill, Adubato and Fratello — maneuvering garbage cans around in efforts to prove their points in a heated basketball argument. All seven men eventually would go on to coach in the NBA, five as head coaches.

"We'd always argue about basketball," Adubato said. "We'd argue about how to play the pick-and-roll, how to attack certain zone defenses, how to start and finish certain plays."

While in the tavern that night, they transformed the salt-and-pepper shakers into players to demonstrate their points. But after the tavern closed, there were no salt-and-pepper shakers available in the street.

"Rubbish collection was the next day," said Adubato. "We couldn't find anything else to continue our friendly discussion, so we gathered up some of the garbage cans. With the cans rattling and voices raised, it got pretty loud."

Soon the cops from nearby Hackensack, East Rutherford and Lodi arrived on the scene. Lights flashed. Laughter ensued.

"There must have been five of those cops who had played basketball for us at various towns in New Jersey," Adubato said. "We got a good laugh out of it, talked with them, put the garbage cans back, and left."

A decade later, in 1978, the NBA came calling for both Fratello and Adubato, who had bounced around in various collegiate coaching positions with continuing success. Again, Adubato received a telephone call from Fratello. He figured his old friend was calling to congratulate him on getting into the NBA as an assistant under Vitale, who had just been hired as head coach in Detroit. He was. But Fratello had something else to add.

"By the way," Fratello told Adubato, "I'm going to the NBA, too. Hubie (Brown) is taking over (as head coach) in Atlanta, and he's taking me with him."

Not long thereafter, the Pistons were hosting the Hawks in the Pontiac Silverdome before a crowd of about 20,000. Vitale, who had an explosive temper, had been tossed from the game, leaving Adubato as the head coach.

"There was a discrepancy in the clock," said Adubato, "and Hubie sent Mike over to the scorer's table to check it out. I go over there, too, and you could just tell the crowd thought we were getting all over each other, arguing about what the clock should be.

"What we really were doing was saying to each other, 'How about us two Jersey guys standing here in front of 20,000 people like this at an NBA game? How did we get here? How did we do it?' "

Fratello did it through hard work and countless late nights during which he picked basketball brains such as Adubato's and Brown's. After five years as an assistant with the Hawks and Knicks, Fratello the understudy became Atlanta's head coach in 1983. A year earlier, he interviewed for the vacant Chicago Bulls' head coaching position — and Bulls vice president Jonathan Kovler wanted to know how the 5-6 Fratello planned to handle players who were mostly a foot or more taller.

"I told him that you don't get respect, you earn it," Fratello said. "Either the players think you know what you're talking about or they don't. If they think you do, they'll respect you. If they don't, they won't. Your size has nothing to do with it."

During seven seasons in Atlanta, Fratello proved he knew what he was talking about. The Hawks won 50 or more games four consecutive seasons from 1985 through 1989 — even though they kept running into greatness in the form of Boston and Larry Bird or Detroit and Isiah Thomas in the playoffs, much the same way the Cavs under Wilkens had kept running into greatness in the form of Michael Jordan. Atlanta under Fratello never lasted past the second round of the playoffs, and following a 41-41 record in the 1989-90 season, he left for many of the same reasons Wilkens left the Cavs after the 1992-93 campaign.

A few days before his first season as the 11th head coach of the Cavaliers began, an envelope arrived in the mail for Fratello from Marv Albert, his former NBC broadcast partner. In it was a NBC patch, the kind worn by announcers on their suitcoats during broadcasts.

"Keep this close to your heart," Albert wrote. "You may be wearing it sooner than you think if things don't work out."

In a development that shocked the sporting world, Michael Jordan announced his retirement on October 6, 1993. Training camps around the NBA, which were about to open in preparation for the 1993-94 season, took immediate notice. It was no different in Cleveland, where the Cavs had long felt their path to a championship was blocked by one obstacle for which they had no solution. The obstacle's name was Michael Jordan.

When Jordan subsequently announced his intentions to pursue a major-league baseball career with the Chicago White Sox, one could not help noting the new divisional alignments for baseball put the White Sox in the same division — the Central Division, no less — as the Cleveland Indians.

The running joke in Cleveland: Sure, the Indians have a promising team, but why bother playing the 1994 season? Jordan is destined to come to the plate in the bottom of the ninth, final game of the season, teams tied for the divisional lead, Sox down by three to the Tribe, two outs, two strikes, bases loaded . . . and rip the first grand slam of his major-league career, costing the Indians their first championship of any kind since 1954. As improbable as it sounded, embittered fans in Cleveland did not discount this scenario as a real possibility.

But at least Jordan was removed from the basketball scene, leaving the Central Division path clear for the Cavaliers' taking. Or so it seemed. Fratello said the team "takes no joy in Michael announcing his retirement. I look at it this way: We felt all along that we were going to be a fine team, a championship contender, no matter who we had to go against. You always want to beat the best. That's what competition at this level is all about. We're not looking at it as, 'Thank goodness, Michael is out of the NBA and out of our way now.'"

Yet, as Gerald Wilkins and others so duly noted, "The opportunity is there. We know it, but so do some of the other teams out there. We can't take anything for granted."

Except for bad luck and injuries. The Cavs should have known to take those two factors for granted. Shortly after training camp opened, backup point guard Terrell Brandon, coming off a very promising second season, came down with mono-nucleosis. He missed all of camp, the first nine games of the regular season, and would not seem 100 percent until late in the year. Larry Nance also encountered a sore right knee in camp, limiting him to few practices and only three of eight preseason games. He played 20 minutes in the season opener — a disappointing 94-91 loss to Milwaukee at the Coliseum — and promptly went on the injured list. After undergoing arthroscopic surgery on his right knee November 9, he missed the next seven weeks and 24 games.

The team stumbled out of the gates, losing 14 of its first 21 games for the franchise's worst start since the 2-19 beginning under George Karl nine years earlier. There was grumbling from the players about Fratello. Several openly argued with him on the sidelines, their loud and abusive exchanges laced with expletives for even those seated 10 rows up in the stands to hear.

During one such early-season exchange, Fratello loudly and repeatedly berated Gerald Wilkins for not getting back quickly enough on defense. Wilkins took offense and engaged in an on-court shouting match that culminated with him yelling at the coach, "You're not a bitch, but you're acting like one!"

When beat writers for several area newspapers reported the incident in the next day's editions, Fratello became furious with the offending reporters. Never mind that the exchange between he and Wilkins was loud enough to be heard by fans sitting several rows up in the stands.

"You guys shouldn't have written about that. I feel like my privacy has been invaded," he said, incredibly. "That's exactly why you guys aren't allowed into practices."

Fratello also threatened to move the writers from their court-side seats "up into the stands" to teach them a lesson. This after he already had them moved from close to the Cavaliers' bench, where they had sat without incident for the previous 23 seasons, to more toward the middle of the scorer's table, lest they overhear and write about anything he might say to his players during a time-out huddle.

Later, after Isiah Thomas broke his hand during a fight with teammate Bill Laimbeer in a Pistons practice and the Detroit-area media reported the incident, Fratello admitted he would have lied about it if such an injury occurred during one of his practices.

"But, Mike," said one reporter, "wouldn't the fans, your paying customers, have a right to know the truth about what had happened?"

"No," replied Fratello flatly.

One former Cav reported that the current players were "in shock" over the dramatic switch in coaching styles from Wilkens to the more volatile Fratello. "They're having a tough time handling it," he said. "A coaching change is one thing. That probably was needed. But going from one extreme to the other, like they did, is a lot to ask a player to go through."

There was griping from fans, who questioned the coaching change during area radio talk shows and in letters to newspapers. There also was an immediate vote of confidence from Embry, who urged everyone to be patient.

"I think with any team there always is going to be a mixture of personalities," he said. "You bring any new personality into the mix, and there is going to be a period of adaptation. Given that most of our players have known only one coach in their careers, I think that has prolonged the period of adjustment. Plus we've had some injuries. That's all it is."

Embry also made it clear who was in charge, should the players begin to think their sniping about Fratello would carry any weight with the front office. "Mike is very direct with the players in regards to what he wants from them and what he expects from them," Embry said. "I think, as a player, that's all you can ask for. He's entitled to his own style, his methods, his ways of getting the job done. He's the coach. The players, they're getting paid to play the game."

Throughout, at least Fratello maintained his quick wit and keen sense of humor. He took abuse from opposing fans about his height nightly. "I don't mind if a guy says something clever or original," Fratello insisted. "I can appreciate a good line."

One night in his native New Jersey, a fan yelled, "Hey Fratello! Is it true you rode Secretariat?" Not bad. But another night in Miami, a fan screamed, "Hey Fratello! Stand up!"

Fratello wheeled on the fan in the middle of action on the court and retorted, "That's real original, pal. Never heard that one before. If that weak shit is all I could come up with, I wouldn't even bother coming to the games."

The fan was effectively silenced for the remainder of the night.

Meanwhile, the injuries and illnesses kept coming for Fratello and the Cavs. Gerald Madkins, a free-agent guard signed in the offseason, broke his right wrist. Five-time All-Star center Brad Daugherty, who was not playing at all like an All-Star, found out why when he was diagnosed with "benign positional vertigo," an inner ear disorder affecting his balance.

Tyrone Hill, a key offseason acquisition who was just beginning to display All-Star-like abilities at power forward, suffered a severely sprained left thumb in late December and was sidelined for nearly six weeks. Daugherty got over the vertigo and came down with a viral infection, causing him to lose a total of 15 pounds in a matter of days.

On and on it went. The team, though, eventually became oblivious to all the pain and suffering around it. With so many players hurt, others began to step up, including previously little-used third-year veteran Bobby Phills, forward-turned-center John "Hot Rod" Williams, the flamboyant Wilkins and promising rookie Chris Mills, the team's first-round draft pick from the previous summer.

With Fratello repeatedly saying he would not accept using injuries or illnesses as excuses for losing, the Cavs began winning despite all their problems. They tied a club record at one point, winning 11 consecutive games. From December 19 through March 8, they posted a 29-10 record that ranked as one of the best in the entire league over that period of time.

As the Cavs struggled to right themselves, the Hawks under Wilkens were flying high the entire season in Atlanta, battling the New York Knicks tooth and nail for best record in the Eastern Conference. They visited Richfield for the first time on December 14. "It's going to be very strange staying in a hotel room in Cleveland ... wearing another uniform in that building ... sitting on the other bench," said Ehlo prior to the game, a 103-92 victory for the Hawks. "I just hope I don't make five or six turnovers by forgetting who I play for and throwing it to the guys in the Cavalier uniforms."

Wilkens admitted it was strange returning to the Coliseum after seven years working there. "But they had a security guard posted to make sure I didn't go to the wrong locker room," he joked.

On a more serious matter, Ehlo discussed the Cavs' image as a soft team — and couldn't help bringing up the fact that no one rose to his defense when Philadelphia's Charles Barkley roll-blocked him almost into the front row at the Spectrum during Game 5 of the Cavs' first-round playoff series vs. the Sixers in 1990. This, he said, would not happen in Atlanta. As an example, Ehlo talked about how in a recent game he got tangled up with New York's John Starks.

"I fell to the ground, and Starks tried to kick me in the head," Ehlo said. "Next thing I knew, the whole (Atlanta) team was at my side, coming to my defense. And when we went to the huddle (for an ensuing timeout), about five different guys came up to me and said, 'Send him my way. I'll be happy to crush him with a pick.' There are ways to get even with guys within the rules of the game, and sometimes I think you have to do those kinds of things or else people will think they can walk all over you."

Ehlo also talked about how Wilkens was having such a positive impact on the Hawks, stressing team defense and sharing the basketball on offense.

"What's really opened my eyes is that we're using the same system, the same terminology, that we did in Cleveland," he said. "But it's true that things had grown stale there somehow. I know it means more to me now to hear him say something that maybe he's said over and over again and I had started to tune out in Cleveland. It's new to these guys. Maybe I had grown a little bored with it in Cleveland and quit paying attention like I should. Maybe all of us did a little bit."

Later in the season, after the Hawks had beaten the Cavs again in Atlanta, Ehlo reminisced some more about his days in Cleveland. A reporter asked what he would remember most about the Coliseum, which would soon be closed for good.

"I remember hitting a last-second shot to win a great game against Utah. That was my best memory," he replied. "Of course, I also remember the shot Michael (Jordan) hit over me to knock us out of the 1989 playoffs. But I've tried to forget it."

Ehlo also was asked about guarding Jordan the night in 1990 when Michael scored 69 points in Richfield, the most he ever scored in the NBA. "Hey, don't pin that one on me. I only gave up his average, which was about 34. He got the other 35 off someone else," Ehlo said. "What gets me is that now I play my son, Austin, in one-on-one and you know who he pretends to be? Yep, Michael Jordan. I can stop this Michael Jordan, though."

And finally, Ehlo was asked to comment on the Cleveland franchise's incredible run of poor luck and wide-ranging injuries over the last several years. By this time, Daugherty was out for the season with two herniated disks in his lower back, and Nance had just undergone his second arthroscopic surgery on the same knee in 4 1/2 months.

"Well, now you know it wasn't me or Lenny bringing the team bad luck," Ehlo said. "I can't explain it. Are you sure that the Coliseum wasn't built on a landfill or something? Maybe they should check into that."

As the playoffs approached, the Cavs actually were playing some pretty solid basketball. Daugherty and Nance remained out. Hill was in and out of the lineup, though he played extremely well when available. And the likes of Williams, Mills, Phills, Gerald Wilkins and Mark Price appeared to be picking up the rest of the slack.

On April 23, for the next-to-last regular-season contest at the Coliseum, the club turned back the clock and wore their old wine-and-gold uniforms for a game against visiting Washington. The Bullets also wore uniforms circa 1976, with the idea being to commemorate the classic Miracle of Richfield playoff series of nearly two decades earlier.

Adding a final touch of class to the night, most of the Cavs wore their sweatsocks pulled high and inscribed via black magic marker with No. 22, in honor of Nance, their truly beloved teammate who it appeared had already played his final game in a Cleveland uniform. The Cavs won, 117-96.

"It was the socks that did it," Wilkins said. "They were real sweet, even if they did make my legs go numb toward the end of the game. We wanted to go all the way, and that's how they wore them back then. Heck, that's how Larry still wears 'em — but we all figured that's because he's so old he probably played way back then. In fact, I told Larry they didn't have to make a (wine-and-gold) uniform for him like they did for the rest of us. He still has his hanging in his closet at home."

Returning for an entire weekend of festivities were such Cavs legends as Nate Thurmond, Bingo Smith, Campy Russell, Austin Carr, Jim Chones, Foots Walker and others. The fans loved it. For a weekend, at least, forgotten were all the bad times at the Coliseum — Ted Stepien threatening to warm up with the team his first game as owner; Bill Fitch and Nick Mileti feuding at what should have been the team's finest hour; George Karl's 1984-85 club getting off to a 2-19 start. The good times of the Miracle year were relived down to the most minute detail.

As fun as that was, the current Cavs did not fully appreciate all the hoopla. "Why did they call it a Miracle year?" Bobby Phills asked *Akron Beacon-Journal* reporter Michael Holley. "Didn't that team win only one playoff series?" Phills meant no disrespect. He just didn't understand. And he also was focusing on the present, which included the Cavs' upcoming playoff series against — you guessed it — the Chicago Bulls. Only this time the Bulls would be without Jordan, and the Cavs were brimming with self-confidence and sporting a newfound aggressiveness.

Three days prior to the opening of their first-round series against the surprising Bulls, who proved they were more than just Michael Jordan by winning 55 games in the regular season, the Cavs received some devastating news. John "Hot Rod" Williams, who had subbed superbly for Daugherty at center over the last 29 regular-season games, suffered a broken bone in his right thumb during practice. He would miss the entire playoffs.

"This is a blow," said Wilkins, "but we aren't dead meat. Not yet. We've been going through stuff like this all year and haven't given up. We're not going to give up now."

They didn't. But try as they might, this latest injury was too much to overcome. They lost the best-of-five series in three consecutive games, increasing their postseason losing streak to the Bulls to nine over the three previous seasons. The games were close, the undermanned Cavs could not be faulted for lack of effort... but when you have to start a journeyman like Tim Kempton at center in a do-or-die situation like Game 3 at the Coliseum, you aren't going to go far in the playoffs.

Kempton, whose biggest claim to NBA fame was once downing a Burger King Whopper in one bite on a dare from

Charlotte teammate Kurt Rambis, actually played reasonably well in his first start of the season. Heck, he had only been with the team for three weeks, signed after a stint in the Italian League when Jay Guidinger went on the injured list with a damaged knee.

Kempton, it should be noted, played ahead of forgotten Danny Ferry in the playoffs despite his brief orientation with the team's playbook. Ferry logged a total of just four minutes the entire series, costing the team a potential 10-point swing during those four minutes. That was in Game 1, after which Fratello never called on Ferry again.

Playing well in Game 3 vs. Chicago was Mills, whom Fratello inserted into the starting lineup along with Kempton. Playing in the biggest game of his life, Mills came up with 25 points, 10 rebounds, five steals and three assists. "Chris Mills, what can I say about him?" Fratello said afterward. "He's only a rookie, but I think I can safely say he's got a bright future in the NBA as long as he doesn't get hurt."

Doesn't get hurt? Playing for the Cavs? Was Fratello serious?

He was. He figures the team's luck has to change for the better someday. He also said the three-game sweep by the Bulls should not put a damper on what became a 47-35 overachieving season in light of all the adversity the Cavs had to overcome.

"This closes the book on our season," said Fratello. "But I can honestly say I'm proud of these guys."

It also closed the book on the Coliseum in Richfield. The Cavs will move to downtown Cleveland and the Arena at Gateway for the 1994-95 season, their 25th in the NBA. Built on 312 acres of property in rural Richfield for $36 million in 1974, future plans for the Coliseum remain uncertain.

But George and Gordon Gund clearly made out on their purchase of the building for $300,000 and other minor considerations in 1981, after banks that had loaned $32.5 million to Mileti for the project had given up on collecting the remainder of what was owed them. By 1984, the building was turning a profit and continued to do so for the next 10 years.

The Gunds agreed to leave it only for a sweetheart deal with the city on the downtown arena, which cost them merely an approximate $4 million out of their own deep pockets. The

Gateway arena itself cost $124 million to build, with taxpayers picking up the bulk of the remaining cost. Gordon Gund also forked out $14 million for naming rights to the Arena over the next 20 years, changing it from Gateway Arena to Gund Arena.

Obviously, then, the Gunds continue to make money hand over fist in this business venture they affectionately call the Cleveland Cavaliers. But Gordon Gund wants something else, too. So do the taxpayers who helped finance his team's new arena.

What they want is a championship.

"We've got some exciting young players with strong character who have helped us position ourselves to be pretty good in the future. We're determined to build a championship team," Gund said.

So were Bill Fitch and Nick Mileti before him. So were Ted Stepien, Bill Musselman and Don Delaney, although it may not have looked like it. And Harry Weltman, Tom Nissalke and George Karl, as well as Lenny Wilkens. This is the nature of sports. This is the nature of the NBA in which the Cavs have resided, and often floundered, for the past quarter-century.

"There are only two stages for a team to be in," Fratello said. "Either you are in a rebuilding mode, or you are trying to win a championship. There really is nothing in between. Building toward contending for a championship should be every team's ultimate goal."

What happens in between, though, is in reality so much more than nothing. It is what makes up a team's rich and colorful history. If the Cavaliers have proven anything over the last 25 years, it's that you don't have to win a championship to produce some memories worth holding onto and others, accompanied by pain, that simply won't fade away.

ALL-TIME STATISTICAL LEADERS

Games Played
1. Bingo Smith, 720
2. Austin Carr, 635
3. John Williams, 587
4. Brad Daugherty, 548
5. Mark Price, 534
6. Craig Ehlo, 513
7. Phil Hubbard, 469
8. Jim Brewer, 462
9. Larry Nance, 433
10. Foots Walker, 427

Points Scored
1. Brad Daugherty, 10,389
2. Austin Carr, 10,265
3. Bingo Smith, 9,513
4. Mark Price, 8,786
5. John Williams, 7,575
6. Larry Nance, 7,257
7. Campy Russell, 6,588
8. World B. Free, 6,329
9. Jim Chones, 5,729
10. Mike Mitchell, 5,217

Assists
1. Mark Price, 4,460
2. John Bagley, 2,311
3. Foots Walker, 2,115
4. Brad Daugherty, 2,028
5. Austin Carr, 1,820
6. Craig Ehlo, 1,803
7. Geoff Huston, 1,630
8. Bingo Smith, 1,566
9. Jim Cleamons, 1,549
10. Ron Harper, 1,158

Blocked Shots
1. John Williams, 1,099
2. Larry Nance, 1,087
3. Jim Chones, 450
4. Roy Hinson, 430
5. Brad Daugherty, 397
6. Jim Brewer, 353
7. Mark West, 270
8. Elmore Smith, 267
9. Mel Turpin, 233
10. Ron Harper, 219

Scoring Average
(Min. 125 games)
1. World B. Free, 23.0
2. Ron Harper, 19.4
3. Mike Mitchell, 19.3
4. Brad Daugherty, 18.8
5. Lenny Wilkens, 18.5
6. Cliff Robinson, 17.7
7. Larry Nance, 16.8
8. Mark Price, 16.5
9. Austin Carr, 16.2
10. Campy Russell, 16.1
    Randy Smith, 16.1

Rebounds
1. Brad Daugherty, 5,227
2. John Williams, 4,162
3. Jim Chones, 3,790
4. Larry Nance, 3,561
5. Jim Brewer, 3,551
6. Bingo Smith, 3,057
7. Phil Hubbard, 2,360
8. Craig Ehlo, 2,267
9. Campy Russell, 2,107
10. Austin Carr, 1,929

Steals	All-Time Leader in:
1. Foots Walker, 722	F.G. PCT: Mark West, .553
2. Mark Price, 699	F.T. PCT:Mark Price, .906
3. Craig Ehlo, 661	3-pointers: Price, 699
4. Ron Harper, 530	3-Pt. PCT: Steve Kerr, .472
5. John Williams, 504	Minutes: Daugherty, 20,029
6. John Bagley, 474	Fouls: Bingo Smith, 1,752
7. Jim Brewer, 419	Turnovers: Daugherty, 1,511
8. Austin Carr, 418	
Campy Russell, 418	
10. Phil Hubbard, 408	

Coaching Records

1. Lenny Wilkens, 1986-93 (316-258, .551)
2. Bill Fitch, 1970-79 (304-434, .412)
3. George Karl, 1984-86 (61-88, .409)
4. Tom Nissalke, 1982-84 (51-113, .311)
5. Mike Fratello, 1993- (47-35, .573)
6. Stan Albeck, 1979-80 (37-45, .451)
7. Bill Musselman, 1980-82 (27-67, .287)
8. Chuck Daly, 1981-82 (9-32, .220)
9. Don Delaney, 1981-82 (7-21, .250)
10. Gene Littles, 1985-86 (4-11, .267)
11. Bob Kloppenburg, 1981-82 (0-1), .000

Team's Year-by-Team Results

Year	Record	Playoffs	Coach
1970-71	15-67	--	Fitch
1971-72	23-59	--	Fitch
1972-73	32-50	--	Fitch
1973-74	29-53	--	Fitch
1974-75	40-42	--	Fitch
1975-76	49-33	6-7	Fitch
1976-77	43-39	1-2	Fitch
1977-78	43-39	0-2	Fitch
1978-79	30-52	--	Fitch
1979-80	37-45	--	Albeck
1980-81	28-54	--	Musselman, Delaney
1981-82	15-67	--	Delaney, Kloppenburg, Daly Musselman
1982-83	23-59	--	Nissalke
1983-84	28-54	--	Nissalke
1984-85	36-46	1-3	Karl
1985-86	29-53	--	Karl,Littles
1986-87	31-51	--	Wilkens
1987-88	42-40	2-3	Wilkens
1988-89	57-25	2-3	Wilkens
1989-90	42-40	2-3	Wilkens
1990-91	33-49	--	Wilkens
1991-92	57-25	9-8	Wilkens
1992-93	54-28	3-6	Wilkens
1993-94	47-35	0-3	Fratello